The Chartered Institute of Marketing

Professional Certificate in Marketing

Assessment Workbook

Marketing Essentials
Assessing the Marketing Environment
Marketing Information and Research
Stakeholder Marketing

For exams in 2008/2009

First edition October 2008

ISBN 9780 7517 5159 8

British Library Cataloguing-in-Publication Data
A catalogue record for this book
is available from the British Library

Published by

BPP Learning Media Ltd
Aldine House, Aldine Place
London W12 8AA

www.bpp.com/learningmedia

Printed in United Kingdom

We are grateful to the Chartered Institute of Marketing for permission
to reproduce in this text the syllabus, tutor's guidance notes and past
examination questions

Authors: Kate Machattie, Dr Kellie Vincent, and Claire Wright

CIM Publishing Manager: Dr Kellie Vincent
Photography: Terence O'Loughlin

Your learning materials, published by BPP Learning Media Ltd, are
printed on paper sourced from sustainable, managed forests.

Contents

Introduction

• Aim of the Assessment Workbook • The Professional Certificate Syllabus
• A guide to the features of the Assessment Workbook • A note on Pronouns

Sections

Review form & free prize draw

1 Aim of the Assessment Workbook

This Assessment Workbook has been designed to help you with the range of assessments you will have to complete to obtain your Professional Certificate in Marketing qualification.

In previous syllabus years you may have been able to choose between an examination or an assignment route to qualification however with the 2008 new syllabus the CIM now stipulate how you will be assessed (a mixture of exams and assignments). This workbook uses the sample assessments provided by the CIM to help you revise for exams and to prepare assignments. The workbook does not aim to teach you the content that you need to know in order to pass (this is covered in our Study Texts) but to arm you with strategies to pass professional qualification exams and write good quality assignments. To do this we:

- Give CIM specific advice in terms of what is expected of students within professional qualifications.

- Provide hints and tips based on our understanding of CIM examiner requirements.

- Use the sample assessments to provide advice about how to tackle the tasks using example answers based on hypothetical case companies.

2 The Professional Certificate Syllabus

The Professional Certificate in Marketing is aimed at anyone who is employed in supporting marketing role such as Marketing Co-ordinator or Executive. You may also be a manager with a senior role within in a small or medium sized company where marketing only forms part of a wider work remit. Possibly you may be looking to move into your first marketing role or you wish to become more specialist.

The aim of the qualification is to provide a strong foundation for marketing knowledge. You will develop the breadth of knowledge of marketing theory but also appreciate issues faced within the organisation as CIM qualifications concentrate on applied marketing within real work-places.

The complete qualification is made from four units which are assessed in different ways:

- **Unit 1 Marketing Essentials** – 3 hour examination comprising 10 short answer questions and a case study with three longer answer questions. All questions are compulsory.

- **Unit 2 Assessing the Marketing Environment** – 3 hour examination with a case study sent to you before the exam.

- **Unit 3 Marketing Information and Research** – A research-based project assignment. There are two compulsory parts to the assessment with tasks based on research within an organisation you are familiar with.

- **Unit 4 Stakeholder Marketing**- A work-based project style assignment where you are able to choose between two alternative topics to research within your own organisation and complete the compulsory tasks.

The CIM stipulate that each module should take 40 guided learning hours to complete. Guided learning hours refer to time in class, using distance learning materials and completing any work set by your tutor. Guided learning hours do not include the time it will take you to complete the necessary reading for your studies or indeed your assessment work. Generally when this figure should at least be doubled in order to fully account for the time you are likely to take to successfully complete this qualification.

The syllabus for each unit as provided by the CIM can be found in each of the corresponding unit sections of this workbook.

3 A guide to the features of the Assessment Workbook

Each of the chapter features (see below) will help you to break down the content into manageable chunks and ensure that you are developing the skills required for a professional qualification.

Feature	Relevance and how you should use it	Corresponding icon
Chapter topic list	Use this as a route map or mini contents for each section.	–
Format & Presentation	Outlines a key marketing presentation format with reference to the Magic Formula	
Concept	Key concept to learn with reference to the Magic Formula	
Application	An example of applied marketing with reference to the Magic Formula	
Evaluation	An example of evaluation with reference to the Magic Formula	
Activity	An application based activity for you to complete	
Key text links	Emphasises key parts to read in a range of other texts and other learning resources	
Exam / Assignment tip	Key advice based on the assessment	

4 A note on Pronouns

On occasions in this Assessment Workbook, 'he' is used for 'he or she', 'him' for 'him or her' and so forth. Whilst we try to avoid this practice it is sometimes necessary for reasons of style. No prejudice or stereotyping accounting to sex is intended or assumed.

5 Additional resources

5.1 The CIM's supplementary reading list

We have already mentioned that the CIM requires you to demonstrate your ability to 'read widely' . The CIM issue an extensive reading list for each unit. Within our study texts we have identified the essential chapters for you to read and have highlighted a range of sources that you could refer to.

5.2 Study materials from BPP Learning Media

To help you pass the entire Professional Certificate in Marketing we have created a complete study package. Individual **Study Texts** have been written for each of the four units for the Professional Certificate level.

Our A6 set of spiral bound **Passcards** are handy revision cards are ideal to reinforce key topics for the Marketing Essentials and Assessing the Marketing Environment exams.

5.3 BPP Learning Media's Online Material

To complement this Assessment Workbook, study texts and Passcards we have also produced some online materials for both students and tutors. These materials have not been designed to remain static but we will be developing more and adding to the content over time. If you have purchased a product within our CIM range then you will be able to access the online materials for free at:

www.bpp.com/lm/cim

Typical content will include:

- Links to the most useful websites for marketers
- Syllabus links to key marketing developments and 'big news' stories
- Pro forma's for key marketing documents such as Marketing Plans, Research Proposals etc
- Tutor only content including slides and case studies

Section 1

An Overview of
CIM Assessments

Topic list

1 What is the CIM looking for in students?

There are a few key points to remember as you study and prepare for your CIM assessment with regard to the CIM's expectations of you. To put this into context try to remember the following:

(a)   You are studying for a **professional** qualification. This means that you are required to use professional language and adopt a business approach in your work. Ten percent of the available marks are awarded for the 'format and presentation' of your work.

(b)   You are expected to show that you have 'read widely'. Make sure that you read the quality press (and don't skip the business pages), read Marketing, The Marketer, Research and Marketing Week avidly. Adding real life examples into you work helps not only show that you have read widely but you are demonstrating that you understand how marketing works. One way to show you are well read is to make full use of the CIM's online Knowledge Hub. Your student membership entitles you to full access to this goldmine of both academic and non-academic press. The Knowledge Hub is an access point to lots of good sources you can use to demonstrate you have read widely in order to answer the specific assignment question posed. Also on the CIM's website, you will find a 'Shape the Agenda' section. This is another good source which enables you to show you are familiar with current CIM research programmes. Within the 'Shape the Agenda' pages you will find highly relevant and recent papers on current topics of importance to the CIM. New agenda papers are published every six months and in recent years topics have included: market segmentation; managing marketing; marketing metrics; relationship building communications and; social marketing.

(c)   Become aware of the marketing initiatives you come across on a daily basis, for example, when you go shopping look around and think about why the store layout is as it is, consider the messages, channel choice and timings of ads when you are watching TV. It is surprising how much you will learn just by taking an interest in the marketing world around you. This will help you build a portfolio of real like marketing examples to use in your assessment work.

(d)   Get to know the way CIM write their exam papers and assignments. They use a specific approach which is referred to as The Magic Formula to ensure a consistent approach when designing assessment materials. Make sure you are fully aware of this as it will help you interpret what the examiner is looking for (a full description of the Magic Formula appears later in this section).

(e)   Learn how to use Harvard referencing. This is explained in later in this section and is important to master because it is a key requirement of the CIM that you use it (in assignments). Harvard referencing refers to a system that helps you to organise and cite your source materials. Paraphrasing somebody else's ideas or directly quoting from a textbook or research paper, news report or article should all be clearly cited. The CIM requires you to use Harvard referencing for a number of reasons. Firstly, they need to ensure that your assignment is your own and an original piece of work. Plagiarising from someone else's work is a serious offence and if you were found to be copying from someone else or another source such as a textbook then you would fail. It is for this reason that the CIM requires assignments to be presented as both paper and electronic versions so that they can run your work through anti-plagiarism software.

The second reason for insisting on Harvard referencing is to demonstrate that you have read widely around the syllabus. It is important that you use a variety of sources in your assignments to justify and back up your ideas. In exams, although you are not expected to include references, if you can at least remember and add the names of key authors and sources then it adds more depth to your answers.

(f)   Ensure that you read very carefully all assessment details sent to you from the CIM. They are very strict with regard to deadlines, completing the correct paperwork to accompany any assignment or project and making sure you have your CIM membership card with you at the exam. Failing to meet any assessment entry deadlines or completing written work on time will mean that you will have to wait for the next round of assessment dates and will need to pay the relevant assessment fees again.

Required skills at the Professional Certificate level

The CIM has also identified key skills that you are expected to develop throughout your studies. These are:

- Communications
- Information management
- Numeracy
- Involving and working with others
- Networking
- Providing and obtaining feedback
- Prioritising
- Analysing
- Monitoring

2 The CIM's Magic Formula

The Magic Formula is a tool used by the CIM to help both examiners write exam and assignment questions and you to more easily interpret what you are being asked to write about. It is useful for helping you to check that you are using an appropriate balance between theory and practice for your particular level of qualification.

Contrary to the title, there is nothing mystical about the Magic Formula and simply by knowing it (or even mentioning it in an assessment) will not automatically secure a pass. What it does do however is to help you to check that you are presenting your answers in an appropriate format, including enough marketing theory and applying it to a real marketing context or issue. After passing the Professional Certificate in Marketing, if you continue to study for higher level CIM qualifications, you would be expected to evaluate more and apply a more demanding range of marketing decisions. As such the Magic Formula is weighted with an even greater emphasis on evaluation and application as you move to the Professional Diploma and Postgraduate CIM levels.

Graphically, the Magic Formula for the Professional Certificate in Marketing is shown below:

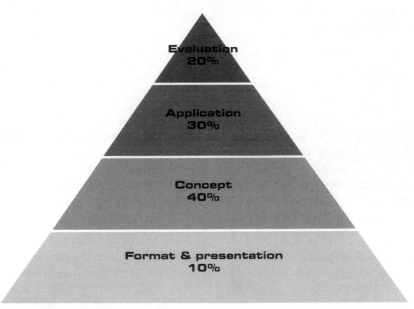

Figure 1 The Magic Formula for the Professional Certificate in Marketing

You can see from pyramid that for the Professional Certificate marks are awarded in the following proportions:

- ## Presentation and format – 10%

  Remember, you are expected to present your work professionally which means that it should ALWAYS be typed and attention should be paid to making it look as visually appealing as possible even in an exam situation. It also means that the CIM will stipulate the format that you should present your work in. The assessment formats you will be given will be varied and can include things like reports to write, slides to prepare, emails, memos, formal letters, press releases, discussion documents, briefing papers, agendas, and newsletters.

- ## Concept – 40%

  Concept refers to your ability to state, recall and describe marketing theory. The definition of marketing is a core CIM syllabus topic. If we take this as an example, you would be expected to recognise, recall, and write this definition to a word perfect standard to gain the full marks for concept. Understanding marketing concepts is clearly the main area where marks will be given within your assessment.

- ## Application – 30%

  Application based marks are given for your ability to apply marketing theories to real life marketing situations. For example, you may be asked to discuss the definition of marketing, and how it is applied within your own organisation. Within this sort of question 30% of the marks would have been awarded within the 'concept' aspect of the Magic Formula. You will gain the rest of the marks through your ability to evaluate to what extent the concept is applied within your own organisation. Here you are not only using the definition but are applying it in order to consider the market orientation of the company.

- ## Evaluation – 20%

  Evaluation is the ability to assess the value or worth of something sometimes through careful consideration or related advantages and disadvantages or weighing up of alternatives.. Results from your evaluation should enable you to discuss the importance of an issue using evidence to support your opinions.

  Using the example of you being asked whether or not your organisation adopts a marketing approach, if you were asked to 'evaluate' this, it would be expected that you would provide reasons and specific examples why you thought they might take this approach but to also consider issues why they may not be marketing orientated before coming to a final conclusion.

3 Revision

3.1 Revision

When it comes to actually revising, there are some essential strategies to address. Firstly, revision should not be left to the last minute and really starts the moment that you study a topic and complete your reading. Once you have completed the required topics, you should make sure that you fully understand the implications to a range of different contexts. Now is the time to start collecting examples of marketing practice by making notes of observations you have made through your own work and on relevant articles you have read within the business and marketing press. This will be an invaluable exercise when you get to your final stage of revision.

Practice, practice, practice is key to passing CIM exams and throughout your course you should have been completing past exam papers. Attempting the questions in this workbook along with the additional practice topics in our online materials at www.bpp.com/lm/cim. You should also check your learning by completing the quick quizzes in the study texts.

3.2 Key steps in revision

This is a very important time as you approach the exam. You must remember three main things, which we will then break down into more detailed advice.

Point 1 Use your time sensibly

1   Be honest with yourself about h**ow much study time you have**? Remember that you must EAT, SLEEP, and of course, RELAX.

2   **How will you split that available time between each subject**? What are your weaker subjects? They will need more time.

3   **What is your learning style**? AM/PM? Little and often/long sessions? Evenings/ weekends?

4   Are you taking regular breaks? Most people absorb more if they do not attempt to study for long uninterrupted periods of time. A five minute break every hour to make coffee or watch the news headlines can make all the difference.

Do you have quality study time? Unplug the phone. Let everybody know that you're studying and shouldn't be disturbed.

Point 2. Set yourself realistic goals

1   Have you set a clearly defined objective for each study period?
2   Is the objective achievable?
3   Will you stick to your plan? Will you make up for any lost time?
4   Are you rewarding yourself for your hard work?
5   Are you leading a healthy lifestyle?

Point 3 Believe in yourself

Are you cultivating the right attitude of mind? There is absolutely no reason why you should not pass this exam if you adopt the correct approach.

*   **Be confident** – you've passed exams before, you can pass them again
*   **Be calm** – plenty of adrenaline but no panicking
*   **Be focused** – commit yourself to passing the exam

3.3 Scrapbook technique

When it comes to starting final revision, one of the most useful exercises you could do before the exam is to carry out what we like to call the scrapbooking activity. This will help you to remember the key theories but also to prepare bank of good marketing examples that may be easier to remember once you get into the exam room. To complete the activity you will need:

*   A large piece of paper or a flipchart
*   Some coloured pens
*   Newspapers, marketing magazines, blog examples etc

Step 1 - Outline theories (list, mind maps, diagrams)

Aim to create one sheet per topic for the module you are revising. For example, if you are revising for Marketing Planning, you may have a sheet for pricing strategies. This is where you will need to think about how you like to remember information, so, for example, do you remember visually or do you list items in your mind, do you like diagrams, or pictures to words. If you are not sure, then think about how you might direct somebody to your house, would you be more likely to write a list of directions, draw a detailed map or a more basic diagram. The important point is that there are many books which tell you how to create mind maps or similar memory aides but at this stage you will not have time to master this and you need to be spending your time actually revising. Therefore, go with whatever works best for you, and get everything that you can think of about individual topics down on that piece of paper. Be creative with your colours if you wish, for instance, you may find it easier to colour code different subtopics.

Step 2 – Review your outline and add more detail

At this stage, you should go back to your notes and texts and add in more detail especially in terms of adding little bits of information about the good and bad points, advantages and disadvantages and contexts in which activities may be more or less appropriate. Now, complete this process for all the topics on the modules syllabus.

Step 3 – Adding examples

Move onto the example creation stage. Pull together as many copies of news reports, marketing press and business journals that you can from the last year. You will need scissors and some glue. You have probably guessed by now what you will be doing, well, yes, go through and stick as many examples as you can find about each of the topics onto your relevant sheets.

The result

By the time you have finished, you should have a huge bank, not only of the key theories and topics, but some good examples to add depth to your answers.

Once you reach the final stages of your revision, you will need to reach the point where you are checking that you remember enough for your time in the exam room. It is here that you will want to be completing whole mock exams to check that you have written in enough depth. You should also be testing yourself to check that you remember key theories and can commit them to memory. You would find BPP Learning Media's Passcards useful in this respect. Here, the sort of information you have included in your own flipchart scrapbook will have been reduced down to hand sized cards which you could use for a last minute memory jog. You may find it useful to write key words to trigger your scrapbooked marketing examples at the bottom of the relevant Passcard page.

4 Writing assignments and work based projects

The Assignment based units offer you considerable scope to produce work that provides existing and future **employers** with **evidence** of your **ability.** It offers you a **portfolio** of evidence which demonstrates your abilities and your willingness to develop continually your knowledge and skills. It will also, ultimately, help you frame your continuing professional development in the future.

The units in which you are required to submit an assignment type piece are:

Unit 3- Marketing Information and Research

Unit 4- Stakeholder Marketing

It does not matter what type of organisation you are from, large or small, as you will find substantial benefit in this approach to learning. In previous years, some CIM Professional Certificate students could choose between exam and assignment routes to their qualification. There were several cases where students made their own organisation central to their assessment and produced work to support their organisation's activities, resulting in subsequent recognition and promotion: a success story for this approach. This is a key reason why the CIM and the employers they worked with to develop the 2008 syllabus decided that fifty per cent of the final qualification should be assessed in this way. The CIM wanted to develop a syllabus that would train marketers to directly move into a supporting marketing role and perform from day one.

So, using your own organisation can be beneficial (especially if your employer sponsors you). However, it is equally valid to use a different organisation, as long as you are familiar enough with it to base your assignments on it. This is particularly useful if you are between jobs, taking time out, returning to employment or studying at university or college.

4.1 Structure and process

The **assignments** that you will undertake during your studies are normally set **by CIM centrally** and not by the study centre. All assignments are validated to ensure a structured, consistent, approach. This standardised approach to assessment enables external organisations to interpret the results on a consistent basis.

The purpose of each assignment is to enable you to demonstrate your ability to research, analyse and problem-solve in a range of different situations. You will be expected to approach your assignment work from a professional marketer's perspective, addressing the assignment brief directly, and undertaking the tasks required. Each assignment will relate directly to the syllabus module and will be applied against the content of the syllabus.

All of the assignments clearly indicate the links with the syllabus and the assignment weighting (ie the contribution each task makes to your overall marks). You will also be given information regarding the assessment criteria (we will cover this more fully later).

Once your assignments have been completed, they will be marked by the CIM. After this, all marks are forwarded to you by CIM in the form of an examination result.

4.2 Preparing for Assignments: general guide

The whole purpose of this guide is to assist you in presenting your assessment professionally, both in terms of presentation skills and overall content. The Magic Formula shows that 10% of the available marks are awarded for format and presentation. It will therefore be helpful to consider how best to present your assignment. Here you should consider issues of detail, protocol and the range of communications that could be called upon within the assignment.

4.2.1 Presentation of the Assignment

You should always ensure that you prepare **two** copies of your assignment, keeping a soft copy on disc. On occasions assignments go missing, or second copies are required by CIM. The CIM also requires you to submit an **electronic copy** which may be scanned through anti-plagiarism software. You should save your assignment using the following convention for the title:

Centre name_ Unit title (abbreviated eg MIR/SM)_ CIM student registration number

You should also ensure that:

- Each assignment should be clearly marked up with your study centre, your CIM Student registration number and ultimately at the end of the assignment a word count. Do not under any circumstances put your name on the assignment because the CIM may not accept it. You cannot use fancy folders to present your work and should simply use a treasury tag in the top left hand corner. You will need to complete and attach a copy of the CIM's 'Assignment Front Sheet and Declaration Form' otherwise your work will not be accepted.

- The assignment presentation format should directly meet the requirements of the assignment brief, (ie reports and presentations are the most called for communication formats). You **must** ensure that you assignment does not appear to be an extended essay. If it does, you will lose marks.

- A word or page limit will be included in the assignment brief. These are specified by CIM and must be adhered to. Students who are +/- 10% risk their work failing. The word count does not include headings, references, bibliography, appendices or tables. Tables will however be counted if they are thought to constitute most or all of your assignment. When slides are presented, any word count will apply to the accompanying notes and not the slides. The word count is required at the end of your document.

- Appendices should clearly link to the assignment and can be attached as supporting documentation at the end of the report. However failure to reference them by number (eg Appendix 1) within the report is the key problem with many appendices. Only use an Appendix if it is essential and clearly adds value to the overall assignment and remember that you cannot gain marks directly for items in the appendix. The Appendix should never act as a waste bin for all the materials you have come across in your research, or a way of making your assignment seem somewhat heavier and more impressive than it is.

4.3 Time management for Assignments

One of the biggest challenges we all seem to face day-to-day is that of managing time. When studying, that challenge seems to grow increasingly difficult, requiring a balance between work, home, family, social life and study life. It is therefore of pivotal importance to your own success for you to plan wisely the limited amount of time you have available.

Step 1   **Find out how much time you have**

Ensure that you are fully aware of how long your module lasts, and the final deadline. If you are studying a module from September to December, it is likely that you will have only 10-12 weeks in which to complete your assignments. This means that you will be preparing assignment work continuously throughout the course.

Step 2   **Plan your time**

Essentially you need to **work backwards** from the final deadline, submission date, and schedule your work around the possible time lines. Clearly if you have only 10-12 weeks available to complete three assignments, you will need to allocate a block of hours in the final stages of the module to ensure that all of your assignments are in on time. This will be critical as all assignments will be sent to CIM by a set day. Late submissions will not be accepted and no extensions will be awarded. Students who do not submit will be treated as a 'no show' and will have to resubmit for the next period and undertake an alternative assignment.

Step 3   Set priorities

You should set priorities on a daily and weekly basis (not just for study, but for your life). There is no doubt that this mode of study needs commitment (and some sacrifices in the short term). When your achievements are recognised by colleagues, peers, friends and family, it will all feel worthwhile.

Step 4   Analyse activities and allocate time to them

Consider the **range** of activities that you will need to undertake in order to complete the assignment and the **time** each might take. Remember, too, there will be a delay in asking for information and receiving it.

Always build in time to spare, to deal with the unexpected. This may reduce the pressure that you are faced with in meeting significant deadlines.

Warning!

The same principles apply to a student with 30 weeks to do the work. However, a word of warning is needed. Do not fall into the trap of leaving all of your work to the last minute. If you miss out important information or fail to reflect upon your work adequately or successfully you will be penalised for both. Therefore, time management is important whatever the duration of the course.

4.4 Tips for writing Assignments

Everybody has a personal style, flair and tone when it comes to writing. However, no matter what your approach, you must ensure your assignment meets the **requirements of the brief** and so is comprehensible, coherent and cohesive in approach.

Think of preparing an assignment as preparing for an examination. Ultimately, the work you are undertaking results in an examination grade. Successful achievement of all four modules in a level results in a qualification.

There are a number of positive steps that you can undertake in order to ensure that you make the best of your assignment presentation in order to maximise the marks available.

Step 1   Work to the brief

Ensure that you identify exactly what the assignment asks you to do.

- If it asks you to be a marketing manager, then immediately assume that role.
- If it asks you to prepare a report, then present a report, not an essay or a letter.
- Furthermore, if it asks for 2,500 words, then do not present 1,000 or 4,000.

Identify whether the report should be **formal or informal**; who it should be **addressed to**; its **overall purpose** and its **potential use** and outcome. Understanding this will ensure that your assignment meets fully the requirements of the brief and addresses the key issues included within it.

It would be a good idea at this point to check your understanding of the assignment with your tutor. Studying with a CIM centre means that you should expect a minimum **one hour** of tuition time specifically with the assignment in mind.

Step 2   Address the tasks and pay attention to the Assessment Criteria

It is of pivotal importance that you address **each** of the tasks within the assignment. **Many students fail to do this** and often overlook one of the tasks or indeed part of the tasks.

The Assessment Criteria that the CIM will use to assign marks is clearly shown on the assignment briefs. Make sure that you look at the criteria and think about whether you have fully addressed them. Likewise, make it easier for your examiner to identify where you are attempting to meet the criteria by wherever possible using similar terms for individual sections of you assignment. For example, within the MRI assignment brief a stated assessment criteria may be: *recommendations for field force guidelines* and you could directly use this a section heading within your work.

Step 3   Information Search

Many students fail to realise the importance of collecting information to **support** and **underpin** their assignment work. However, it is vital that you demonstrate to the CIM your ability to **establish information needs**, obtain **relevant information** and **utilise it sensibly** in order to arrive at appropriate decisions.

You should establish the nature of the information required, follow up possible sources, time involved in obtaining the information, gaps in information and the need for information.

Consider these factors very carefully. CIM are very keen that students are **seen** to collect information, **expand** their mind and consider the **breadth** and **depth** of the situation. In your *Personal Development Portfolio*, you have the opportunity to complete a **Resource Log**, to illustrate how you have expanded your knowledge to aid your personal development. You can record your additional reading and research in that log, and show how it has helped you with your portfolio and assignment work.

Step 4   Develop an Assignment Plan

Your **assignment** needs to be structured and coherent, addressing the brief and presenting the facts as required by the tasks. The only way you can successfully achieve this is by **planning the structure** of your Assignment in advance.

Earlier on in this unit, we looked at identifying your tasks and, working backwards from the release date, in order to manage time successfully. The structure and coherence of your assignment needs to be planned with similar signs.

In planning out the Assignment, you should plan to include **all the relevant information as requested** and also you should plan for the use of models, diagrams and appendices where necessary.

Your plan should cover your:

- Introduction
- Content
- Main body of the assignment
- Summary
- Conclusions and recommendations where appropriate

Step 5   Prepare Draft Assignment

It is good practice to always produce a **first draft** of an assignment. You should use it to ensure that you have met the aims and objectives, assignment brief and tasks related to the actual assignment. A draft document provides you with scope for improvements, and enables you to check for accuracy, spelling, punctuation and use of English.

Use the **'week in a drawer'** trick which involves completing your first draft and then not looking at it for at least a week. When you return to the draft areas where you are not entirely clear will be very apparent to you now. Your study centre tutor is only allowed by the CIM to give feedback on your written work once. It would therefore be advisable to make the most of this opportunity once you have reflected on areas of improvement after this week .

Step 6   Prepare Final Document

In the section headed 'Presentation of the Assignment' in this unit, there are a number of components that should always be in place at the beginning of the assignment documentation, including **labelling** of the assignment, **word counts**, **appendices** numbering and presentation method. Ensure that you **adhere to the guidelines presented**, or alternatively those suggested by your Study Centre.

4.4.1 Writing reports

Students often ask 'what do they mean by a report?' or 'what should the report format include?'.

There are a number of approaches to reports, formal or informal: some report formats are company specific and designed for internal use, rather than external reporting.

For Continuous Assessment process, you should stay with traditional formats.

Below is a suggested layout of a Report Document that might assist you when presenting your assignments.

- *A Title Page* includes the title of the report, the author of the report and the receiver of the report

- *Acknowledgements* – this should highlight any help, support, or external information received and any extraordinary co-operation of individuals or organisations

- *Contents page* provides a clearly structured pathway of the contents of the report – page by page.

- *Executive summary* – a brief insight into purpose, nature and outcome of the report, in order that the outcome of the report can be quickly established

- *Main body of the report divided into sections, which are clearly labelled.* Suggested labelling would be on a numbered basis eg:

  - 1.0   Introduction

  - 1.1   Situation Analysis

  - 1.1.1 External Analysis

  - 1.1.2 Internal Analysis

- *Conclusions* – draw the report to a conclusion, highlighting key points of importance, that will impact upon any recommendations that might be made

- *Recommendations* – clearly outline potential options and then recommendations. Where appropriate justify recommendations in order to substantiate your decision

- *Appendices* – ensure that you only use appendices that add value to the report. Ensure that they are numbered and referenced on a numbered basis within the text. If you are not going to reference it within the text, then it should not be there

- *References / Bibliography* – whilst in a business environment a bibliography might not be necessary, for an **assignment-based report it is vital**. It provides an indication of the level of research, reading and collecting of relevant information that has taken place in order to fulfil the requirements of the assignment task. Where possible, and where relevant, you could provide academic references within the text, which should of course then provide the basis of your bibliography or list of references. A list of references is often preferable to a bibliography because it is more obvious that you have actually used the sources you have stated (see A brief guide to Harvard referencing).

5   Writing a company background

One item required within the appendix to accompany your assignment is a background to your organisation. In the sample assessment materials produced by the CIM, they stipulate in both Unit 3 Marketing Information and Research and Unit 4 Stakeholder Marketing that unless it has been covered already elsewhere in your work, you should include a

"*brief background to the organisation, it's customer base and product/service range if not previously described (2 sides A4 maximum, no marks allocated)*".

Even if you think that you may have covered this previously it may be worth adding it to the appendix. CIM examiners have said on many occasions that candidates frequently struggle to write clear and concise company backgrounds.

It is useful to first think about why you are being asked to provide this background. Imagine for a moment that you are an examiner faced with a few hundred scripts. Each candidate is likely to refer to a different company or division, the large majority of which will be unknown to the examiner. Unless the examiner is directly familiar with the company you are referring to, it is quite possible that they may take your responses out of context or misinterpret your meaning because they do not know the specifics or nature of your organisation. Think about when you first move to a new job, to begin it is difficult to see how the bigger organisational picture fits together because you may not know much about the industry, the culture of the organisation and key factors of influence. The same situation is true for the examiner and so your company background serves the purpose of your company background is to provide a brief induction document into these issues that will help put your answer into context.

Two points need to be remembered;

(1)   The examiner may use your company background to put the rest of your answer into context.
(2)   Your background should be clear, concise (no longer than two pages of A4) and well structured.

5.1 What should be included in the company background?

The following can be used as a checklist to ensure that you have included sufficient detail without rambling.

The organisation

*   Organisations name including a parent company or more recognised brand.

*   Type in terms of size, sector and ownership and legal structure.

*   When established and major historical events.

*   Growth and broad strategic aims.

*   Mission statement

*   Broadly outline any other details specific to the organisation which are important to the assignment tasks eg. culture, staff, structure, supply chain partners of importance etc

The market

*   Market overview and the organisations position within the market eg market leader
*   Approximate size of the market
*   Key competitors
*   Customer groups and their characteristics
*   Broad key trends eg rapidly growing market...etc

Product/service range

*   Description of the product/service range
*   Key feature, associated benefits and unique selling proposition
*   Historical developments of the product/service range
*   Details of complementary products
*   Details of substitutes

You are likely to find that not all of these points are relevant to your organisation but it will be useful to at least run through it in order to think about the key implications that will help put your company into an appropriate context for the examiner. Frequently when we work within organisations much of the knowledge we possess is unconscious. You may find it helps to show your final company background to someone who is not familiar with yours. Ask them to read your background and then in their own words to describe your organisation back to you- you will find this helps you to see whether you have produced a realistic impression.

6 A brief guide to Harvard Referencing

6.1 What is Harvard referencing?

Harvard referencing is the preferred method of the CIM for you to clearly state the materials you use to complete your written assessments. Referencing serves two purposes, firstly, it enables readers of your work to find the source documents for themselves to read further into the topic and secondly, it avoids the problems of plagiarism (it is more difficult for you to be accused of copying another's work and passing it off as your own if you have outwardly acknowledged their contribution).

Sometimes Harvard referencing is referred to as 'The Author, Date Method' and although it is the most commonly used and highly structured method, you will find that there are slight variations amongst guides about the exact way to state references. For example, some suggest book titles should be written in italics whilst others state that they should be underlined. Whichever convention you choose is fine so long as you stick to the same throughout.

6.1.1 When and how do you reference within your paragraph?

Any time that you refer to the writing of another, their thoughts, theories, drawings or sayings, you should clearly cite their work. In practice this means that there are two instances when you should state your reference. The first is within the paragraph where you are referring to their work and the second is at the end of your document where you should provide a list of references.

To demonstrate how you cite a source within the paragraph you can consider the following example. It is likely that at some point in your CIM studies that you will want to refer to the work of marketing guru Philip Kotler. You may find yourself writing something similar to:

Kotler (1994) outlined that the process of marketing involves stages of analysis, planning, implementation and control

There are a few things to note from this:

(1)   The author Philip Kotler's name is used as part of the sentence. This means that their surname (Kotler) is used and is then followed by the year of publication (1994)which is shown in brackets

(2)   If there were two authors then you would write Kotler and (year).

(3)   If there were more than two authors then you would only use the surname of the first and refer to all others as et al. For example in this case if Kotler had co-authors then you would write Kotler et al. (1994).

If it did not seem appropriate to use the author's name within the sentence, you should still refer to them at the end of the sentence, for example you might have written:

The marketing process involves four essential stages; analysis, planning, implementation and control (Kotler, 1994). Should it be ; and then , - is this direct from Kotler – would have thought should be commas throughout?

Here you will see that before the final sentence full stop, you should have included in brackets the author's surname followed by a comma and then the year. There may be occasions that you find the same point is raised within more than one source. For example, you will be hard pressed to find a marketing text book which doesn't identify one of the key roles of marketing as identifying and meeting customer needs. Rather than trying to identify which is the most appropriate to use you should use as many as is necessary. For example, you may write:

Marketing should encompass the notion that there is a need to identify and satisfy customer needs (Blythe, 2007; Hill and O'Sullivan, 2004; Kotler, 1994).

You should notice that the order of the sources is alphabetical according to author surname and that they are separated by a semi colon.

If you take a <u>direct quote</u> from the author, it should be referenced as shown in the example below: ***"Marketing means working with markets to actualize potential exchanges for the purpose of satisfying human needs and wants"*(Kotler, 1994 p.12)**

Again, you should use the author's surname and date within brackets following the italicised quote, but as it is a direct quote then you should provide more information to enable to reader to find it, for example by including a page reference.

Now that you have cited the source at the point that you refer to it, you should remember to add the entry to your reference list placed at the end of your document.

6.1.2 How do you cite different types of material within a reference list?

At the point within the sentence/ paragraph where you cite your source, you will always use the author's surname and date regardless of whether the source was a book, newspaper or website. When you come to compile your reference list however, the nature of the material will determine how you structure your reference.

Examples of a number of types of materials are shown below along with examples of the convention being put into practice. As the convention is summarised, make sure that you pay attention to the use of underlining, italics, bold and grammatical marks.

A Book

Author surname, Initial. (Year) Book title, Edition if more than one, Publisher, City.

Kotler, P. (1994) Marketing Management: Analysis, Planning, Implementation and Control, Eighth Edition, New Jersey, Prentice Hall.

Blythe, J. (2006) Principles and Practice of Marketing, Thompson, London.

Hill, L. and O'Sullivan, T. (2004) Foundation Marketing 3rd Edition, Prentice Hall, Oxford.

An edited book

Editor surname, Initials (ed) (Year) Book title, Edition if more than one, Publisher, City.

Bateson, J.E.G. (ed) (1991) Managing Services Marketing: Text and Readings, Second Edition, The Dryden Press, Orlando.

A Chapter or readings in a book

Author surname, Initials (Year) 'Chapter, reading, article title' In Editor surname, initial (ed) Book title, Edition if more than one, Publisher, City, pages.

Chase, R.B (1991) 'Where does the customer fit in a service operation?' In Bateson, J.E.G. (ed) Managing Services Marketing: Text and Readings, Second Edition, The Dryden Press, Orlando, pp171-177.

A newspaper or magazine

Author surname, Initials or Anon (Year) 'Article title' Journal or Newspaper, Date

Cowlett, M. (2007) ' PR Leagues' Marketing, 23rd May

An academic journal

Author surname, Initials (Year) 'Article title' Journal, Volume, (Issue or Special Edition), pages.

A website

Author, initials (Year) 'Title' [Online] Company/ website owner details, Available at: web address [accessed date].

Boots Group Plc., (2003). 'Corporate social responsibility'. [Online]. Boots Group Plc.
Available at: http://www.Boots-Plc.Com/Information/Info.Asp?Level1id=447&Level 2id=0 [accessed 23 July 2005].

A blog etc.

Author, Initials., (Year). Title of document or page. [type of medium]. Website Address Locating details(eg. Breadcrumb) [Accessed date]

Jay, S. (2008) 'Good affiliates are just ahead of the curve' [Online blog], available at: http://www.thedigitalmarketingblog.co.uk/2008/02/index.html [accessed 12.3.08].

A recorded broadcast

Author, Initials, (Year). Title of document or page. [type of medium]. Locating details [Accessed date]

Anon (2007) 'The Edwardian Larder' [Television programme] BBC 4, [First Aired Monday 11 June 2007 10.50pm-11.50pm]

An annual report

Corporate author, (Year). *Full title of annual report*, Place of Publication: Publisher

Advertising Standards Authority (2006) ASA Annual Report, London: Advertising Standards Authority.

All references should be placed in alphabetical order. If you are referring to more than one source written by the same author, references should be listed in chronological order (earliest first).

6.1.3 How to work practically with Harvard Referencing

There are software packages available such as Endnote which can be used to file, sort, organise, insert within your text and automate your final reference list. Microsoft Word 2007 also now has referencing functionality which will do the same. Although these packages will make referencing appear easier, for the size of documents you will be working probably wouldn't warrant the investment. With this said, you will need to become highly organised as you read and start to make citations.

A few tips worth trying :

(1)   Create a separate master document in which you complete the full reference list style citation in table format as shown below as you refer to the source;

Author/Year	Reference
Kotler (1994)	Marketing Management: Analysis, Planning, Implementation and Control, Eighth Edition, Prentice Hall, New Jersey,
Hill, L. and O'Sullivan, T. (2004)	Foundation Marketing 3rd Edition, Prentice Hall, Oxford.
Anon (2007)	The Edwardian Larder' [Television programme] BBC 4, [First Aired Monday 11 June 10.50pm-11.50pm]
Jay, S.(2008)	*'Good affiliates are just ahead of the curve'* [Online blog], available at: http://www.thedigitalmarketingblog.co.uk/2008/02/index.html [accessed 12.3.08].

Open a blank table in a separate document which you call References for question x (the specific question you are working on), As you insert a citation into your work, copy and paste the reference from your master document.

When you have finished your answer, sort the table alphabetically, merge the cells, tweak any line breaks etc and make sure that you clear the border lines from around and within the table. The reference list below was formatted this way.

References

Anon (2007) The Edwardian Larder' [Television programme] BBC 4, [First Aired Monday 11 June 10.50pm-11.50pm]

Hill, L. and O'Sullivan, T. (2004) Foundation Marketing 3rd Edition, Prentice Hall, Oxford.

Jay, S.(2008) *'Good affiliates are just ahead of the curve'* [Online blog], available at: http://www.thedigitalmarketingblog.co.uk/2008/02/index.html [accessed 12.3.08].

Kotler (1994) Marketing Management: Analysis, Planning, Implementation and Control, Eighth Edition, Prentice Hall, New Jersey.

6.1.4 So what is the difference between a list of references and a bibliography?

A bibliography will include all items that you have read throughout your studies which have helped to shape your thinking to be able to answer a particular question. A reference list will include only those sources which you directly cite.

A bibliography should be placed directly after a reference list. This is not as relevant to your work and so you may wish to only use a list of references.

Useful online guides to referencing

Anglian Ruskin University (2008) '*Harvard System of Referencing Guide*' [Online] available at:
http://libweb.anglia.ac.uk/referencing/harvard.htm?harvard_id=40#40 [accessed 20.3.08].

Sheffield University (2008) '*Harvard Referencing Guide*' [Online] available at: http://www.shef.ac.uk/library/libdocs/hsl-dvc1.pdf [accessed on 20.3.08].

Professional Certificate in Marketing Assessment Workbook

Section 2
Marketing Essentials

Topic list

1 Unit overview and syllabus

1.1 Unit characteristics

The aim of this unit is to provide a detailed explanation of the key theories and practice behind marketing as an exchange process and a business function, but also as a means of creating customer value in the short to medium term. This unit introduces individuals to the importance of the marketing planning process and the role of marketing across the organisation.

The unit also aims to provide knowledge of the key marketing tools to support an innovative range of marketing activities. Students will be taught the nature and implications of the use of marketing tools as both independent tools and tools that are often integrated to maximise the impact of the marketing proposition.

On completion, students should be able to explain how to utilise all elements of the marketing mix and how they can be co-ordinated to create a value proposition that reflects the organisation's objectives.

1.2 Overarching learning outcomes

By the end of this unit, students should be able to:

- Explain how marketing has evolved and the importance of market orientation in creating customer value

- Assess the importance of marketing, its cross-functional role and the contribution it makes to the organisation and society

- Identify and explain the stages in the marketing planning process

- Assess the key elements of the internal and external marketing environment that impact upon the organisation, it objectives and its activities

- Identify and describe the characteristics and applications of each element of the marketing mix (7Ps)

SECTION 1 – The nature and scope of marketing (weighting 25%)

1.1	Explain the evolution of market orientation:
	• Product orientation
	• Production orientation
	• Sales orientation
	• Market versus marketing orientation
1.2	Assess the contribution of marketing as a means of:
	• Creating customer value
	• Creating and responding to competition
1.3	Appreciate the different characteristics of a market-oriented approach to business:
	• An exchange process
	• A philosophy of business
	• A managerial function
	• A dynamic operation, requiring analysis, planning and action
	• A catalyst for change

1.4 Identify and evaluate the factors that may make market orientation difficult to achieve within the organisation:

- Lack of committed leadership and vision
- Lack of customer knowledge
- Lack of infrastructure eg, technology
- Autocratic leadership
- Conflict between marketing and other functions
- Preference for production or sales focus
- Transactional approach to business

1.5 Explain the cross-functional role of marketing and its importance to organisational performance:

- The importance of internal relationships and information sharing
- The setting and achievement of common and realistic goals
- Establishing common information and control systems
- Establishing clear company policies in relation to products, branding,   production, etc
- The role of marketing as an internal service provider for other business   departments
- Contribution of marketing to the development of the business strategy

1.6 Evaluate the impact of marketing actions on consumers, society and the environment, and the need for marketers to act in an ethical and socially responsible manner:

- Ethical codes of practice for marketers (CIM Code of Practice)
- Corporate Social Responsibility as a cultural value
- Corporate citizenship – upholding the law and behaving responsibly
- Social awareness of key marketing issues relating to social causes
- Societal marketing

1.7 Explain the significance of buyer-seller relationships in marketing and comprehend the role of relationship marketing in facilitating the attraction and retention of customers:

- Benefits of customer retention
- Drawbacks of customer defection
- Relationship management in B2B and B2C
- The link between degrees of customer loyalty and long-term organisational stability and growth
- The role of technology in enhancing or undermining relationships and thereby affecting retention.

SECTION 2 – Planning within the marketing context (weighting 25%)

2.1 Explain the importance of objectives, the processes for setting them and the influences upon them:

- Objectives as a basis for determining future direction, consistency, motivation and measurement
- Objectives as a basis for determining achievement
- SMART Objectives (Specific, Measurable, Achievable, Realistic, Timebound)
- Internal and external influences on setting objectives

2.2 Identify the different types of organisational objectives:

- Profit
- Sales/Revenue
- Marketing
- Growth e.g. market share
- Technical – technology innovation
- Survival
- Ethically and socially responsible

2.3 Evaluate the importance of the marketing planning process to the market   oriented organisation. Using a marketing plan as a means of:

- Delivering strategies and achieving objectives
- Implementing a marketing project
- Monitoring of timeline progress against schedule
- Managing implementation
- Resource management (human and physical)
- Financial management
- Measurement of successful implementation

2.4 Explain the different stages of the marketing planning process:

- Corporate objectives/business mission
- Marketing audit
- Setting business and marketing objectives
- Marketing strategies
- Marketing tactics/mix decisions
- Implementation
- Monitoring and control

2.5 Explain the concept of the marketing audit as an appraisal of:

- The internal and external environment
- Organisational strengths, weaknesses, opportunities and threats
- Organisational competencies and capabilities
- Organisational resource versus an organisation's capacity to deliver
- Competitor analysis

SECTION 3 – The marketing mix (weighting 50%)

3.1 Explain and illustrate the principles of product and planning:

- Branding
- Product lines/ranges (depth and breadth)
- Packaging eg, sustainability, design eg, re-cyclying
- Service support

3.2 Explain the concept of the Product Life Cycle, (PLC) and its limitations as a tool for assessing the life of the product/services:

- Development
- Introduction
- Growth
- Maturity
- Decline
- Obsolescence
- Limitations including failure of the product to succeed/no measurable outcome

3.3 Explain the importance of new products and services into the market:

- Changing customer needs
- Digital revolution
- Long-term business strategies

3.4 Explain the different stages of the process of New Product Development:

- Idea generation
- Screening new ideas
- Concept testing
- Business analysis
- Product development
- Test marketing
- Commercialisation and launch

3.5 Explain the importance of price as an element of the marketing mix:

- Brings together the marketing mix elements to fulfil customer needs
- Income, revenue and profit generation
- Contributing to the organisation's business and financial objectives
- Limitations of price as a competitive tool

3.6 Identify and illustrate a range of different pricing approaches that are adopted by organisations as effective means of competition:

- Absorption costing
- Cost base and marginal costing
- Cost Plus
- Price skimming
- Penetration pricing
- Loss-leader
- Promotional pricing

3.7 Define the different channels of distribution, and the role they play in a coordinated marketing mix:

- Wholesaling
- Retailing
- Direct marketing
- Internet marketing
- Vending
- Telephone selling
- Franchising
- Digital/e-channels

3.8 Explain the factors that influence channel decisions and the selection of alternative distribution channels:

- Multiple channels
- Location of customers
- Compatibility
- Nature of the goods/services
- Geographic/environmental/terrain
- Storage and distribution costs
- Import/export costs

3.9 Evaluate a range of marketing communications tools that comprise the marketing communications mix and consider their impact in different contexts:

- Direct Response Advertising
- Personal selling
- Sponsorship
- Public relations
- Direct marketing
- Sales promotions
- Digital technologies
- Website

3.10 Evaluate the range of marketing communications media and consider their impact in different contexts:

- TV
- Cinema
- Bill Boards
- Press
- Magazine
- Web-advertising
- Sales promotions

3.11 Explain the importance of a coordinated services marketing mix, its characteristics and implications for the marketing of service products:

- Coordinated approach to people, physical evidence and process
- Characteristics/implications: inseparability, intangibility, variability, perishability and non-ownership

3.12 Explain the different methods used for measuring the success of marketing activities:

- Budget measurement
- Objectives attained
- Sales/revenue, profit/loss
- Efficiency/effectiveness
- Zero defects/returns
- Customer service complaints
- Increased awareness and changing attitudes
- Repeat purchase and loyalty

3.13 Explain the process of product and service adoption explaining the characteristics of customers at each stage of adoption:

- Innovators
- Early Adopters
- Early majority
- Late majority
- Laggards

3.14 Explain the concept of developing a coordinated approach to the marketing mix, as a means to satisfying customers' requirements and competing effectively:

- Designing a mix which is compatible and co-ordinated effectively
- Being mindful of the target market, their needs and expectations
- Being mindful of tactical competitive activities
- Being mindful of the impact of other elements of the marketing mix

2 The Exam Paper

The CIM have outlined the format for this new paper;

Unit 1 – Marketing Essentials: 3 hour examination comprising:

- **Part A worth 40%:** ten short questions of four marks each used to test knowledge and understanding across the syllabus

- **Part B worth 60%**: Case study with three questions requiring extended answers and testing knowledge, understanding, application and evaluation

- **All questions are compulsory**

3 Tackling the specimen paper

To begin, start to look at the specimen paper. We will then provide you with some answers written by us for you to review how they are constructed and the level of detail that is expected from you by the examiners. Along the way we will point out relevant exam tips.

3.1 The specimen paper

Part A

ALL TASKS ARE COMPULSORY (40% weighting)

Task One

Outline the evolution of market orientation. (4 marks)

(Syllabus area 1.1)

Task Two

Identify and explain **FOUR** factors that might restrict the implementation of marketing orientation within an organisation.

(4 marks)

(Syllabus area 1.4)

Task Three

Describe **FOUR** ways in which marketing acts as a co-ordinating function in an organisation. (4 marks)

(Syllabus area 1.5)

Task Four

Explain how the marketing audit is used in the planning process. (4 marks)

(Syllabus area 2.5)

Task Five

Identify **FOUR** limitations of the product lifecycle concept. (4 marks)

(Syllabus area 3.2)

Task Six

Briefly define relationship marketing and identify **THREE** benefits of relationship marketing to an organisation. (4 marks)

(Syllabus area 7.1)

Task Seven

Highlight the differences between an organisation that is **product-oriented** with an organisation that is **marketing-oriented**, using examples to illustrate your points. (4 marks)

(Syllabus Reference 1.1)

Task Eight

Briefly explain the different stages of the process for new product development (NPD). (4 marks)
(Syllabus Reference 3.4)

Task Nine

Explain the differences between **price skimming** and **penetration pricing**, using examples to illustrate your points.

(4 marks)

(Syllabus Reference 3.6)

Task Ten

Your employer is a producer of sports equipment. Use examples from this business to explain **TWO** factors that might influence the setting of the organisation's marketing objectives. (4 marks)

(Syllabus area 2.1)

PART B – CASE STUDY

ALL TASKS ARE COMPULSORY (605 weighting)

Virgin Galactic

In October 2005, a new record was set. SpaceShipOne, a privately-funded re-useable spacecraft, entered space for the second time inside a week, and in so doing won the Ansari X prize of $10 million. This was not a particularly profitable venture – the backer, Microsoft co-founder Paul Allen, had reputedly spent $20 million on the development of the spacecraft. Aviation pioneer Burt Rutan, whose company designed and built the craft, believed that the craft would open the door to space tourism.

Richard Branson, founder of the airline Virgin Atlantic, agreed, and has set up a company called Virgin Galactic, offering space travel. He contracted Rutan to start work on a larger, passenger-carrying version of the spacecraft, and placed an order for five of these to be delivered by 2010. He also announced that flights on the spacecraft would cost around $200,000, and began to accept deposits from prospective passengers. In January 2008 the final design for the spacecraft was unveiled, and Branson announced that 200 people had already paid deposits, and a further 85,000 had registered an interest in travelling into space.

Flights are expected to start in 2010: six passengers and two pilots will blast off for a two-and-a-half-hour ride into space. At $200,000 per ticket the flight is hardly cheap, but it is still within the reach of quite a large number of people – and it is certainly the trip of a lifetime! It is also substantially cheaper than the $20 million currently being charged by the Russian Space Agency for trips to the International Space Station.

The flight cannot take place without a spaceport. New Mexico, in the USA, is the chosen place for this: local residents have voted for a 0.25% increase in sales taxes to fund the building of Spaceport America, presumably with a view to the long-term economic gains for the state. The chosen site already has a NASA testing facility, and was part of the test area for the first atom bomb.

Other entrepreneurs are looking to get involved in space tourism. Amazon.com founder Jeff Bezos has his own scheme, as has the Paypal founder, Elon Musk. Richard Branson believes that a commercial success with space flight could unlock huge investments, on the scale of those in the mobile telephone or Internet markets. Branson is, at present, by far the best known of the entrepreneurs involved.

People will not be able simply to turn up at Spaceport America and fly. Virgin Galactic will provide each prospective astronaut with three days' training, including atmosphere flights in a simulated spaceship, and will accommodate the astronauts in the comfort to which most of them will be accustomed. They will have to undergo medical checks, although Virgin Galactic do not believe that many people would fail the medical, and there will of course be an opportunity for a celebration when they return to earth.

In the longer term, as competitors enter the market, the price of tickets will probably fall considerably. At present, Branson and Virgin Galactic have the lead over the others, and since they have sole rights to SpaceShipTwo (and Rutan's other designs) they should be able to maintain a technical lead for some time to come.

The above data has been based on a real-life situation, but details have been changed for assessment purposes and may not be an accurate reflection of reported news.

Tasks

You are to assume the role of a Marketing Assistant for Virgin Galactic. Produce a report for your Marketing Manager that addresses the following tasks.

Task One

Identify and explain **FIVE** ways in which Virgin Galactic can add value to the customer experience. (15 marks)

(Syllabus area 1.2)

Task Two

Evaluate the importance of the marketing planning process to Virgin Galactic and how this will help them to achieve the company's objectives. (20 marks)

(Syllabus areas 2.2, 2.3, 2.4)

Task Three

Explain the importance of a co-ordinated services marketing mix (7Ps), its characteristics and implications for Virgin Galactic's marketing of space travel. (25 marks)

(Syllabus areas 3.3, 3.5, 3.6, 3.9, and 3.13)

(Total 60 marks)

3.2 Example answers to Part A Short Questions

Task One

Outline the evolution of market orientation. (4 marks)

The historical trend has been for organisations to move from a focus on producing as much as possible to a focus on producing what the market actually wants. In other words, organisations have become increasingly market oriented. The stages of development are as follows:

The emphasis with a production orientation is upon making products that are affordable and available – efficiency of production processes is the key. This usually prevails in conditions where demand exceeds supply.

A product orientation is found in an organisation which concentrates on the product itself. It takes the view that if the product is right it will sell itself. There are also still many companies that have a product orientation, based on the notion that because an idea looks good to the producer it will satisfy the customer.

A sales orientation is found in an organisation where the selling function is dominant. It is typically found where capacity exceeds demand and where the organisational aim is to sell what it makes, rather than what the market wants. Underlying this philosophy is a belief that a good sales force can sell just about anything to anybody, and that sales 'transactions' rather than customer 'relationships' are the key to business success.

Arriving at a marketing orientation, we find organisations that place a priority upon determining what customers want, and then setting about providing those goods or services which meet customers' wants and needs.

It is worth noting that the total marketing concept may not necessarily represent a real shift in philosophy. Perhaps it simply reflects the fact that the business environment is now much more sophisticated, as are consumers, with more information, better education and greater expectations. The growth of the organic food market provides one such example. It could be argued that so-called 'modern marketing techniques' are the same old process of persuasion, more cleverly disguised.

(Syllabus area 1.1)

 EXAM TIP concept

This is a very full answer but it gives the key features of each orientation and follows the requirements of the question in that it presents the marketing orientation as the 'ultimate' orientation, while making it clear that the other orientations can still be found. The question in the final paragraph as to whether or not there has actually been a shift in philosophy is an interesting one.

Task Two

Identify and explain FOUR factors that might restrict the implementation of marketing orientation within an organisation. (4 marks)

The organisation should understand that major organisational, structural and cultural changes will be required. The organisation will have to consider the four Ps, with the customers' needs as the priority – if this is absent, a market orientation is difficult to achieve.

(1) Problems may arise within the *structure* of the company. Sales and product oriented firms do not require the same degree of 'working together' as a marketing oriented company. Conflict between various functions will also inhibit the ability to work effectively together.

(2) When progressing to marketing orientation, *effective communication* is vital to prevent confusion and provide reassurance. The various operating divisions and departments of the Organic Food Company, for example, need to communicate well on such issues as stock levels, customer service, competitor activity and product development.

(3) The necessary *infrastructure* needs to be in place. Problems will arise if senior managers do not commit to a marketing philosophy and build it into their systems and culture. Commitment and vision from management will filter down to other staff.

(4) Reinforcement is needed through *HR policies*: staff recruitment, training, appraisal and reward systems. Otherwise, changing to a market oriented organisation is not possible.

Without care, a marketing orientation itself can have adverse consequences.

- Organisations may develop a bias that favours marketing activities at the expense of production and technical improvements which could offer a more appealing product.

- Focusing new product development on satisfying immediate customer perceptions of what is needed can stifle innovation. Organisations should devote at least some of their expertise to *future* customer requirements.

(Syllabus area 1.4)

  EXAM TIP   concept

This answer concentrates upon structural, cultural/communications, managerial and staffing factors that can be a barrier to the establishment of a marketing orientation.

Task Three

Describe FOUR ways in which marketing acts as a co-ordinating function in an organisation. (4 marks)

In order to implement the marketing concept, market-orientated companies need proper co-ordination between market needs, production decisions and financial control. That requires good cross functional communication between marketing and the people responsible for development, design and manufacturing, and finance. Relationships with other departments need to be developed and managed to ensure that all departments are working towards the same overall goal.

Although every organisation is different, common patterns appear in the structure of organisations. Marketing departments have often evolved from sales departments. In traditional sales or production orientated organisations, marketplace issues were the responsibility of a sales director reporting to senior management. With fuller recognition of the marketing approach to business, sales and marketing may become a single department, with sales as a sub-group within marketing.

Marketing managers have to take responsibility for planning, resource allocation, monitoring and controlling the marketing effort, but it can also be claimed that marketing involves every facet of the organisation's operations. If the philosophy of a market orientation is regarded as a prerequisite for success, the marketing department naturally becomes the main co-ordinator, maintaining relationships and ensuring that all relevant information is shared with whoever else in the organisation might legitimately need it.

Extreme care should be taken not to understate the role of finance, production, personnel and other business functions. To reduce the potential for conflict, senior management should ensure that departmental heads have clear instructions as to the organisation's goals.

(Syllabus area 1.5)

EXAM TIP

Bear in mind that in the truly market-oriented organisation, marketing is not an activity that can be pigeon-holed as the responsibility of the marketing department. All of the company's activities must be co-ordinated around the needs of the customer, and policies enforced. That is the main theme behind this question and an important syllabus topic.

Task Four

Explain how the marketing audit is used in the planning process. (4 marks)

A marketing audit is a systematic and comprehensive review of a firm's current marketing activities and capacity, used in marketing planning. It performs a dual role in checking both where the company is, and where it has come from.

In order to exercise proper strategic control a marketing audit should satisfy four requirements.

- It should take a comprehensive look at every product, market, distribution channel and ingredient in the marketing mix.

- It should not be restricted to areas of apparent ineffectiveness such as an unprofitable product or a troublesome distribution channel.

- It should be carried out according to a set of predetermined, specified procedures.

- It should be conducted regularly, usually on an annual basis.

A marketing audit will evaluate six aspects of marketing: environment, strategy, organisation, systems, productivity and functions.

The marketing audit should look at both the organisation's micro environment and its macro environment (PEST factors).

(Syllabus area 2.5)

EXAM TIP

The short answer is that the marketing audit 'kicks off' the whole marketing planning process.

Task Five

Identify **FOUR** limitations of the product lifecycle concept. (4 marks)

Criticisms of the practical value of the product life cycle include the following.

(a)   The stages cannot be easily defined.

(b)   The traditional bell-shaped curve of a product life cycle does not always occur in practice. Some products have no maturity phase, and go straight from growth to decline. Others have a second growth period after an initial decline. Some have virtually no introductory period and go straight into a rapid growth phase, while others (the vast majority of new products in fact) do not succeed at all.

(c)   Strategic decisions can change a product's life cycle: for example, by repositioning a product in the market, its life can be extended. If strategic planners 'decide' what a product's life is going to be, opportunities to extend the life cycle might be ignored.

(d)   Competition varies in different industries and the strategic implications of the product life cycle will vary according to the nature of the competition. The 'traditional' life cycle presupposes increasing competition and falling prices during the growth phase of the market and also the gradual elimination of competitors in the decline phase. This pattern of events is not always true.

(Syllabus area 3.2)

Apart from the stages of the product life cycle, this is probably the main question that could be asked in Part A of this paper regarding this particular model.

Task Six

Briefly define relationship marketing and identify **THREE** benefits of relationship marketing to an organisation. (4 marks)

Relationship marketing is the process of creating, building up and managing long-term relationships with customers, distributors and suppliers through two-way communication. It aims to change the focus from getting customers to keeping customers. In a relationship approach, a sale is not the end of a process but the start of an organisation's relationship with a customer. Its features are:

- Focus on customer retention
- Focus upon product benefits
- Long timescale
- High customer service
- High customer commitment
- High customer contact
- Quality is the concern of the whole organisation

Many firms have begun the move towards proactive relationships – even in consumer markets – in order to build customers' loyalty to the brand and cross-sell related products. The lifetime value of a customer to a company can be measured in terms of revenue and profits. Existing, loyal customers are valuable because:

- They do not have to be acquired, or cost less to acquire
- They buy a broader range of products
- They cost less to service as they are familiar with the company's ways of doing business
- They become less sensitive to price over time
- They can recommend by word of mouth to others

(Syllabus area 1.7)

  EXAM TIP

concept

Note that the main justification for relationship marketing comes from the need to retain customers. It has been estimated that the cost of attracting a new customer may be five times the cost of keeping a current customer happy.

Task Seven

Highlight the differences between an organisation that is product-oriented with an organisation that is marketing-oriented, using examples to illustrate your points. (4 marks)

Concept	Focus	Means	Aims
Marketing orientation	Customer needs and wants; long-term customer relationships	Integrated marketing activities	Profitability through customer satisfaction
Product orientation	Assumed customer demand for product quality, performance and features	Continuous product improvements	Profitability through product quality

Using the example of the Organic Food Company, a product orientation would see the company relying solely upon its products' reputation and quality to sell more of its existing range, rather than finding out what products the customers actually want and making and selling those.

(Syllabus area 1.1)

 EXAM TIP

concept

Many companies continue to believe that if the product is right, it will sell itself. For some sectors this might hold true, but if a competing product arrives that 'does the job' better, the market for old models will disappear.

Task Eight

Briefly explain the different stages of the process for new product development (NPD). (4 marks)

The stages of the NPD process are as follows:

The concept for the new product should be tested on potential customers to obtain their reactions

A thorough business analysis is required for each product idea, projecting future sales and revenues, giving a description of the product so as to provide costs of production, providing estimates of sales promotion and advertising costs, the resources required, profits and return on investment.

Money is invested to produce a working prototype of the product, which can be tried by customers. This stage ensures that the product can be produced in sufficient quantities at the right price.

The purpose of test marketing is to obtain information about how consumers react to the product. Will they buy it, and if so, will they buy it again? With this information an estimate of total market demand for the product can be made.

Finally the product is developed for full launch. This involves ensuring that the product is in the right place at the right time, and that customers know about it.

(Syllabus area 3.4)

 EXAM TIP

concept

This process is important for maintaining customer satisfaction through change; refreshing or extending the product range; and adapting to environmental opportunities and threats. These will all contribute towards the success of a company's long term business strategy.

Task Nine

Explain the differences between price skimming and penetration pricing, using examples to illustrate your points.(4 marks)

Price skimming involves setting a high initial price for a new product (in order to take advantage of those buyers prepared to pay a high price for innovation) and then gradually reducing the price (to attract more price sensitive segments of the market).

This strategy is an example of price discrimination over time and is favoured in the following situations.

- Insufficient market capacity, and competitors cannot increase capacity

- Buyers are relatively insensitive to price increases (for example, the organic food market is regarded as dominated by consumers who are prepared to pay a premium price)

- High price perceived as high quality

This is the opposite of penetration pricing. Penetration pricing is pricing a new product low in order to maximise market penetration before competitors can enter the market. The organisation sets a relatively low price for the product or service, to maximise sales by stimulating growth of the market and/or obtaining a larger share of it. This strategy was used by Japanese motor cycle manufacturers, for example, to enter the UK market. It worked! UK productive capacity was virtually eliminated and the imported Japanese machines could later be sold at a much higher price and still dominate the market.

(Syllabus area 3.6)

  EXAM TIP concept

Companies may undertake any of a variety of pricing strategies, depending on their objectives and the industry they operate in. Pricing strategies can be used to pursue a number of marketing objectives.

Task Ten

Your employer is a producer of sports equipment. Use examples from this business to explain TWO factors that might influence the setting of the organisation's marketing objectives.(4 marks)

Objectives can be defined as goals which (usually) can be quantified ("increase profits by 30% over the next 12 months"). They might not always be expressed in financial terms (eg, customer satisfaction or loyalty). Objective setting is a key part of marketing planning. Objectives should set out clearly what the organisation is aiming to achieve, both at the corporate level and at the marketing level.

Marketing objectives may involve targets for the size of the customer base, growth in the usage of certain facilities, gains in market share for a particular product type etc. Marketing objectives will be influenced by a range of factors including:

The strategic objectives of the business as a whole (eg growth, product innovation using sports technology)

The resources (skills, competences, finance, relationships) available

Marketing strategy decisions, eg cost leadership (being the cheapest) or differentiation (having a unique product); how to place the product within the sports equipment market (product/market strategy)

Other functional strategies that need to be aligned with marketing (eg research and development to support marketing activity)

The competitive environment in the industry or specific competitor activity (eg some competitors may introduce new products in the wake of the Beijing Olympics)

Environmental (PEST) factors .

If such factors are taken into account, objectives are more likely to be relevant (to the needs and challenges of the business) and realistic.

(Syllabus area 2.1)

  EXAM TIP

format

Note that the question required only TWO examples. Remember too the influence of SMART criteria when setting objectives.

3.3 Part B – Case Study suggested answers

Task One

  EXAM TIP

concept

'Adding value to the customer experience' is an important aspect of the *Marketing Essentials* syllabus. The creation of customer value is what distinguishes an organisation with a marketing orientation from one that is stuck with a product or sales focus: it uses its marketing expertise to enhance its customers' experience, and its own success. This answer makes use of the 7C's model and gives seven ways that VG can add value – you only need to include five in your answer.

REPORT

To: Marketing Manager

From: Marketing Assistant

Date: December 20X8

The marketing function at Virgin Galactic (VG) must make sure that potential travellers value the organisation and what it has to offer. Each potential customer must be made to realise that VG is currently the best-placed organisation for commercial space travel, at a price that customers are prepared to pay, in a place that is convenient.

Some organisations have realised that they need to shift from the traditional 'P-focus' of the marketing mix, to a 'C-focus' (that is, customer-focused). A new marketing model (called the '7Cs') could look like this when applied to VG.

Ways in which VG 'adds value' to the customer experience

- By giving them a service that satisfies their travel needs better (who else can offer space travel at the present time?). This is called the '**customer solution'**. VG can offer state-of-the-art facilities as it has sole rights to SpaceShipTwo – this gives the company a considerable technical head start on the competition.

- By providing that solution at a competitive **cost**. This will be more relevant in the future as currently VG can charge premium prices, given that its service is further along in development than the competition, and the involvement of Richard Branson lends it great credibility. When more competitors enter the market, fares are likely to fall.

- By **communicating** the 'solution', and what it involves, clearly and comprehensively

- By offering the service in a **convenient location** – New Mexico has been chosen as the site for the spaceport, as this has some of the necessary infrastructure already in place, and the USA is easy to get to for most of the customers who would be involved

- By making sure that the people involved in the delivery of the service are capable of performing that delivery to very high standards (given that potential customers are very likely to be accustomed to a high standard in most aspects of their daily lives). This is called '**customer consideration'**. This is a very niche market, with a small volume of very high value transactions, and so the process of servicing the customer has an extremely high profile.

- By **co-ordinating** the entire experience, from initial interest and payment of a deposit to the space flight itself and any after-parties – people will not simply turn up and fly. Amongst other services they will need training, a very high standard of accommodation, and medical checks. This aspect of the experience may have to be sensitively managed as the training may be rigorous.

- By **confirming** that potential astronauts are on the programme – many deposits have been taken and these customers will need regular communication and updates on the status of their booking and the likely date of their flight.

Task Two

  EXAM TIP   concept

The first part of the question requires you to explain the benefits of the marketing planning process in the context of Virgin Galactic. As such the answer should have identified all of the steps of the marketing planning process: addressing controllables and responding to external environment; the relationship with corporate and business objectives; SWOT analysis; marketing strategies planned to achieve objectives; identification of segments and positioning for the unique service; marketing tactics/mix decisions developed; the plan should be monitored and controlled and fed back into next year's plan. Make sure that you consider the importance of undertaking each stage.

To: Marketing Manager, Virgin Galactic

From: Marketing Assistant

Date: Dec 20X8

Importance of the marketing planning process

A marketing plan is a specification of all aspects of an organisation's marketing intentions and activities. It is a summary document, providing a framework that permits managers and specialists to undertake the detailed work of marketing in a co-ordinated and effective fashion.

The creation of a good marketing plan is likely to be a time-consuming exercise, since it should deal wit both current circumstances and plans for the future.

(a)   It should be based on detailed knowledge of both the target market (a select few very wealthy individuals!) and the company.

(b)   It should give sufficient detail of intentions to support the design and operation of all marketing-related activities.

Planning enables organisations to be effective, not just efficient. Information is gathered and used to develop a corporate plan which acts as a framework within which specific functions such as marketing can develop their own objectives and plans.

The benefits of using such a plan at Virgin Galactic are detailed below at each stage of the marketing planning process:

1.0 *Mission Statement/Corporate Objectives*

This involves the statement to customers about your promise to them, and objectives as a company. This could involve 'Be the first in space!' or 'Unsurpassed luxury and comfort for the discerning space traveller'. This communicates to your customers that you are committed to these issues as a philosophy for the company.

2.0 *Marketing Audit*

This involves looking at the changes in the macro environment, Political, Economic, Social and Technological issues. This is beneficial for developing a marketing strategy for what is a highly unique and innovative service: technological investment will be at the forefront of the corporate strategy, and the marketing of these unique space flights may choose to focus upon the amazing technology that has brought space travel to the 'ordinary' man. The marketing audit also requires a company to research internally as well as externally – thus an internal audit of the current marketing practices is required.

3.0 *SWOT Analysis*

This involves considering Virgin Galactic's internal strengths and weaknesses, and external opportunities and threats. It is like a prioritised summary of the marketing audit.

4.0 *Business Objectives*

These include objectives for the future, such as investment in more spacecraft or the development of linked services. This will encourage the company to monitor and achieve these objectives.

5.0 *Marketing Objectives*

These include marketing objectives such as objectives relating to market share, passenger numbers, advance bookings and the profitability of what is a huge investment. The benefit here is that this objective can be evaluated on an annual basis, and this will help in terms of deciding to change (where necessary) the strategy and tactics to achieve objectives.

6.0 *Marketing Tactics*

This involves the application of the marketing mix to determine the strategy to be used. Consideration therefore of price, product, place, promotion, people, physical evidence and processes is important. This is a unique service and will need a unique marketing approach.

7.0 *Marketing budget*

Marketing expenditure will depend on resource allocation decisions at corporate level, but any marketing plan will include, as a matter of course, a statement of the budget required and the way it is to be spent. Quantified monetary plans will be vital for such a capital intensive project: sales/revenue forecasts, costs/expenditure budgets, forecast profit and loss statements. Also covered here is the allocation of other resources such as time, staff and assets.

8.0 *Timetable for implementation*

Detailed timescales for implementation of plans

9.0 *Monitoring and control*

Once the marketing plan is implemented, the task of management is to monitor and control what happens. Monitoring means checking that everything is going to plan. Control means taking corrective action as early as possible if things are not going to plan. Progress and results will be monitored, reviewed and measured against objectives and the budget.

Task Three

 EXAM TIP

application

This is quite a comprehensive answer which has included all of the characteristics of services. The answer has been contextualised and references to Virgin Galactic have been included throughout. The answer highlights the key extended mix elements and highlights not only some of ways in which VG should address these areas, but also the problems if they do not.

REPORT

To: Marketing Manager

From: Marketing Assistant

Date: December 20X8

This report highlights the characteristics of services, their implications for the marketing of space travel and the importance of the extended marketing mix.

Characteristics and implications of service provision

There are five characteristics of a service, which are described below:

- Perishability. A service cannot be stored or saved. It has an immediacy that cannot be held over until sometime in the future. The space flight that the customer is paying for takes place, and is over. If seats on the space flight are not consumed, they 'perish'. They cannot be used later. They cannot be 'produced' in advance, to allow for peaks in demand.

This presents specific marketing problems. Meeting customer needs depends on staff being available as and when they are needed. Anticipating and responding to levels of demand is, therefore, a key planning priority for Virgin Galactic, in order to avoid:

- Inadequate level of demand accompanied by substantial variable and fixed costs

- Excess demand resulting in lost custom through inadequate service provision

- Intangibility. You cannot touch or feel the service offering as it has an abstract delivery. Unlike a product which you can touch (and smell and see) a service has no physical presence. This can give problems since customers can only make a judgement based on experience. As it is very likely to be their only space flight (due to limitations of cost and the fact that the waiting list may stretch months or even years into the future) then Virgin Galactic needs to make the experience tangible with luxury additions to the service: a special photograph, a party at the end, other types of high-end souvenir.

Dealing with intangibility may therefore involve the following.

- Increasing the level of tangibility. Use physical or conceptual representations/illustrations to make the customer feel more confident as to what it is that the service is delivering: the 'physical evidences' component of the extended marketing mix.

- Focusing the attention of the customer on the principal benefits of consumption. Communicate the benefits of purchasing the space flight, so that the customer visualises its use and feels that it is less 'risky'. Promotion and sales material could provide images or records of previous customers' experience.

- Differentiating the service and reputation-building. Enhance perceptions of customer service and customer value by offering excellence in the delivery of the service. This reputation can be easily attached to the Virgin brand.

- Inseparability. Services often cannot be separated from the provider. Think of having dental treatment or taking a space journey. Neither exists until they are actually being experienced/consumed by the person who has bought them. The customer has to be present for the service to take place.

Space travel customers are likely to be very demanding individuals, used to the best of everything, and Virgin Galactic will only have one chance to impress them. This points up the need for excellence and customer orientation, and the need to invest in high quality people and high quality training: the 'people' component of the extended marketing mix.

- Heterogeneity. The delivery of the service will vary each time to the customer. This is because a service is dependent on the unique interaction of the provider and the customer which will vary depending on the interaction between the two individuals. The variability is created by the influence of human behaviour in the transaction, and consistency can become a difficult problem to manage. In terms of marketing policy, heterogeneity highlights the need to develop and maintain processes for:

- Consistency of quality control, with clear and objective quality measures

- Consistency of customer service and customer care

- Effective staff selection, training and motivation

- Monitoring service levels and customer perceptions of service delivery

- Non-ownership. Ownership of a service remains with the provider. The traveller does not take SpaceShipTwo home with him. There are two basic approaches to addressing this problem.

- Promote the advantages of non-ownership, although not many people would expect to own a space rocket!

- Make available a tangible symbol or representation of ownership such as a certificate, voucher or luxury merchandise item (maybe a quality scale replica of the spacecraft). This can come to embody the benefits enjoyed.

The Extended Marketing Mix

The extended marketing mix is comprised of People, Process and Physical Evidence

- People. There should be a strong emphasis on staff training to ensure a consistently high quality of provision. This can include such areas as personal presentation, dealing with enquiries, providing quotations and maintaining technical competencies in line with current developments.

- Physical Evidence. The image of Virgin Galactic, and any correspondence that is sent out in response to enquiries, including from the website, needs to be consistent and include company brand identity such as the famous Virgin logo. The service can be presented in tangible (and promotional) physical form: consider how travel tickets could be presented in branded envelopes (or more sophisticated document wallets), with vouchers for added services, information leaflets and other added value elements – despite the fact that all the customer has purchased is the promise of a future benefit.

Note that physical evidence can be used as a marketing communications tool: staff uniforms, interior decoration, tidiness and signage should reflect a common and consistent quality image. All promotional literature and website content should be regularly updated to provide the latest technological developments and current thinking on space travel.

- Process. As part of customer service, efficient administrative processes underpin a high quality of provision. The level and quality of service which is available to customers of Virgin Galactic is especially sensitive. Process issues include the following.

Capacity utilisation: matching resource/staff utilisation to anticipated demand, to avoid delays and bottlenecks
Managing customer contacts and expectations: keeping people realistically informed and empowering staff to respond to changing needs.

3.4 Part A- Short Question Practice

As there are currently few practice questions available, we developed our own practice examination questions for you to try. These are written along the same lines as the specimen paper and within the examination format you will encounter.

To try to be realistic, we have written the answers with an organisation in mind, the following case study is used as an example to highlight answers. In section 1 we highlighted the importance of creating a company background for your own organisation. Although you are not expected to recreate this in the exam, it is useful for you to read our version of a background so you can see how we integrate our knowledge of a real scenario into our answers.

Company background

Case Study - The Organic Food Company

Background

The production and retailing of organic foods is a growing area. Under European Community (EC) law, an authorised body must rigorously inspect the production of food that can be marketed and sold as organic.

The organic food market in the UK is worth about £1 billion, reflecting concerns over genetically-modified (GM) foods and other scares over food safety. Organic foods are believed to contain higher levels of vitamin C and essential minerals. Major supermarkets now stock organic lines, and there is some evidence that the demand for organic products is increasing at a faster rate than UK growers can currently supply. It takes time to convert land to organic practices, and some farmers are reluctant to invest the time and money in what they see as a passing fad. Indeed it is forecast that organic produce will remain a market sector only in rich countries, to meet the demands of those consumers who are prepared to pay a premium.

The Organic Food Company

The Organic Food Company was established by two environmentally conscious former supermarket managers, and started trading in April 2005. It bulk buys organic produce from a range of suppliers, and retails organic produce grown in the UK and overseas. It procures its overseas-grown produce from a number of organic wholesalers. It has established business links with organic farms and organic dairies, and a fast-expanding customer base.

The company is continuously expanding not only the product range, but also the range of routes to the market for organic produce. These currently include selling through the Internet and opening shops in key cities, as well as more traditional routes such as its mail order business and selling at local markets. With the growing availability of organic food in supermarkets, the latter is becoming less profitable, even though it is a good way of promoting the mail order business.

The company has maintained its high reputation as a quality producer and the perception by its customers is that the company is one of the leading producers and distributors of organic produce.

Aside from the large supermarkets, there are a number of small, mainly local companies, selling organic produce, as well as a small number of similar Internet and mail-order businesses operating in the UK and Europe.

The challenges facing The Organic Food Company are twofold.

- To have attractive products that are competitively priced
- To have different routes to the market, in order to retain customers in the face of the supermarket threat

The company has a loyalty scheme to retain its customers, offering them discounts for introducing new customers. The company's loyalty scheme also entitles customers to discounts as their cumulative order value increases during each calendar year.

The mail order business

Due to the growth in demand and healthy sales, The Organic Food Company has generally achieved around only 90% of despatches on time. It has always had difficulties keeping up with its growing customer base and the problems of recruiting staff to meet increases in demand. The threat to customer satisfaction levels is obvious, and the company has recently recruited a customer service manager.

Internet trading

The Organic Food Company appointed a local IT company and set up a website in mid-2007 which would allow customers to view the ranges and prices of products available and to order on-line.

When The Organic Food Company started Internet trading in December 2007, it had not expected a high level of demand and was taken by surprise. In the first three weeks in December, Internet orders equalled those of the preceding six months. This success has continued into 2008 but there is some evidence that the website in its current form is struggling to cope with the level of orders.

The Organic Food Company shops

During early 2007, the first Organic Food Company shop was opened in the suburbs of a major city. A second shop was opened in February 2008. Despite attracting a number of regular customers, turnover has been slower than anticipated and the first shop is not forecast to break even until the end of 2008. This is due to the relatively high rent and staff costs. Additionally, the level of waste has increased at the shops due to the short shelf life of some products. The shops manager has spent the agreed marketing budget on promoting and launching the shops, but is adamant that he needs to undertake more meticulously planned marketing activity.

Product range and suppliers

Market research has identified that an increasing number of new customers are purchasing organic produce for the first time, and that they want to be able to purchase not only the produce itself but also ranges of prepared meals, bottled sauces and other organic produce such as fresh bread. A product development manager is responsible for selecting, preparing and trialling recipes. A range of organic wines was introduced in late 2006 and these have proved popular with regular customers and achieve a gross margin of over 40%.

The Organic Food Company's team of suppliers includes 150 organic food producers, several food preparation companies and bulk manufacturers. The Organic Food Company has always worked closely with all of its suppliers, and the company has especially close links with the key farmers who supply 100% of their produce to The Organic Food Company.

First supermarket order

In February 2007, The Organic Food Company signed its first contract to regularly sell some of its bottled own brand packaged goods to one of the large UK supermarket chains. The brand name of The Organic Food Company was starting to get really well established, and all of the Directors agreed that this was a good opportunity, especially as it would increase demand for other products by customers who liked the limited range that had been contracted for by the supermarket.

The supermarket chain was not prepared to negotiate terms at all with The Organic Food Company and simply treated it as another of its many suppliers and imposed its standard terms.

Expansion plans

At the end of 2007, The Organic Food Company employed 265 full-time employees and up to 50 part-time staff on a temporary basis to meet peak demand, particularly at busy times such as Christmas. It had a customer base of over 40,000 customers, with an average order value of £80. The customer service manager is considering putting together a customer service plan that will focus upon customer retention, aware that a number of other organic retailers are now offering Internet-based retailing.

With the increase in the volume of orders from the Internet business, the company has almost outgrown its warehouse and distribution centres. It operates from four different rented sites, all geographically close, with around 95% of its prepared organic foods sub-contracted to a variety of food manufacturers.

The company is planning to move to a large purpose-built site on the edge of a major city during 2008 that will accommodate all of the company's needs until 2012. The proposed site, together with the cost of the food preparation areas and bottling and packaging areas, is forecast to cost £18 million. Although a site had been identified, the company had not yet made any firm commitment.

Competitive position in 2008 and beyond

Over the last four years, organic produce has been available in an increasing number of stores and also from a number of Internet-based companies. There is an ever-increasing number of products available, and more retailers are stocking organic produce in its various forms. The Organic Food Company has been at the leading edge of some of the retailing initiatives, including returnable packaging for dairy products. This not only cut down on the packaging costs but also helped the company to appear to be environmentally friendly by recycling some of its packaging. The company has also developed and uses a unique 'tamper-proof' seal. While the cost of developing these seals, and the additional cost of packaging is higher than some of its competitors, it is a feature that has enhanced The Organic Food Company's brand reputation as a high quality food producer.

As the main supermarkets have increasingly stocked more ranges of organic produce, the retail price has fallen and The Organic Food Company has had to realign its prices to stay competitive. Additionally, due to the limited amount of organic produce that can be produced (referred to at the beginning of this article), there is an element of 'scarcity value'. This has helped maintain prices at a higher level than will continue in the future if more farming land in the UK becomes licensed as organic. Therefore, in the medium term it is expected that prices, and levels of profitability, will fall. To offset this, however, is the continued high growth in the demand for organic produce, partly fuelled by food scares, and also by the increasingly selective consumer.

The above data has been based upon a real-life situation, but details have been changed for assessment purposes and may not be an accurate reflection of reported business news.

3.5 Part A questions

Task One

Briefly define **FOUR** different channels of distribution.(4 marks)

The term channels of distribution refers to the methods by which goods or services are transferred from producers to consumers. The Organic Food Company participates in several distribution channels.

- Retailers are traders operating outlets which sell directly to households. The Organic Food Company has its own shops.

- Distributors and dealers contract to buy a manufacturer's goods and sell them to customers. The Organic Food Company acts as a distributor for a range of organic suppliers.

- Multiple stores (eg supermarkets) buy goods for retailing direct from the producer, sometimes under their 'own label' brand name. The Organic Food Company sells some of its products to a large supermarket chain.

- Direct marketing methods include e-commerce (Internet trading via online marketing)

(Syllabus area 3.7)

EXAM TIP

When thinking about channels of distribution, it may help to think about a business with which you are familiar and brainstorm all the channels that you think it may be involved in.

Task Two

Identify examples of marketing objectives, covering each of the SMART criteria. (4 marks)

Specific	Stating exactly what has to be achieved: 'Increase Internet sales in 2008'
Measurable	Quantified, so that that you can tell if the objective has been achieved. If you were aiming for a 10% increase in Internet sales and gained a 15% increase, you can tell that you have exceeded your objective.
Achievable	The objective has to be realistic in the circumstances, given the resources that are available. For example, the Organic Food Company should be well placed to increase its Internet sales if it can sort out the ability of its website to cope with the level of orders.
Relevant	The objective must relate to the wider objectives of the organisation. Increasing Internet sales, for example, will be directly relevant for a retailing organisation in the modern age.
Time bounded	There should be deadlines and timeframes for achieving the objective. This might be controlled by having milestones throughout the year to assess progress towards the target.

(Syllabus area 2.1)

EXAM TIP

concept

The ability to relate the SMART mnemonic to specific marketing objectives will distinguish a good answer from a weak one that restricts itself to defining 'SMART' in general terms.

Task Three

Explain how the marketing planning process assists with resource management. (4 marks)

In developing strategy, most organisations will be required to make important resource allocation decisions. Marketing plans and strategies need to be developed within an overall strategic framework and will be very closely linked with plans for other functions of the organisation. This approach ensures that resources available within the organisation are used as effectively as possible. Resources are sometimes described as the five Ms.

- Men: its human resources and organisation

- Money: its financial health

- Materials: supply sources and products

- Machines: production facilities, fixed assets, capacity. For example, the Organic Food Company has outgrown its current warehouse and distribution centres and needs to invest in additional capacity.

- Markets: its reputation, position and market prospects

(Syllabus area 2.3)

The five Ms model is a useful way of remembering the resources that are employed by most organisations. This question puts the marketing function, and marketing planning in particular, within the overall strategic context.

Task Four

Outline the key features of societal marketing. (4 marks)

The societal marketing concept holds that the key task of the organisation is to determine the needs and wants of target markets, and then to adapt the organisation to delivering the desired satisfactions more effectively and efficiently than its competitors. This should be done in a way that preserves or enhances the consumers' and society's well-being. Activities need to be carried out in a sustainable way if customers' needs are to be met in the longer term. An organisation such as the Organic Food Company, which has a stake in the continued development and adoption of organic farming practices, can be said by the very nature of its business to be promoting societal marketing – selling environmentally sustainable food products to an increasing number of consumers, using environmentally friendly packaging.

(Syllabus area 1.6)

 EXAM TIP concept

This topic area does not appear on the Specimen Paper, but that does not lessen its importance. Along with the impact of advances in information and communication technologies, modern awareness of environmental, social and ethical concerns is of direct and practical importance for the marketing professional.

Task Five

Give FOUR Items of financial information that can be used to measure marketing performance. (4 marks)

Financial information for measuring marketing performance could include:

- Total profits and sales

- Increase / decrease in profits and sales over the preceding period, comparing 'like-for-like' (in the case of the Organic Food Company, this means for example stripping out the effect of new shop openings)

- Sales and profits in each major business segment that the company operates in. The Organic Food Company would be interested in comparing sales from Internet trading, mail order, the city shops and selling at local markets.

- Levels of debt, and interest rates on that debt. The new capacity required by the Organic Food Company could cost it as much as £18 million, which is likely to come from bank borrowing.

Sales are generally subject to the most scrutiny. This could include comparison with forecast sales, unit sales analysis, comparison with competitors' sales, sales by geographic area, comparison with sales in the industry and sales by product group.

(Syllabus area 3.12)

 EXAM TIP concept

Measuring the success of marketing activities is always going to have a financial slant, and the analysis of sales is fundamental within that. Other, non-financial, methods for measuring the success of marketing activity might include quality considerations, customer complaints, customer awareness and customer loyalty. These may be more difficult to measure.

Task Six

Explain the importance of the introduction of new products and services into the market. (4 marks)

New product development is important for maintaining customer satisfaction through change; refreshing or extending the product range; and adapting to environmental opportunities and threats. These will all contribute towards the success of a company's long term business strategy. It is important for example to:

- Meet the changing needs/wants of customers – such as the introduction by the Organic Food Company of a range of prepared meals and bottled sauces

- Match competitors: responding to innovations and new product lines

- Respond to environmental threats and opportunities: in the case of the Organic Food Company, developing 'green' alternatives such as returnable packaging

- Extend the product/brand range as part of a product development strategy: new products (such as organic bread or organic wine) can bring new customers to the brand and enable cross-selling of products

(Syllabus area 3.3)

  EXAM TIP concept

This is a different slant on new product development and requires a bit more thinking than the more familiar question on the NPD process. Use a company or product that you know well and consider how that company might benefit from introducing new products to its customers. It is also fruitful to think about the product life cycle when talking about NPD – many companies simply have to innovate to keep their product range fresh as products reach maturity and eventual obsolescence (companies manufacturing high technology products in particular).

Task Seven

Explain the key features of promotional pricing. (4 marks)

Promotional pricing is pricing that is related to the promotion of a product, generally over the short term only. Pricing and promotion are often co-ordinated. There are four main types of promotional pricing.

- Price leaders – products that are sold at or below cost to attract customers. This tactic is often used in department stores and supermarkets when two or more products in the line are complementary – one of the products will be priced at a low margin in order to attract customers and demand for the higher priced product.

- Special event pricing – pricing that is linked to an event or a holiday to increase sales volume. An example is the 'Buy 2, get the 3rd free' often seen at Christmas. The Organic Food Company is likely to have special prices for the Christmas and other festive periods.

- Everyday low pricing – this involves the reduction of prices for a prolonged period, supported by cutting costs elsewhere in the operation (such as distribution costs, or cutting down on other promotions).

- Experience curve pricing – the fixing of a low price that competitors cannot hope to match, in order to increase market share. A company can do this when it has been able to reduce manufacturing costs through improvements in processes that have been accumulated through experience.

(Syllabus area 3.6)

  EXAM TIP concept

Make sure that you know the key features of the various pricing techniques that are listed in the syllabus. They are a rich source of material for short questions, as evidenced by their appearance on the Specimen Paper.

Task Eight

Outline the principles of a marketing orientation as a 'philosophy of business'. (4 marks)

An organisation that follows a marketing orientation is one which implements the marketing concept as a philosophy behind its operations - first of all by determining what customers want, and then setting about providing those goods or services which meet customers' wants and needs (at the right price, at the right time, at the right place) and communicating effectively with these customers. The organisation will do this in a way consistent with achieving its own objectives, but always with the customer at the forefront. At the same time, a market oriented organisation avoids short-term sales-focused relationships.

- It focuses on meeting the needs of customers, which have been clearly identified and fully understood.
- Its structure and processes are designed to meet the needs of customers.
- All activities are co-ordinated around the needs of the customer.

Underlying all of this is the belief that a market orientation is fundamental to the continuation and competitiveness of the organisation. When customers' needs change, as they surely will, or whenever better solutions emerge that more closely meet customers' needs, the organisation adapts and responds. Otherwise the organisation does not survive. The Organic Food Company has been careful to innovate in its product lines to make sure that customers continue to be interested, and it has made sure that its products are available through a variety of channels.

(Syllabus area 1.3)

  EXAM TIP

concept

This looks like a tricky question at first but if you focus upon outlining the principles of the marketing orientation, the 'philosophy of business' part falls into place. By describing what a market oriented organisation is all about, and why a market orientation is best suited to meeting customer needs, therefore helping to ensure organisational success, the question of how market orientation relates to business success is answered.

Task Nine

Identify examples of **FOUR** factors that influence the selection of distribution channel. (4 marks)

In setting up a channel of distribution, the organisation has to take several factors into account.

Customers	The number of potential customers, their buying habits and their geographical proximity are key influences. Different distribution strategies may be adopted for consumer and industrial markets. Industrial channels tend to be more direct and shorter.
Nature of the goods or services	Some product characteristics have an important effect on design of the channel of distribution (eg perishability, level of customisation). The Organic Food Company has discovered that the perishability of some of its products has had a detrimental effect upon the performance of its city stores, as products cannot be kept on the shelves for an extended period.
Distributor characteristics	The location, customer base, performance and reliability, promotion and pricing policies of different types of distributor, and specific distribution outlets, will all be relevant to the decision.

Competitors' channel choice	For many consumer goods, a brand will sit alongside its competitors' products. For other products, distributors may stock one name brand only (eg cars). The Organic Food Company is likely to find its products on supermarket shelves along with those of competitors.
Costs	In addition to the costs of importing goods from overseas suppliers, or exporting to overseas customers, products will often need to be transported, stored or held somewhere awaiting sale or collection.
Organisation's characteristics	A strong financial base gives the organisation the option of buying and operating their own distribution channel. The market position of the organisation is also important: distributors are keen to be associated with the market leader, but other brands may experience distribution problems.

(Syllabus area 3.8)

  EXAM TIP   concept

Only four factors were needed here. Channel choices are influenced by factors within the market itself: customers, competitors, costs, product features and characteristics of the organisations involved.

Task Ten

Use examples from a business of your choice to explain how websites can be used in marketing communications. (4 marks)

Web advertising is generally acknowledged to be when an advertiser pays to place advertising content on another website. The Organic Food Company could use web advertising to drive visitors to its own website, perhaps by placing advertisements on the website of a supermarket or a related company (such as an organic clothing manufacturer) and it has its own interactive website that enables the placing of orders.

The ability to reach customers directly is a prime goal for most organisations. The use of the Internet as a communications medium is attractive, because of its interactive nature.

The benefits of using the Internet for marketing communications have been described as the '5Ss':

- *Sell* goods and services online, to a global market. While the market for organic produce may not necessarily be global, the selling of products online certainly opens up the market beyond the immediate local area.

- *Serve* customers in new and better ways

- *Save* money, with fewer of the overheads that are associated with traditional ways of doing business

- *Speak* to customers directly

- *Sizzle* with a well designed and informative website that can engage and entertain the visitor. Customers can view the product range and prices. The website must be able to cope with the number of visitors to avoid the risk of 'crashing'.

(Syllabus area 3.10)

  EXAM TIP   concept

The use of web advertising and the Internet in modern marketing is going to be a regular topic in exams. The number of businesses with transactional websites, as opposed to purely informational ones, is growing all the time.

4 Part B- Case Study Question Practice

4.1 Case study

Botswana Telecommunucations Corporation (BTC)

The telecommunications sector in Botswana, Africa, is characterised by a growing, unsatisfied demand for telecommunications services in both urban and rural areas and among businesses as well as households.

Botswana Telecommunications Corporation (BTC) is a state-owned enterprise incorporated under the BTC Act of 1980 to provide public telecommunications services in Botswana. Currently it has over 100,000 customer access lines in service.

BTC has a telecommunications infrastructure that is one of the most modern in Africa. Its network, composed of an all-digital microwave and fibre optic system with digital exchanges at the main centres, provides a reasonable level of service.

Current services provided include national and international telephony, managed and data networks, leased circuits, toll-free services, Internet, paging, public telephones, voice messaging, telex, telegraph and customer premises equipment. International access is provided from Botswana to almost every country in the world.

Since the introduction of cellular networks in the country through two other companies, BTC has also supplied the backbone networks to facilitate cellular communications throughout the country.

During the past two years, access lines to customers have increased by 19% to exceed 102,000. This has significantly reduced the waiting period for services which had been observed in most parts of Botswana. This increased penetration of the market means that there are now 6.4 telephones for every 100 people in the population.

The Corporation's commitment to bringing telecommunications services to rural areas continues with the implementation of programmes in Barolong and the northern Tuli areas. These were undertaken with Government financial assistance.

The telecommunications industry in Botswana is expected to experience massive growth during the next five years. The mobile telecommunications industry represents a major challenge to BTC. The Corporation knows that it will need to consider this challenge from a market orientation perspective, as previously it has been more product oriented.

Indeed, BTC anticipates that the main challenges facing it are as follows:

- Large investment in networks and development of new services
- Introduction, development and support of new products and services
- Customer care and responsiveness at all levels within the organisation
- Streamlining of processes and work procedures to address customer concerns
- Competing resources in balancing rural and urban telecommunications requirements nationwide.

In Botswana, BTC intends to maintain its position as the primary network provider of choice. BTC is confident that introducing a new customer care policy and billing system will help to attain corporate targets. The company states that it is dedicated to meeting customer and investor expectations.

Tasks

You have been asked to help BTC in meeting the challenges which face it. Produce a report for the marketing manager of BTC which addresses the following tasks.

Task One

Identify, with reasons, the steps for introducing a marketing orientation within BTC, and explain how it will contribute towards the development of BTC's business strategy.   (20 marks)

(Syllabus areas 1.1, 1.3, 1.5)

Task Two

Explain the concept of a product as a 'bundle of benefits' that delivers customer value, and the key differences between services and products. Discuss the problems that these differences may present to BTC.   (20 marks)

(Syllabus areas 3.1, 3.11)

Task Three

Identify the various stages of the marketing planning process for BTC, and explain the concept of the marketing audit as an appraisal of its external marketing environment. (20 marks)

(Syllabus areas 2.3, 2.4, 2.5)

(Total 60 marks)

4.2 Suggested answers

Task One

 EXAM TIP

concept

This unit is very focused upon the importance of the marketing orientation and the way that it co-ordinates business functions. It will come up as a topic in every exam sitting in Part A, Part B or both. You must appreciate its importance and be familiar with the range of issues that could be asked in an exam question. Here, the slant is on how a marketing orientation can contribute towards the development of a business strategy. You need to be familiar with this to be able to place marketing activities within the context of business activity.

To: Marketing Manager, BTC

From: Marketing Consultant

Date: December 20X8

Terms of reference

Due to the changing technological environment in which the telecommunications industry now operates, Botswana Telecommunications Corporation needs to reappraise its position within the market. Therefore, this report will identify the steps required for introducing a marketing orientation within BTC and how the effective use of information technology may contribute. It will then go on to explain the key differences between services and products and the problems that these differences may present to BTC. The final section of the report will then discuss the elements of the marketing mix which BTC will need to consider when marketing its services.

Introduction – defining 'marketing orientation'

At present, as outlined in our company's Annual Report, we as a company are product orientated. Therefore, being able to produce certain products and services, we sell these to our customers whether or not they fit the needs of our customers.

As this is the case, a marketing orientation is necessary. Theodore Levitt suggests that a marketing orientation is superior to a production orientation. Therefore, no longer can an organisation expect to concentrate on efficient production. The concept suggests that the organisation needs to be customer focused and market driven in order to succeed in today's competitive environment. Marketing orientation is a co-ordinated marketing effort that involves many things such as market research, market led product/service development, etc. An organisation that follows a marketing orientation is one which implements the marketing concept - first of all by determining what customers want, and then setting about providing those goods or services which meet customers' wants and needs (at the right price, at the right time, at the right place) and communicating effectively with these customers. The organisation will do this in a way consistent with achieving its own objectives, but always with the customer at the forefront.

The steps involved in becoming marketing orientated

Marketing orientated organisations put the customer first, therefore, this means that the customer will need to become central to all business and marketing decisions and planning. The customer has to be taken into consideration before any other aspect.

The main steps are as follows:

Assessing customer requirements

Before any decisions are made, BTC needs to assess their customers and decide what their needs and wants are and how they will meet those needs. This can be done by looking through past records and any networks and customer access lines. The corporation already knows that access lines to customers have increased by 19% to over 102,000 in the last two years. This is essential in a marketing orientation as the customer comes first and their needs need to be met and exceeded in order to be successful.

Levels of customer satisfaction should be tested and analysed to identify the areas where the organisation is failing the customer. Areas such as complaints systems, down-time technical reports, new customers gained and old customers lost should be identified and analysed.

Making sure management is committed to customer requirements

There must be support from senior management that marketing orientation is important and it is essential to ensure that the orientation is widespread throughout the whole of the corporation. If management levels are customer focused, then it is inevitable that the orientation will filter throughout the rest of the corporation. Indeed, this should lead to the planning of a change in the organisation's internal culture.

Focus the whole of the corporation

This can be done by introducing Total Quality Management systems. Here, systems need to be set in place to make sure the whole staff knows what your objectives are and how you intend to meet these objectives. BTC are already aware that customer care and responsiveness at all levels within the organisation is one of their main challenges. To ensure this, every member of staff needs to be aware of what you are aiming for, how you intend to do it and why. Feedback needs to be passed back to management from the TQM system and evaluation needs to take place on a regular basis.

Departments must work together, breaking down any barriers that exist currently between them. Effective and efficient communication is vital for marketing orientation.

Setting service standards

Using customer feedback from the analysis undertaken (see 3.1) should allow service standards to be agreed which the internal systems will fulfil. For instance, one service standard might be concerned with the length of time customers are expected to wait to access services. If the waiting period is caused because BTC cannot install lines quickly enough, measures must be put in place which will rectify this situation and keep the customer fully informed at all times.

Identify staff training requirements

BTC's new philosophy and culture needs to be communicated to all staff. Areas where staff are unable to deliver the required levels of service because of the lack of training need to be identified. A training plan must be put in place to resolve the situation. This could include such things as delegation and empowerment training, technical product training and customer handling skills. Reward schemes and staff motivation should also been considered as this will help with the success of the new culture. Staff are in prime positions to give feedback about customers as they are dealing with them at front of house or moment of truth situations.

BTC's model for marketing orientation

The following model will help in the implementation of such a programme:

Determine CUSTOMER NEEDS

↓

Top management commitment

↓

Invest in resources

continuous

assessment

Develop service standards

↓

Staff training and customer care

programme launched

↓

Marketing the services

↓

Monitor and control through

customer feedback

Potential problems

Adopting a marketing orientated approach is a time consuming, process and training and costs need to be invested, therefore it may be difficult to convince top management about the benefits as they will be long term rather than quick fixes in relation to the investment made. Therefore, there may be a resistance to change within BTC. Barriers may exist between departments that are tough to break down.

Contribution towards business strategy

Kotler wrote that the marketing orientation is all about 'achieving organisational goals depends on determining the needs and wants of target markets and delivering the desired satisfactions more effectively and efficiently than competitors'. For BTC, it can be seen from the above analysis that a transition to a marketing orientation will enable the business to focus upon what drives it and how its goal of maintaining its position as the primary network provider of choice can be met, both currently and in the future.

Task Two

  EXAM TIP  concept

This question is set in a primarily service-focused environment, although BTC does get involved in product development as well. You must remember that services are an important area of the international economy and account for more employment than the manufacturing sector. They are likely to feature regularly on exam papers.

Products as 'bundles of benefits'

A product is a bundle of benefits which satisfy a set of wants that customers have. Products have:

- A physical aspect, which relates to the components, materials and specifications (colour, size etc) of the product
- A functional aspect, which describes how a product performs and for what purpose it is likely to be bought
- A symbolic aspect which represents the qualities the product suggests to, or offers, the buyer

Customers buy the product that they believe offers the highest customer delivered value. This is the difference between total customer value and total customer cost. The customer value includes the product, services, personal and image values, whereas the total customer cost includes the monetary cost as well as time and energy spent. It is the 'bundle of benefits' that delivers consumer value. For instance, a product such as a telephone system will have certain expectations as to functionality in performance. Understanding the customer's combined preferences is an important consideration for BTC.

Many organisations have recognised that they have to provide customer value as a bundle of benefits in products and services. This value is reflected in the specific customer requirements within each customer segment.

BTC recognises that there is a growing and unsatisfied demand for telecommunications services, with penetration of telephone services still very low when compared to more developed economies. It has committed to bringing the benefits of improved public telecommunications services as well as investment in new products and customer service initiatives. This will require a greater customer focus than previously, and will force the company to really think about what Botswanans want from their telephone services –what 'bundle of benefits' they seek.

The difference between marketing services and products

There are five major areas where services differ from products and they present challenges to the company, which can be overcome by the use of effective marketing.

- **Heterogeneity**

    This means that services can differ from time to time and from person to person who is delivering the service. The same telephone operator can provide an excellent service to one customer then provide a poor level of service to the next customer, dependent on how the member of staff is feeling at the time. Service involves human contact, which introduces the problems of human effort and human behaviour which is difficult to control precisely. Therefore, ensuring continuity of service standards is difficult.

    To counter this BTC should ensure that there are delivery standards which are monitored closely, taking customer feedback to support the research.

- **Inseparability**

    The service cannot be separated from the provider – the producer of the service is also the retailer of it, unlike products which can be made in a factory and then sold to the end-customer in a different country. BTC needs to consider this to ensure that the service provided is consistent with the brand values that they want to project. This could have implications for standards of delivery where the reputation of the organisation is at stake each time the customer takes up the service – known as 'moments of truth'.

    Vigorous control of the standards to ensure excellent delivery is required here. Careful recruitment, staff training and a rewards philosophy are required to ensure that quality staff are delivering the service.

- **Perishability**

    This means that the service cannot be kept to use later, it must be consumed at the time that it is offered. There is no second chance – each customer interaction must meet customer requirements. This can produce difficulties for the organisation in ensuring that both the service and the staff to deliver it are available, when the service is most in demand. Overstaffing leads to wasted resources, but understaffing leads to customer frustration.

    BTC should use promotional techniques effectively to increase off peak demand, such as reduced rates. This should go some way to evening out demand fluctuations.

- **Intangibility**

    Services are intangible, ie there is nothing physical to hand over to the customer, unlike a product. This means that customers will judge BTC more on the personal experience they get from each interaction with BTC, so it is imperative that a consistently high level of service is provided from each member of staff within BTC.

    Therefore promotion methods should be used to illustrate the value and benefits of the service or brand. Testimonials from satisfied customers are useful here to add value to the service.

- **Ownership**

   Ownership of services is sometimes complicated. For example, a business may pay BTC to provide telephone and Internet services to their office premises. BTC retains ownership of this service and can change the timing or layout of the service as they like. The business does not receive anything until BTC chooses to deliver the service.

Promoting BTC's services

Promotional objectives for services are not very different to those for products. BTC needs to ensure that its new marketing focus takes the following objectives into account.

- Build awareness and interest in BTC
- Communicate and portray the benefits of BTC's services
- Build and maintain the overall image and reputation of BTC
- Advise customers of new products and services

Task Three

 EXAM TIP concept

Exam tip. Identifying the stages of the marketing planning process should have include an explanation of all of the stages, rather than just offering a list.

When explaining the concept of the marketing audit as an appraisal of the external marketing environment, your answer must consider the macro environment.

(a) The planning process enables a marketer to plan and forecast future events, and the possible route an organisation should follow. The stages of the marketing planning process that could be followed by BTC are described below.

   The Marketing Plan

   (i) **Corporate Objectives**

      Firstly BTC needs to remind itself of the company objectives: maintaining its position as the primary network provider of choice, and meeting customer and investor expectations.

   (ii) **Marketing Analysis**

      It is necessary to examine external and internal market factors. PEST analysis gives a suitable framework:

Political:	These include factors that relate to government at local, national, and international levels. It will include possible legislation that is relevant to BTC's products and services.
Economic:	Trends that influence profit and target consumer groups' disposable income, economic climate and forecast
Social:	Social and lifestyle trends, buyer behaviour and cultural influences
Technological:	Methods of production, service delivery and the impact of new technology in the telecommunications sector

The second part of the marketing auditing looks at SWOT analysis for the company.

INTERNAL	EXTERNAL
Strengths	Opportunities
Weaknesses	Threats

This enables BTC to analyse the strengths (such as its dominant market position) that it can exploit as well as understanding its weaknesses (such as its lack of marketing orientation and experience). It also needs to assess external influences, particularly of possible future competitors if the market in Botswana is thrown open, and how it should plan to convert these into opportunities.

(iii) **Marketing Objectives**

Marketing objectives need to fit with the overall company objectives. They may include profitability, market share or customer awareness levels. These objectives should be SMART, ie Specific, Measurable, Achievable, Realistic and Time related.

(iv) **Marketing Strategy**

This is a broad overview of how BTC wishes to achieve its objectives. The strategy part of the plan is where it decides on its target audience, and how it will position its products and services.

(v) **Marketing Tactics**

This is a more comprehensive breakdown of how the marketing mix is to be adapted for the product.

(1) **Product**: use, features, design

(2) **Price**: pricing policy to adopt, which depends greatly on market position and return on investment

(3) **Promotion**: the communication tools that would most effectively reach out to a far flung and sometimes relatively unsophisticated target audience and the most appropriate mix of advertising, public relations, sales promotion etc

(4) **Place**: this includes determining the logistics and technology required to get the products and services to the customer.

(vi) **Implementation**

This is the logistical activity of co-ordinating all those involved in putting the plan into action.

(vii) **Monitoring and Control**

It is essential to get feedback on whether the plan is successful, and by constantly monitoring the situation react to circumstances so that BTC can achieve its objectives.

(b) A marketing audit is a systematic and comprehensive review of a firm's current marketing activities and capacity, used in marketing planning Marketing audits comprise of two factors: internal audits and external audits. In this case we shall only assess the external audit.

The marketing audit allows the marketer to scan the external environment for factors that may currently affect the organisation or could possibly do so at some time in the future. A tool that aids the scanning process is known as PEST, which stands for Political, Economic, Social/Cultural and Technological factors. These help the marketer at BTC appraise the macro environment over which the organisation has little or no control. The marketer must be aware of activities occurring in the macro environment in order to understand its impact and to develop contingencies from future trends. The wider macro environment represents the greatest opportunities and threats facing organisations.

Political environment

The political framework and processes in Botswanan society will influence the operation of the business. Marketing management must be alert to the changes in the political attitude that are influenced by local, national and international government action. The legislation and policies from these bodies impacts the organisation in many different ways.

Economic environment

Marketing management must understand the effects of the many economic variables that are likely to effect business operations. Economic indicators such as interest rates, inflation and balance of payments are important pointers of future trading prospects and need to be understood and evaluated for every business.

Social/cultural environment

People's basic beliefs, attitudes and values are shaped by the society in which they exist. While Botswana has one of the most modern telecommunications infrastructures in Africa, penetration is still very low and there are outlying rural areas with very little access to even the most basic telephone service. The behaviour of consumers is conditioned to some extent by social attitudes.

Technological environment

Technology is a major environmental influence upon BTC. The impact of new information technology, developments in mobile communications and the Internet are all important external considerations. Technology affects the way in which goods are distributed and promoted.

The market environment of people, organisations and forces within the firm's immediate external environment are also important as part of the environmental scanning activity. These include possible competitors, suppliers and intermediaries.

Competitor environment

The BTC marketer must identify any key competitors, their relative strengths and weaknesses and their objectives and strategies. They must also assess likely new entrants or substitutes into the marketplace and determine if competition could be based on some alternative offering.

Supplier environment

Nearly every firm is likely to have suppliers. These groupings are important in the supply of the final product or service to the customer. The marketer must ensure that the suppliers that it uses commit to the strategic plans of the business and are able to contribute to its implementation. Because of the increasing interdependence of suppliers and their customers it is extremely important that the supplier can align itself to supporting all the marketer's requirements including quality and delivery performance.

Intermediaries

The intermediate distribution system is composed of agents, distributors, wholesalers and retailers that are constantly changing in response to environmental influences.

5 Mock exam

5.1 Mock Exam Paper

5.1.1 Part A Questions

Task One

Explain how a SWOT analysis is used in the marketing audit.   (4 marks)

Task Two

Outline the benefits to a business of customer retention. (4 marks)

Task Three

Identify FOUR different types of organisational objective. (4 marks)

Task Four

Explain the stages of product/service adoption. (4 marks)

Task Five

Explain why personal selling is particularly appropriate in B2B marketing. (4 marks)

Task Six

Identify and briefly explain the characteristics of services that distinguish them from products. (4 marks)

Task Seven

Outline the key features of a production and a sales orientation, and how they contrast with a marketing orientation.

(4 marks)

Task Eight

Explain what is meant by 'budgetary control' in the context of the marketing planning process. (4 marks)

Task Nine

Identify and briefly explain the stages in the product life cycle. (4 marks)

Task Ten

Explain the importance of branding and packaging in the successful marketing of a product for a business of your choice.

(4 marks)

5.1.2 Part B – Case Study Questions - SAMSUNG

All tasks are compulsory (60% weighting)

Samsung Seeks Superiority through Innovation, Screens and Chips

The Samsung Group is South Korea's largest company (or 'chaebol') and the world's second largest conglomerate by revenue. In 2005, it overtook its rivals Sony and Matsushita (responsible for JVC, Panasonic and Technics) as the world's leading consumer electronics brand, and became part of the top twenty global brands overall. A decade ago, Samsung was widely regarded as a supplier of cheap imitations of superior Japanese products. At the time, the focus of its business was on memory chips and low-margin items such as microwave ovens and cheap TVs, which were mainly sold through discount stores. Following a major restructuring of its strategy and operations, it has turned itself into the fastest growing player in the global consumer electronics industry, with sales of US$153.2 billion in 2006. Employing approximately 254,000 people in many countries, the company consists of five main consumer-related business units, the details of which are shown below:

Digital appliance	Digital Media	LCDs	Semiconductors	Tele-communications Networks
Washing machines	TVs and monitors	Large LCD-TFT screens	Memory chips	Mobile phone handsets
Air conditioners and purifiers	VCRs		Digital processors	PDA phones
Microwave ovens	DVDs		Flash cards	Wireless network systems
Refrigerators	Camcorders		DVD and CD drives	Integrated access platforms
Vacuum cleaners	Printers			
	Laptops			

Samsung Electronics Ltd has built up its position through rationalisation and diversification of its activities, together with strong marketing and innovative product design. From its strong position as a manufacturer of essential electronic components, Samsung has built its reputation as the major consumer brand in a range of different product categories. The company is the market leader in the microchip and TFT-LCD screen sectors, and is the world's largest producer of colour TVs, monitors and VCRs. In 2007 Samsung Telecommunication Business reported over 40% growth and became the second largest mobile phone device manufacturer in the world, with 15.6% market share.

Samsung has used its success in the mobile phone business to drive its brand performance, which can be attributed to a strategy of delivering innovative products at premium prices. According to their marketing chief much of their achievement has stemmed from identifying at an early stage that the mobile phone was changing 'from a utility item to a fashion statement'. This led them into the camera phone market, and they became the first producer to equip a cell phone with an MP3 player. In 2008, Samsung Electronics' Telecommunication Business declared its new business strategy focusing on consumers and marketing. Samsung mobile phones are divided into 6 major categories – Style, Infotainment, Multimedia, Connected, Essential and Business.

The change in direction of the company over the last decade is based on a realisation that there was more money to be made from innovating and setting the pace than from producing only me-too products. To do this it has not only been able to draw upon its own extensive manufacturing and R&D capability (more than 20,000 researchers in 15 laboratories worldwide) but has also worked closely with strategic partners, including competitors as well as customers, in establishing new industry standards. The approach which has proved so successful in their mobile phone business is now regarded as the basis for further growth in all customer sectors, with a particular emphasis on the use of wireless technology in the home.

Supporting all of its development has been the extensive use of marketing to communicate with customers and build a brand which is increasingly recognised as a world-leader. However, in order to achieve its ambition of becoming and remaining number one in the consumer electronics market it plans to invest even more in research, development and design and at the same time review its brand positioning. The intention is to invest heavily in integrated communications campaigns, including global advertising (some of it online) and promotions, which will lift brand loyalty to the point where people will say 'I only want a Samsung'.

The above data has been based on a real life organisation, but details have been changed for assessment purposes and do not reflect the current management practices.

Tasks

You work as an assistant in the marketing department of Samsung Electronics. You have been asked by the Marketing Manager to write a report that addresses the following tasks.

Task One

Explain the internal and external factors that the company needs to take into account when setting prices and selecting appropriate distribution channels for its products. (20 marks)

(Syllabus areas 3.5, 3.6, 3.7, 3.8)

Task Two

Explain the importance of setting appropriate objectives, and how the introduction of new products can assist with the achievement of these objectives at Samsung. (20 marks)

(Syllabus areas 2.1, 2.2, 3.3)

Task Three

Explain how building relationships with customers will assist Samsung in growing its consumer electronics business.

(20 marks)

(Syllabus areas 1.5, 1.7)

(Total 60 marks)

5.2 Mock Exam Suggested Answers

5.2.1 Part A Answers

Task One

Explain how a SWOT analysis is used in the marketing audit. (4 marks)

SWOT analysis is a commonly used technique within the overall marketing audit to assess the current situation of the business in its markets.

Strengths and weaknesses are features of the organisation itself and its product/service range.

(a)   Strengths are features from which the company may be able to derive competitive advantage. They are also known as core competences.

(b)   Weaknesses are disadvantages that may have to be remedied. For example a company's growth might be hampered because its people have weak customer handling skills. A training programme could be introduced to help its people develop strong skills.

Opportunities and threats are features of the environment, particularly the immediate competitive or task environment. Effective SWOT analysis does not simply require a categorisation of information, but also requires some assessment of the relative importance of the various factors. By understanding its strengths, weaknesses, opportunities and threats, an organisation can begin to put together plans for making the most of its market.

Here is an example SWOT for the Organic Food Company.

Strength: High reputation as a quality producer and distributor of organic produce

Weakness: Customer satisfaction levels are at risk because of the problems in recruiting adequate numbers of staff to meet strong demand

Opportunity: Likely growth in the market, and Internet sales opportunities

Threat: Retail prices decline as supermarkets stock more and more organic lines

(Syllabus area 2.5)

  EXAM TIP

concept

The question asks how SWOT is used within the marketing audit, so it is important to approach it from a marketing perspective (rather than a general business one). This shows that you appreciated the relevance of SWOT to the work of the marketer.

Task Two

Outline the benefits to a business of customer retention. (4 marks)

The lifetime value of a customer to a company can be measured in terms of revenue and profits. Existing, loyal customers are valuable because:

- They do not have to be acquired, or cost less to acquire
- They buy a broader range of products
- They are familiar with the company's ways of doing business
- They become less sensitive to price over time
- They can recommend by word of mouth to others

Customers who defect may be lost forever, and at the very least will be expensive to lure back. Customers may be lost because of poor service, and they will spread bad experiences through word of mouth. This is why the Organic Food Company needs to make sure that its Internet and mail order businesses are able to fulfil customer orders.

The process of retaining customers for a lifetime is an important one. It is necessary to develop an effective two-way communication process to turn a prospect into a lifetime advocate for the company. The main justification for relationship marketing comes from the need to retain customers. It has been estimated that the cost of attracting a new customer may be five times the cost of keeping a current customer happy.

In terms of competitive forces, relationship marketing attempts to make it harder, or less desirable, for a buyer to switch to another seller.

Relationship marketing also opens channels of communication for marketers to cross-sell related products, solicit feedback for further marketing planning and even make special offers (to boost sales or increase customer loyalty). It is clear that the more loyal customers that a business has, the better its prospects for survival and growth.

(Syllabus area 1.7)

  EXAM TIP

concept

This answer refers to relationship marketing, which is a fundamental part of any customer retention strategy.

Task Three

Identify FOUR different types of organisational objective. (4 marks)

Most commercial organisations will express their primary objective in financial or quantitative terms.

- Profitability
- Sales/Revenue
- Marketing expenditure
- Growth eg market share (as a general rule, most firms want to grow)
- Cash flow

Although a company must make profits, profit on its own is not satisfactory as an overall long term corporate objective because it fails to allow for the size of the capital investment required to make that profit. Other objectives may be more qualitative:

- Levels of technology and product innovation
- Survival
- Ethically and socially responsible aims
- Customer service and satisfaction levels
- Product quality
- Employee/HR practice

(Syllabus area 2.2)

This is a long list of objectives, and the question only requires four. Some discussion of the validity of the various types of objective identified (such as the limitations behind using profit as an overriding objective) should be included in your answer.

Task Four

Explain the stages of product/service adoption. (4 marks)

The diffusion of a new product refers to the spread of information about the product in the market place. Adoption is the process by which consumers incorporate the product into their buying patterns, and these are its stages:

Innovators – these are people who like to own the latest products, and value being the 'first' to have them amongst their group of friends and family members.

Early adopters – these people are open to new ideas, but they prefer to wait and see how the product goes after its initial launch, and to observe the experience of the innovators

Early majority – these will buy the product when they are sure that there is no risk with the product

Late majority – of similar numbers to early majority, the late majority will only buy the new product when most other people already have one

Laggards – these people adopt products only when they have no choice but to do so

Innovators and early adopters are thought to operate as 'opinion leaders' and are therefore targeted by companies in order to influence the adoption of a product by their friends.

The main problem with this model is that the categories appear to add up to 100% of the target market. This does not reflect marketers' experience. Some potential consumers do not adopt/purchase at all. It has consequently been suggested that an additional category is needed: non-adopters, or non-consumers. In the case of the Organic Food Company, it is certainly the case that there will be some consumers who are not interested in either the philosophy or the expense of organic food.

(Syllabus area 3.13)

 EXAM TIP

concept

This is one of the most familiar models in marketing theory and one that you should know well. It can be easily applied to technological products in particular, but the adoption of all kinds of products and services seems to follow the same basic pattern. It is important to be aware of its limitations (even though this was not strictly required by the question).

Task Five

Explain why personal selling is particularly appropriate in B2B marketing.

(4 marks)

Personal selling encompasses a wide variety of tasks including prospecting, information gathering and communicating as well as actually selling. It involves the presentation of products and persuasive communication to potential clients by sales staff.

The salesperson's job begins before meeting the buyer. Preparation could include finding out about the buyer's personal characteristics, the history of the trading relationship, and the specific requirements of the buyer and how the product being sold meets those requirements. In this way, the salesperson can frame sales presentations and answers to objections.

At the other end, the selling process does not finish when the sale is made. Indeed, the sale itself may only be the start of a long-term relationship between buyer and seller.

Personal selling is very appropriate in B2B markets, where there are fewer, higher-value customers who are looking for a more complex total offering tailored to a more specific set of requirements. Personal selling communicates a larger amount of technical and complex information than would be possible using other promotional methods, and there is greater ability to demonstrate a product's functions and characteristics.

(Syllabus area 3.9)

 EXAM TIP   format

Start by defining what personal selling is, and then explain what makes it so suitable for B2B markets.

Task Six

Identify and briefly explain the characteristics of services that distinguish them from products. (4 marks)

The following characteristics of services distinguish them from products.

- *Intangibility*: services cannot be touched or tasted
- *Inseparability*: services cannot be separated from the provider
- *Heterogeneity* (or lack of 'sameness'): the standard of service will vary with each delivery
- *Perishability*: services cannot be stored for provision 'later'
- *Ownership*: service purchase does not transfer ownership of property.

(Syllabus area 3.11)

 EXAM TIP   concept

This is a straightforward question that should cause few problems. Think of a service such as a train journey or the receipt of an insurance quote when looking at this list so that it makes complete sense to you.

Task Seven

Outline the key features of a production and a sales orientation, and how they contrast with a marketing orientation. (4 marks)

Concept	Focus	Means	Aims
Marketing orientation	Customer needs and wants; long-term customer relationships	Integrated marketing activities	Profitability through customer satisfaction
Sales orientation	Existing products made by the firm; creating sales transactions	Energetic selling and promoting	Profitability through sales volume
Production orientation	Assumed customer demand for product availability and affordability	Improving production and distribution efficiency	Profitability through efficiency

(Syllabus area 1.1)

The tabular format enables clear presentation of the three different philosophies – their features, how they are approached and what they strive for. In the context of the Organic Food Company, it is clear that a modern food producer and retailer, operating in a fiercely competitive market, will need to have a strong marketing orientation. It is no good producing organic foods that nobody will want to buy however cheap they are, or concentrating on selling existing products without finding out what customers want.

Task Eight

Explain what is meant by 'budgetary control' in the context of the marketing planning process. (4 marks)

A budget is a consolidated statement of the resources required to achieve desired objectives, or to implement planned activities. It is a planning and control tool relevant to all aspects of marketing management activities, because it plans how resources are going to be used in achieving marketing targets.

In terms of measuring marketing effectiveness for the Organic Food Company, budgeted results might comprise:

- Targets for the overall financial objectives and other strategy objectives such as sales targets and growth in the number of sales outlets

- Subsidiary financial targets, including the sales budget and marketing expenditure budget for each part of the business (the local markets, mail order, Internet, shops)

- Product-market strategy targets (such as sales to supermarkets of selected product lines)

- Targets for each element of the marketing mix (product range, price setting, promotional spend, distribution costs)

There are various methods of setting the marketing budget, but two common ones are designing it around the amount felt necessary to maintain a certain brand value, and setting expenditure at a certain percentage of sales or profits. The Organic Food Company appears to have its own marketing budget problems as the shops manager has spent his agreed budget already, but feels that more marketing activity is required. Senior management need to be sure that extra expenditure will be worthwhile.

If budgets are missed, part of any corrective action may well be to adjust the budget for future periods in the light of experience. A poorly constructed budget that cannot be attained is not an effective control mechanism.

(Syllabus area 2.4)

  EXAM TIP concept

Define what is meant by a budget, and then apply it to the marketing context. The use of a company with which you are familiar will help to structure the answer. It is important to be clear as to how budgets are used to control the resources required to undertake marketing activities.

Task Nine

Identify and briefly explain the stages in the product life cycle. (4 marks)

The product life cycle suggests that products are born (or introduced), grow to reach maturity and then enter old age and decline. The profitability and sales position of a product can be expected to change over time.

Introduction. A new product, following development, takes time to find acceptance by consumers and there is slow growth in sales. Only a few firms sell the product, unit costs are high and prices may be high as a result.

Growth. If the new product gains market acceptance, sales will rise more sharply and the product will start to make profits. New customers buy the product and, as production rises, unit costs fall. The Organic Food Company's range of organic wines probably falls into this category.

Maturity. The rate of sales growth slows down and the product reaches a period of maturity, which is probably the longest period of a successful product's life. Most products on the market are at the mature stage of their life.

Decline. Most products reach a stage of decline, which may be slow or fast. Many producers are reluctant to leave the market, although some inevitably do because of falling profits. If a product remains on the market too long, it will become unprofitable and the decline stage in its life cycle then gives way to an 'obsolescence' stage.

(Syllabus area 3.2)

  EXAM TIP   concept

This is a familiar model that you should be very comfortable with. Make sure that you are equally familiar with its limitations as these could easily form the subject of a question. One such appears on the Specimen Paper.

Task Ten

Explain the importance of branding and packaging in the successful marketing of a product for a business of your choice. (4 marks)

The key benefit of branding is product differentiation and recognition. It aids product differentiation by conveying a lot of information very quickly and concisely. This helps customers readily to identify the goods or services and thereby helps to create a customer loyalty to the brand.

- It maximises the impact of advertising for product identification and recognition.

- Branding leads to a readier acceptance of a manufacturer's goods by wholesalers and retailers, such as the major supermarkets stocking Organic Food Company lines

- It reduces the importance of price differentials between goods. Customers may choose Organic Food Company branded products even if they are a bit more expensive, if they are comfortable with and loyal to the brand

- It supports market segmentation, since different brands of similar products may be developed to meet specific needs of categories of uses.

- It supports brand extension. Other products can be introduced into the brand range to 'piggy back' on the articles already known to the customer, such as a range of organic wines to complement existing gourmet foods

Goods which are sold in large numbers, such as food products, promote a brand name by their existence and circulation. If the brand name is associated with quality, as is the case with the Organic Food Company, all goods in the range must be of that standard.

Product packaging fulfils a number of functions.

- Protection of contents from damage or deterioration

- Distribution, helping to transfer products from the manufacturer to the customer

- Selling, as the design and labeling provide information, attract attention and convey the brand image

- User convenience, as an aid to storage and carrying

- Compliance with government regulations eg providing a list of ingredients and contents by weight, as in food packaging

- Promotion, as packs can be used to print sales promotion information

- Management information, as bar codes can be used to track sales

Packaging and branding are related because values integral to the packaging itself (size, environment-friendliness, convenience, attractiveness, protection of product quality) are part of the overall image of the product. The sustainability of resources, and therefore the importance of recycling, is having a major impact upon companies' packaging decisions. The Organic Food Company has been innovative in introducing returnable packaging for dairy products.

Packaging must appeal not only to consumers, but also to distributors. A sales outlet wants a package design which helps to sell the product, but also minimises the likelihood of breakage, or extends the product's shelf life, or makes more economic use of shelf space.

(Syllabus area 3.1)

  EXAM TIP concept

This answer conveys a lot of information – the key point to bear in mind is that packaging and branding are key (and connected) elements of the product part of the marketing mix, promoting awareness and differentiation.

Task One

To: Marketing Director

From: Marketing Assistant

(a) **Factors involved in setting product prices**

Internal

Cost

This is the most important consideration and is generally used by when deciding on the pricing structure for our products. Samsung needs to at least set the lowest viable price at which the company can afford to sell the product. There are at least four different types of costs in regard to a product or service. These include fixed costs, variable costs, total costs and average costs.

(i) Fixed cost – a cost that does not change according to the increase in the number of units produced i.e. rent, rates and insurance for the premises. These fixed costs need to be spread over the forecasted number of products budgeted to be produced each year. This will identify how much cost from each product will be required within the selling price to cover the fixed costs of the organisation.

(ii) Variable costs – a cost that changes according to the number of units produced. These will include direct costs, such as the raw materials of chips and TFT-LCD screens and labour costs and indirect cost such as power and process costs used to make the Samsung products.

(iii) Average cost – this is the total cost divided by the number of units produced

(iv) The total cost is the sum of fixed and variable cost times the quantity produced. The company needs to monitor its costs to produce and sell its products carefully. If they are more than the competitors', Samsung Electronics will have to charge a higher price or make less profit, putting it a competitive disadvantage.

Organisational

Samsung Electronics must decide who within the organisation should set the prices, and the relevant price setting methodologies. Often they are negotiated by the sales force having been set by management. Companies handle pricing in a variety of ways, often delegating the decision to line managers. However, senior management must set the pricing objectives and policies and have operating procedures that give clear guidelines for line managers describing responsibility of approval.

Other internal factors

Our marketing objectives: is our aim profit maximisation or market share leadership?

Our marketing mix strategy: for example, factoring in the cost/ price implications of quality, we might decide that a high quality product demands a higher price to be in line with customer perceptions

Our product portfolio strategies are also very relevant: reference points for new products need to be set, and we may decide to have some 'loss leaders' to support the product range. Samsung prides itself on innovating and setting the pace, and prices need to support that strategy.

External

The market and demand

Forecasted customer demand is considered and calculations are made of how much will be demanded at a certain price using the demand curve. An important element is the premium added to the price to reflect the value of the brand. It is useful to know the shape of the demand curve when setting prices as we can set a higher price if our market is inelastic and attracted to the brand. Marketing communication serves to influence the demand curve to make it more inelastic by promoting the branded range of Samsung Electronics products. As costs increase we must consider year on year inflation, affecting the cost of employment, raw materials and distribution. Finally, it is important for us to consider the disposable income for our segmented target customer and understand the price implication during the economic cycle across the five main consumer-related business units of Samsung Electronics.

Competition

Our competitors of branded consumer products must be taken into account. The marketer looks at competitors, the macro environment, our internal environment and the stage in the product life cycle. An external factor affecting Samsung Electronics' pricing decisions is competitors' costs and prices, and possible competitor reactions to their own pricing initiatives.

A consumer who is considering the purchase of a Samsung product will evaluate its pricing and value against the prices and values of comparable products made by such brands as JVC, Panasonic, Technics, Sony and others. Customer perception and relative price sensitivity is very important. If Samsung Electronics follows a high price, high margin strategy it may attract competition. Conversely a low price, low margin strategy may stop competitors and drive them out of the market. Once Samsung Electronics is aware of competitors' prices and offers for each of its five main business units it can use them as a starting point for its own pricing to position its offer relative to the competition.

Suppliers and intermediaries' objectives

These will have an impacting on Samsung's costs, as they will react to price decisions to protect their own margins.

PEST factors

This is a general framework of external influences but we can point out that economic factors determine affordability, and often lead changing perceptions of 'value'; technology lowers production costs and this might enable us to lower prices for some products.

  EXAM TIP   concept

The examiner expects you to be able to consider the influences on price that will be applicable in a given business situation. Pricing is not just a matter of covering costs (although this is obviously very important): there are strategic considerations too. This question gives you good practice in this area. A detailed understanding of the marketing mix is required for this syllabus: do not forget the influence of the customer.

Factors involved in selecting distribution channels

In setting up a channel of distribution, Samsung has to take several factors into account.

* Samsung's own characteristics

Customers

The number of potential customers, their buying habits and their geographical proximity are key influences. The use of mail order and Internet purchases for those with limited time or mobility (remote rural location, illness) is an example of the influence of customers on channel design.

Different distribution strategies may be adopted for consumer and industrial markets. Industrial channels tend to be more direct and shorter. There have traditionally been fewer direct distribution channels from the manufacturer to the consumer in the consumer market. Even with the advent of e-commerce in some sectors, it is still more usual for companies in consumer markets such as Samsung to use wholesalers and retailers to move their product to the final consumer.

Nature of the goods or service

Some product characteristics have an important effect on design of the channel of distribution. Some fragile or bulky electronic items need extra care, and highly valuable items might be better suited to direct delivery.

Distributor characteristics

The location, customer base, performance and reliability, promotion and pricing policies of different types of distributor, and specific distribution outlets, will have to be evaluated.

Competitors' channel choice

For many consumer goods, a supplier's brand will sit alongside its competitors' products.

Costs

There are considerable costs associated with distribution. In addition to the costs of transporting finished goods, products will often need to be stored (in warehouses for example) or held somewhere (such as on the shop floor) awaiting sale or collection.

Samsung's own characteristics

A strong financial base gives the supplier the option of buying and operating their own distribution channel. The market position of Samsung is also important: distributors are keen to be associated with the market leader, but other brands may experience distribution problems.

Task Two

 EXAM TIP   concept

The setting of appropriate objectives puts marketing into the overall context of the business. Developing objectives generates the 'bigger picture' that the overall business strategy is designed to reflect. This helps with controlling business performance.

New product development is important in this context because it refreshes or extends the product range; and is part of the process of adapting to environmental opportunities and threats. This will contribute towards the success of a company's long term business strategy.

The importance of setting appropriate objectives

- Objective setting is a key part of marketing planning. Objectives should set out clearly what the organisation is aiming to achieve, both at the corporate level and at the marketing level.

- Corporate objectives define specific goals for the organisation as a whole. These may be expressed in terms of profitability, returns on investment, growth of asset base and earnings per share. They may also reflect non-financial goals: innovation, market share, corporate social responsibility, leading employer brand etc. Corporate objectives then need to be translated into market-specific marketing objectives.

What is a new product?

- One that opens up an entirely new market

- One that replaces an existing product

- One that broadens significantly the market for an existing product

- Whatever the category that a new product falls into, it is an important contributor to overall business strategy and growth.

The importance of new product development for Samsung

There are a number of reasons why a company such as Samsung needs to consider extending its product mix with the introduction of new products.

To meet the changing needs/wants of customers: a new product may meet a new need (eg for environmentally friendly alternatives) or meet an existing need more effectively (eg digital cameras, mobile phone technology).

To match competitors: responding to innovations and market trends before or shortly after competitors, so as not to miss marketing opportunities.

To respond to environmental threats and opportunities: capitalising on opportunities presented by new technology, say (digital cameras), or other products (accessories and supplies for digital cameras); minimising the effects of threats such as environmental impacts (developing 'green' alternatives) or safety concerns (developing new safety features).

To extend the product/brand range as part of a product development or diversification growth strategy. New products can bring new customers to the brand and enable cross-selling of products in the mix.

To extend the 'maturity' stage of the PLC for a product, by modifying it to maintain interest, simulate re-purchase (because it is 'new and improved') and/or target as yet unreached market segments.

To refresh the product range, as products go into the decline stage of their life cycle. Some products may become obsolete and need updating. Others will simply be deleted, and the company will need to replace them in the product mix in order to maintain brand presence and profitability.

It can be seen that new product development (NPD) is a very important growth strategy for a company such as Samsung Electronics developing a new mobile cell phone. In the high technology sector, which is becoming increasingly led by the latest fashion, it is extremely important to be seen as the company which is 'setting the pace' with innovative new products.

NPD plays an important part in the company's ability to grow. If a company continues to produce and market the same product to new and existing market sectors it will eventually exhaust the market because all consumers will have purchased the product.

NPD can mean that a totally new mobile phone can be produced that has not been marketed before. Product diversification is a good way of getting into new market segments and obtaining new market share with the production of a product, such as with mobile phones, that has not been targeted to a segmented group of users of this product. NPD can also mean that an existing product is launched but with a modification. For example we have a mobile phone in the marketplace that has a new technology such as a camera. An upgrade of this product would be the introduction of MP3 player technology into the mobile phone.

Task Three

EXAM TIP

application

In this syllabus, it is important that you are able to explain the role of marketing in building and retaining customer relationships, and the concept of relationship marketing. This question is a good test of your ability to apply the theory to a business situation.

Building relationships with customers

Relationship marketing is the process of creating, building up and managing long-term relationships with customers, distributors and suppliers. It aims to change the focus from getting customers to keeping customers.

Under a relationship marketing approach, all the activities of Samsung Electronics are used to build, maintain and develop customer relationships, the objective being to build customer loyalty leading to customer retention.

There are five distinguishable levels with the relationship that can be formed with customers who have purchased a product or service. These are:

Basic	Selling a product without any follow up
Reactive	Selling a product with follow up encouraged on the part of the customer
Accountable	Having sold a product the follow up occurs a short time afterwards to confirm the customer's expectations have been met
Proactive	The sales person contacts the customer from time to time with suggestions regarding improved products
Partnership	The company works continuously with the customer to deliver improved levels of value

Relationship marketing can contribute to an organisation in a number of ways. It can establish a rapport with customers, creating trust and confidence. It allows an opportunity to interact and hence communicate the organisation's commitment to satisfying customers' needs and wants. By creating a notional bond as one of its objectives relationship marketing strives to achieve a sense of belonging, thereby making the customer feel part of the business. It attempts to tailor products and services to cater for specific needs of customers and therefore reduces the need to 'switch'. The use of database management and information communication technology helps to address the customer needs in a very focused manner and can be manipulated to the individual's requirements.

There are significant benefits that can be derived from relationship marketing. It can contribute to cost savings as it is up to five times more expensive to find a new customer than retain an existing customer. It can help to entice new customers away from competitors as a perceived added value activity. It will also make it more difficult for existing customers to switch, as there is an emotional bond that underpins loyalty to the customer and the company

Relationship management is concerned with getting and keeping customers by ensuring that an appropriate combination of marketing, customer service and quality is provided. In order for relationship marketing to work, it is important for Samsung Electronics to recognise that both parties must feel that they can benefit from long-term relationships rather than one-off transactions. A key element of relationship marketing is that development of such mutually beneficial long-term relationships between customers and suppliers is considered by Samsung Electronics. Relationship marketing also widens the concept of exchange to consider all of the parties involved. To ensure successful relationship marketing there needs to be an appropriate supportive organisational culture and everyone in the business must be concerned with generating customer satisfaction.

It is important to recognise that consumers have become more sophisticated and therefore their purchasing behaviour has become more complex. Customers require a more customised offering and therefore require individual treatment. Customers are becoming more susceptible to switching between suppliers, and competition has increased in the marketplace, including the one for high technology products. Focus on trust and loyalty has become key elements of the marketing activity and needs to be recognised by Samsung Electronics.

For consumer products, relationship marketing can be applied through the service encounters at the retailer; by the experience of purchasing online at the point of delivery of the purchase; or with financing or after-sales issues related to the purchase, such as product insurance.

Conclusion

Relationship marketing is a technique that accommodates the broader perspective of building loyal customers in an ever increasingly competitive consumer electronics market place servicing customers with a wide variety of needs.

Section 3

Assessing the Marketing Environment

Topic list

1 Unit overview and syllabus

The aim of this unit is to provide an understanding of the nature and scope of the internal and external marketing environment with broad consideration of the impact of international and global marketing.

The unit seeks to provide an overview of the significance of the marketing environment within the confines of the PESTEL model, but with consideration of issues including environmental and economic sustainability.

The unit addresses the key characteristics of the marketing environment and assesses the impact of market forces that are uncontrollable and how an organisation responds to them. At the same time, some consideration should be given in terms of how the factors within the micro and internal environment can be manipulated to the benefit of the organisation and its customers.

On completion, students should be able to demonstrate a detailed understanding of the internal, micro and macro environment. This should include consideration of the key controllable and uncontrollable drivers of change, and the challenges posed to market oriented organisations in today's volatile and dynamic business and marketing environment.

Overarching learning outcomes

By the end of this unit students should be able to:

- Explain the nature and scope of the internal marketing environment, including the resource perspective

- Distinguish between the types of organisation within the public, private and voluntary sectors and understand the different influences and challenges they face and how their objectives differ as a result

- Identify and explain the different characteristics of the micro environment and recognise the sources of information required to gain a good understanding of it together with its drivers and challenges

- Assess the importance of and potential impact on a market oriented organisation of key trends in political, economic, social, technological and legal/ethical/regulatory environment

- Consider the implications for organisations pursuing both economic and environmental sustainability as part of its agenda for CSR

SECTION 1 – The nature of the organisation (weighting 15%)

1.1 Evaluate the different characteristics of the internal marketing environment, and consider the challenges facing the organisation in developing the customer value proposition including:
- Resource capability
- Competency
- Internal politics
- Objectives
- Key internal drivers

1.2 Explain the classification of public, private and voluntary sector organisation in terms of:
- Legal forms
- Organisational characteristics, influences and challenges
- Divorce of ownership and control

1.3 Explain how organisational objectives differ across a range of different sectors and consider the influences upon setting these objectives and the challenges they represent:

- Identifying stakeholder needs

- Satisfying stakeholder needs

- The increasing need to address corporate social responsibility issues

1.4 Assess the comparative strengths and weaknesses of small/medium and large/global organisations in the context of the marketing environment:

- Business/local focus versus global focus (ie, standardisation versus adaptation

- Organisational constraints:

- Objectives

- Resources

- Risks

- PESTEL

- Shareholders

- Stakeholders

- Niche versus mass marketing

SECTION 2 – Planning within the marketing context (weighting 30%)

2.1 Evaluate the stakeholders that constitute the micro environment within which organisations operate and their importance to the marketing process:

- Company

- Customers

- Competitors

- Suppliers

- Distributors

2.2 Evaluate the micro environmental factors that have a bearing on an organisation's ability to meet customer expectations and generate customer satisfaction:

- The importance of continuous marketing research

- Product/service portfolio analysis

- The link between service quality and customer satisfaction

- Extended marketing mix

2.3 Explain the nature of the interactions between the organisation and its various stakeholders including shareholders, employees, customers, local communities, suppliers, channel members and competitors:

- Understanding and managing stakeholder power and interest

- Developing relationships with partners, pressure groups, consumer groups etc

- Competition for customers

- Consumer protection legislation

2.4   Evaluate the different types and sources of information required to gain an in-depth understanding of the micro-environment:

- Company reports
- Department of Trade and Industry
- Central Office of Statistics Office
- Research organisations eg, Dunn and Bradstreet, MINTEL, etc
- Industry journals

2.5   Examine the nature, scope and impact of competition policies on the organisation and its marketing environment:

- Legislation, regulatory bodies and watchdogs
- Monopolies and mergers
- EU Competition Policy
- Bilateral international competition relationships (Europe, Japan and the USA)
- Fair trade policies (local versus international)
- Patents
- Trademarks

2.6   Explain the process for undertaking a detailed competitor analysis and how the analysis influences the marketing decision making process:

- Competitor identification
- Competitor strengths and weaknesses
- Competitor strategies
- Competitor response patterns (tactics)
- Key success factors (KSF)
- Company capability profiling

SECTION 3 – The macro environment (weighting 40%)

3.1   Explain the importance of the macro environment to the marketing process:

- PESTEL market performance indicators
- Identification and implications of market turbulence, complexity and dynamism
- Effects of changing markets within the world arena

3.2   Identify key sources of information useful in analysing the macro-environment.

- Government statistics
- Economic indicators
- Business confidence indicators
- Internet
- Trade publications, etc

3.3   Explain the social, demographic and cultural environments and, in general terms, their influence on and implications for marketing including:

- Social cultural behaviour and change
- Demographic/population trends, etc
- The need for social responsibility and marketing ethics
- The growth of consumerism

3.4 Explain the economic environments within an international context and, in general terms, their influence on and implications for marketing, including consideration of:

- Interest rates
- Exchange rates
- GDP
- GNP
- Effects of demand and supply
- Economic growth and unemployment
- The effect of changing economies eg,
  - The single European Market (EU)
  - Market driven economies in Eastern European
- European Monetary Union
- Business cycle

3.5 Explain the political and legislative environments and, in general terms, their influence on and implications for marketing:

- Political activities resulting in legislative changes
- Green legislation
- Customer protection legislation
- Employment legislation, etc

3.6 Explain the natural environment and, in general terms, its influence on and implications for marketing including:

- Policies relating to emissions and waste, etc
- Governmental and pressure group influence on environmental priorities
- Pollution and waste management
- Moral and ethical responsibility
- Green marketing – 5Rs (ROI, Reach, Responsibility, Reputation, Revenue)
- Social responsibility and sustainability

3.7 Assess the potential significance of environmental challenges to marketing in the future:

- Globalisation
- Global warming/emissions/carbon footprints
- Environmental decline
- Shortage of natural resources
- Reducing waste
- Increasing re-cycling
- Alternative energy sources (wind power, solar power, electric/gas cars, etc)
- Alternative transportation

3.8 Explain the evolution of the technical and information environments and consider its actual and potential impacts on organisations, employment, marketing and communications:

- The technical diffusion process
- Technology and the workforce
- Technology and the impact of social change
- The convergence of technology ie, telecommunications linked with media communications
- Digital superhighways
- Credit transfer
- The internet and other technology based communication tools

3.9   Evaluate the impact of economic and environmental sustainability on an organisation's CSR agenda including the impact it has on the organisation, its vision, mission and objectives:

- Environmental information systems
- Impact analysis
- Codes of conduct
- Social/conscience marketing/human rights
- Ethics
- Environmental sustainability
- Shareholder activism (Green shareholders)

3.10   Evaluate different methods for undertaking analysis of environmental trends:

- Environmental audits
- Quantitative and qualitative forecasting techniques
- Trend impact analysis
- Scenario building
- Delphi method

3.11   Review the emergence of social marketing as an increasing trend in establishing social values associated with CSR:

- Growth of social and cause related marketing
- Traceability/Transparency
- Fair trade/Local product policy
- Government initiatives eg, packaging, labelling, recycling, etc

SECTION 4 – Undertaking a marketing audit (weighting 10%)

4.1   Explain the process of undertaking the internal and external market   environment audit:

- Environmental scanning
- Collecting internal and external marketing information
- PESTEL analysis
- A competitor comparison of key competitors
- Assessing opportunities and threats
- Reviewing environmental and resource constraints

4.2   Describe the meaning and role of various analytical tools in the marketing auditing process:

- PESTEL
- Five Ms
- Ansoff's Growth Strategy Matrix
- SWOT

2   The exam paper

This examination is unique within the Professional Certificate level because it is the only paper in which you are given a case study **five weeks** before your exam to prepare some analysis of the marketing situation in advance. This analysis will include a **SWOT and PESTEL** analysis which should not exceed four A4 pages. You are to take your analysis along to assist you in the exam and submit this along with your exam answers. You are not awarded any marks within the marking scheme for this preparatory analysis however you will find the examination significantly easier if you have prepared effectively.

On the day of the exam you are given questions to respond to about the case study and a clean copy of the case study.

The examination will last for **three hours**. All the tasks will relate to the pre-seen case study and are divided into two compulsory parts.

Part A- comprises **five** compulsory **short answer** tasks. This is worth 40% of the final mark.

Part B- comprises **three** compulsory **extended answer** tasks. This is worth 60% of the final mark.

3 How to prepare the pre-seen case

3.1 What the Case Study is and how it differs from other CIM papers

Case studies represent **real organisations** and describe the marketing challenges they face. Often, cases are also set in real time and so you may well be faced with a very topical issue. You will be given a large amount of information and will need to spend a significant amount of time working through it.

  EXAM TIP application

Whilst writing the cases for 2008 and 2009 the global financial crises and UK recession may feature within the case study given their importance to the marketing environment. You should be wary however about jumping to conclusions and making too many assumptions about a given situation. The case material that you are given may refer to a time prior to a recession for example and you need to demonstrate that you are immersed in the actual case environment rather than being distracted by real life events. You should not let real life events (however unexpected) unnecessarily colour your interpretation of the situation (even through you can state certain assumptions) the trick is to stick to the details of the situation as outlined in the case.

3.2 Procedure

You will be given the case study **five weeks prior to the exam** date. You then have time to complete your analysis of the marketing environment and **prepare PESTEL and SWOT analyses**.

In the exam room, you will be faced with specific questions relating to the case.

You are expected to take into the exam a limited number of pre-prepared pages of analysis summary. We will say more about how to prepare for these later in this section.

3.3 The value of Case Study in the work place

There are few short cuts when it comes to tackling a case study and it is a time-consuming exercise, but you will find the process extends your knowledge and improves skills which have immediate relevance to your work.

Case Study is a very **practical** examination. A knowledge of marketing theory on its own will not be sufficient to gain you an exam pass. You have to be able to apply that theory in the context of a real business issue and situation. This means that you must:

(a)   Know the framework for assessing the marketing environment
(b)   Be able to apply the various tools of analysis
(c)   Be able to make marketing decisions based on the marketing environment
(d)   Be able to condense detailed analysis into a summarised maximum of four pages of A4
(e)   Have the skills to present your views and ideas in a convincing way

Even experienced marketers often pay little more than lip service to assessing the environment effectively. Faced with the pressure of an impending examination, many candidates are amazed at the depth and quality of analysis they are able to conduct, even with the limited information supplied in a case. This experience can be a useful benchmark for marketing planning in your own business.

Some students get concerned about not being expert in the sector of the exam case study. It can seem daunting if you have services marketing experience and are suddenly faced with an FMCG challenge, like Cadbury (the sample assessment). This may seem unrealistic and less representative of life in the business world. However, in our experience, it is a very real reflection of the situations faced by marketing consultants. Marketers expertise is *marketing*, and the disciplines and concepts of marketing travel well between sectors. If anything, lack of detailed industry or product knowledge makes it easier to avoid the myopia so often characteristic of those who are product focused.

Besides the chance to practise analysis and decision-making skills, the case study also provides the opportunity further to develop **team-work skills**. Unless you are studying independently, you will probably be tackling the case as part of a formal syndicate or study group. This is an excellent idea as it provides a time efficient way of tackling analysis as well as providing a forum for brainstorming and creative thinking. However, to make a syndicate work, you need to have and use team working skills and be disciplined in how you communicate with other members. Again, these are practical skills highly valued in the workplace.

 EXAM TIP format

WARNING!

If you are working with peers to analyse the case study, make sure that the final SWOT and PESTEL analysis taken into the exam are **your own work**. The CIM's 'Important notes for candidates' are very clear in their requirement for individual work only.

3.4 Case problems and challenges

Case study brings with it its own set of problems and challenges which you need to be aware of before beginning your studies.

3.4.1 Exam technique

In practice, relatively few candidates fail examinations because of lack of knowledge. **Much more common is a lack of exam technique**. This results in any one of a number of common problems including failing to **manage time** or answer the question set. Similarly, with the Case Study exam, it is often a failure of technique not knowledge which causes exam failure. Exam technique is rather different for a case exam, but none the less requires practice and the development of a wide range of skills already alluded to, from analysis to persuasive communication, skills which you would expect to find in a **competent, practising junior marketer**.

Exam technique for the case study starts when the exam case is **issued**. Finding enough time for preparation and using that time effectively is all part of case technique. The seeds of success or failure are sown during this important preparation time, so **preparation is key**.

3.4.2 Valuable information

The exams may seem like a long way off, but it is never too early to start planning for them. Check out the date of your exam. **The exact date should be available on the CIM website**. Calculate back five weeks from this date. This is the latest date the case should be issued to you. By this date, you want to have broadly completed your studying of the unit, completed any assignment work for other units and have begun your revision for Marketing Essentials examination.

- Avoid planning too many events for those pre-exam weekends
- Talk to your employer about taking some study leave
- Book holiday time for study if necessary

Don't forget that the time you spend before the exam should also be dedicated to topic revision before you can begin to *apply* your knowledge using the case study. We have included additional question topic practice at the end of this section which you can work through at your early stage of revision or as you progress through your learning before you receive the case materials.

3.4.3 Planning

Using your preparation time well is the next case challenge. **Sharing the workload** by being part of a study group is to be advised whenever possible. There is no doubt that cracking a case study alone is hard and lonely work, but, whether working alone or as part of a group, you need a timetable and plan of action. Some candidates fail to meet the challenge of analysis. They do too little or too much. Both are recipes for failure. Watch out for indications of which trap you are most likely to fall into.

The Too Little Analysis Candidate	The Too Much Analysis Candidate

The Reader. Confuses reading the case with analysis of it. Does not see the importance of spending time really considering the details of the case.	**The Analysis Addict**. Suffers from the complaint we know as **Analysis Paralysis**. The symptoms are fear of decision-making and finding comfort in the safe activity of analysis.
The Too Little Analysis Candidate	**The Too Much Analysis Candidate**

The Juggler. Typically puts off tackling the Case analysis till the week before the exam. With so much other revision to do, it is easy to not take the case seriously. Sadly what might seem straightforward and obvious at the first read often proves much more complex after detailed analysis.	**The Detail Fanatic**. It is easy to get hung upon detailed aspects of the industry you have been given and the company itself. You are not expected to contact the case company or look for additional information. There may be inconsistencies but successful candidates do not let this distract them. They keep focused on the bigger picture, and where necessary, they make assumptions and move on.

Adequate analysis will ensure you have a sound grasp of the case issues and have the facts and figures needed to support your recommendations and convince the examiner of their commercial credibility.

3.5 The specimen case study

The following information is the sample (specimen) material provided by the CIM when this syllabus was launched. Step 1 is to read it!

Cadbury Schweppes

Cadbury Schweppes' origins date back to the founding of Schweppes, a mineral water business, by Jacob Schweppe in 1783, and the opening of a shop that sold cocoa products, by John Cadbury in 1824. The two businesses were merged in 1969 to create Cadbury Schweppes plc. Many of their key brands are long-established, having been launched in the late 19th and early 20th centuries, most notably Cadbury Dairy Milk and Dr Pepper.

Cadbury Schweppes' principal businesses are confectionery and non-alcoholic beverages. It has the largest share of the global confectionery market with broad participation across all categories and by geography. In beverages, the company has strong regional presences in North America and Australia.

Confectionery

Cadbury Schweppes' confectionery strategy is to significantly grow its share of the global confectionery market through organic growth and acquisition. In 2004, Cadbury Schweppes had the number one share of the global confectionery market (source: Euromonitor), having substantially grown share through expansion both geographically and in product participation.

In 2005, Cadbury Schweppes had the largest share of the global confectionery market at 10% (source: Euromonitor). This compares with a market share of 5.3% in 2001. The company has strong positions in many of the world's important confectionery markets, and a leading market share of all its geographic regions. It reported that profit from operations had increased from £825 million in 2004 to £1003 million in 2005.

Beverages

Cadbury Schweppes' beverage strategy is to concentrate on strong regional beverages businesses, focusing on the Americas and Australia. In 1999, Cadbury Schweppes sold its beverages businesses in around 160 countries to focus on those regions where the company had, or could build, a sustained competitive advantage.

In 2005, Cadbury Schweppes concluded that growth and returns could be better increased through focus and investment in its advantaged global confectionery business, and American and Australian regional beverages operations rather than by further investment in Europe Beverages. Therefore, Cadbury Schweppes decided it would be in the best interests of its shareholders to sell the Europe Beverages business. The sale, for €1.85 billion, was completed on 2 February 2006.

In the Americas, Cadbury Schweppes has increased the scale of its operations and expanded its brand portfolio, particularly in the non-carbonated sector of the beverages market. In 2005, Cadbury Schweppes grew its share of the US carbonated soft drinks market, the world's largest, to 17%. In Australia, Cadbury Schweppes has the number two position in the soft drinks market.

Together, its US beverages and confectionery businesses make Cadbury Schweppes the 10th largest food supplier to the US grocery trade. Similarly in Australia, Cadbury Schweppes' combined confectionery and beverages businesses make it the largest supplier of food products to the grocery trade.

Goals and Priorities

Cadbury Schweppes' strategic goals for 2004 – 2007 are to:

- Deliver superior shareowner performance
- Profitability and significantly increase global confectionery share
- Profitably secure and grow regional beverages share
- Ensure capabilities are best in class
- Reinforce reputation with employees and society

The company believes that it can consistently deliver superior shareowner performance by profitably growing its global confectionery and regional beverages businesses: ensuring that its team and capabilities are 'best in class', and ensuring that it has strong relationships with its employees and the communities in which it does business.

Regions and functions

The company is organised into four business segments called regions. Each region is focused on commercial operations in its geographical and product area. The four regions are:

- Americas Beverages
- Americas Confectionery
- Europe, Middle East and Africa
- Asia Pacific

Competition

The confectionery and soft drinks industries are highly competitive. Cadbury Schweppes' brands compete with those of many other multi-national, national and regional companies and private label suppliers in various markets. The company competes actively in terms of quality, taste and price of products and seeks to develop and enhance brand recognition through the introduction of new products and packaging, and extensive advertising and promotional programmes.

It is the world's leading confectionery group by sales value. Chocolate confectionery is primarily a branded market. Four groups account for around 44% of the world market, each with market share built on regional strengths. Its 7.8% chocolate share is built on strong positions in the UK, Ireland, Australia, New Zealand and India. The sugar confectionery market is significantly more fragmented, with a greater presence of local and regional brands and private label products, but a 6.9% share makes Cadbury Schweppes the global market leader. Gum is also a branded market. It is more global in nature with brands and products more consistent across geographies. Two groups account for approximately 62% of the global total. Cadbury Schweppes' number two position is built on strong market shares in the Americas, parts of Continental Europe, Japan and Thailand.

The soft drinks industry includes a number of brand owners that act as licensors of branded products. Through Dr Pepper/Seven Up, Cadbury Schweppes is the third largest carbonated soft drinks group in the US by sales volume. In Australia, it is the second largest beverages company and the fourth largest supplier of edible products to the grocery trade.

Industry trends

Both the confectionery and beverages markets in which Cadbury Schweppes operates are growing. The main drivers are population growth and increased consumer wealth (particularly in developing markets), and product innovation, affecting both developed and developing markets.

According to Euromonitor, the global confectionery market grew in value by 3.9% in 2004. It forecasts a similar rate of growth continuing for the foreseeable future. Within the overall confectionery market, chocolate grew at 4.1% in 2004, sugar by 2.4% and gum by 6.5%. In gum, consumers are switching from sugared to sugar-free products; 70% of Cadbury Schweppes' gum is sugar-free.

Overall, developing markets are growing faster than developed markets. Around 30% of Cadbury Schweppes' confectionery sales are generated in developing markets around the world. Its key developing markets are Mexico and Brazil in the Americas Confectionery region; Russia, Poland, Turkey, Egypt and South Africa in the EMEA region; and India and Thailand in the Asia Pacific region.

Its main beverages market is the US. According to AC Nielsen, the US refreshment beverages market, which includes non-alcoholic carbonated and non-carbonated soft drinks, grew by 2% in volume and 6% in value in 2005. Carbonated soft drinks (CSDs) volumes have been flat or declining in recent years, and fell by 3% in 2005. The decline has been attributed to a combination of above inflation pricing and consumers switching to non-carbonated products, primarily sports drinks and bottled water. Within the carbonated market, products sweetened with sugar (regular) declined 5% in 2005, while those sweetened with low calorie sweeteners (diet) grew slightly by 1%. Cadbury Schweppes has six out of the top 10 non-cola diet CSDs in the US, including Diet Dr Pepper, Diet A&W, Diet Sunkist and Diet Rite. In 2005, diet CSDs accounted for 24% of its US CSD sales and grew by 4%. The company does not participate in the sports drinks market in the US, and has only a small presence in the bottled water market. The non-CSD categories in which it participates grew by 2% in volume in 2005.

Many of Cadbury Schweppes' businesses are seasonal. Their seasonality is primarily influenced either by the weather, or by religious festivals and holidays. Within the Group, its businesses have different seasonal cycles throughout the year depending on their geographical location and the timing of festivals and holidays, which also may vary from year to year. For the Group as a whole, the second half of the year is typically the larger half.

Consumers and customers

Cadbury Schweppes' products are primarily impulse products and are sold to the consumer through many different outlets, ranging from grocery stores to petrol station kiosks and fountain equipment at leisure, food and entertainment venues. In many markets, sales to the large multiple grocery trade accounts for less than 50% of sales. No single customer accounts for more than 10% of its revenue in any period presented. It has a variety of programmes in place to ensure that consumer insights are built into its commercial strategy.

Raw materials and suppliers

Cadbury Schweppes uses a wide range of raw materials in manufacturing its products; the main ones being cocoa beans, sugar and other sweeteners (including polyols and artificial sweeteners such as aspartame), dairy products including milk, and fruit and nuts.

It buys its raw materials from about 40,000 suppliers around the world. No single supplier accounts for more than 10% of its raw material purchases. It developed a Human Rights and Ethical Trading (HRET) policy in 2000, and seeks to minimise the impact of price fluctuations and ensure security of supply by entering into forward agreements and long-term contracts wherever available.

The company imports cocoa beans from West Africa and the Far East. West Africa accounts for over 60% of world production. It buys cocoa beans and cocoa butter from a range of suppliers, and tries to minimise the effect of cocoa price movements and secure its future requirements by entering into forward and future contracts.

It purchases most of its sugar at prices essentially set by the European Union or maintained by various national governments through quotas and duties. Only a relatively small proportion is purchased at fluctuating world prices. It has not experienced difficulty in obtaining adequate supplies of sugar for its operations, and does not anticipate any future difficulties, given the many available sources.

Corporate and Social Responsibility (CSR)

Cadbury Schweppes believes that corporate social responsibility is an integral part of being an effective, value-creating business. It always seeks to manage the business in a way that is both profitable and responsible and adds value to shareowners and to the wider society. This commitment is explicitly stated as one of its businesses five goals; "nurture the trust of colleagues and communities".

To sustain its success in different and changing markets and diverse cultures, the Board of Cadbury Schweppes is committed to achieving superior levels of business integrity, ethics and professionalism, working to high international standards of corporate and social responsibility and corporate governance across all its activities. Cadbury Schweppes is a signatory to the UN Global Compact and endorses its ideals.

The CSR committee oversees an agenda covering five activity areas:

- Human rights and employment standards
- Ethical sourcing and procurement
- Marketing Food and Consumer issues
- Environment, health and safety
- Community.

Human rights and employment standards

Cadbury Schweppes' Human Rights and Ethical Trading (HRET) policy has been developed taking into account international standards – such as the International Labour Organisation conventions, the UN Declaration of Human Rights, and OECD guidelines – as well as cultural and industry best practice from its local markets. Adopted by the Main Board in 2000, it covers core labour rights and dignity at work; health and safety in the workplace; fair remuneration; diversity and respect for differences and opportunity for development.

Ethical sourcing and procurement

Ethical sourcing and sustainability are two key drivers of Cadbury Schweppes' Global Supply Chain. Ethical Sourcing Standards for the Group based on the learning from pilot studies completed in five countries (China, Ghana, Indonesia,

Mexico and Turkey), were put in place in 2002. These standards are being underpinned with a system for supplier evaluation, training for employees and a programme of engagement with its suppliers.

Marketing Food and Consumer issues

Cadbury Schweppes' Food Issues Strategy Group drives the global strategy to ensure that the company is innovating, investing and managing its business to keep abreast of, understand and meet the needs of consumers with respect to the way it develops, produces and markets its products.

In 2005, the company rolled out a 12 Point Action Plan in response to consumer health concerns, embracing a global marketing code of advertising, including special reference to children, and an extensive series of policies on matters related to food and its content. A particular area of focus is the development of sustainable solutions to obesity and poor lifestyles.

Building CSR into its brands is a top priority for Cadbury Schweppes covering areas such as labelling, consumer information, ethical sourcing, responsible advertising and cause-related marketing. It also has an active engagement with the World Health Organisation and non-governmental organisations (NGOs) on matters of importance to consumers.

Environment, health and safety

Cadbury Schweppes' Environment, Health and Safety (EHS) Steering Group deals with environmental issues related to the manufacturing of its products, protecting bio-diversity and the eco-systems from which it sources raw materials, the management of its supply chain and the distribution, sale and consumption of its products. Sustainable agriculture is an important opportunity for the company, as well as for the farming communities the company works with.

Community

Cadbury Schweppes aims to create prosperous, educated, sustainable and healthy communities in the countries and cultures in which it operates. With a focus on education and enterprise, health and welfare and the environment, the company develops targeted programmes for local communities.

External Ratings

Cadbury Schweppes' CSR performance is rated by various external organisations' indices. These include:

- Dow Jones Sustainability World Index. In 2005, the company was scored at 73%, up from 71% in 2004

- FTSE4Good and FTSE4Good Supply Chain Labour Standards Criteria. Cadbury Schweppes is included in these indices, which measure performance of companies that meet globally recognised CSR and supply chain labour standards

- The Carbon Disclosure project included Cadbury Schweppes in their Climate Leadership Index for the second year running

- UK's Business in the Community Corporate Responsibility Index. In 2005, Cadbury Schweppes was rated at 89%, up from 87% in 2004

Source: Cadbury Schweppes Annual Report 2005

Supporting Data: Cadbury Schweppes

Number of No. 1 or No. 2 Positions in the Top 50 Confectionery Markets by Geography

	Cadbury Schweppes	Nestle	Kraft	Mars	Wrigley	Hershey
No.1 Position	16	6	5	2	5	1
No.2 Position	8	10	5	6	3	1
Total Confectionery	24	16	10	8	8	2

Source: Euromonitor 2004

Market Share in the Global Confectionery Market (US dollar share)

	Global confectionery market	Chocolate	Sugar	Gum
Cadbury Schweppes	10.0%	7.8%	6.9%	26.0%
Mars	9.2%	15.2%	3.1%	0.2%
Nestlé	7.8%	12.3%	3.6%	–
Hershey	5.8%	8.4%	3.1%	1.7%
Wrigley	4.9%	–	0.3%	36.0%
Kraft	4.9%	7.3%	2.7%	0.5%

Source: Euromonitor 2004

Sales Contribution by Product

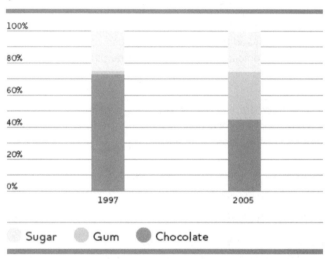

Sales Contribution by Geography

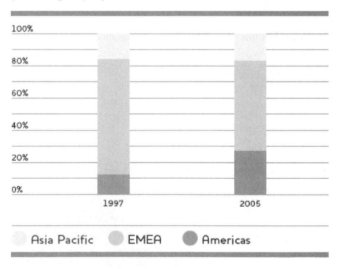

Revenue by region

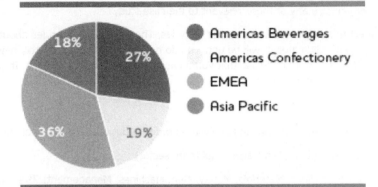

Underlying Profit from Operations

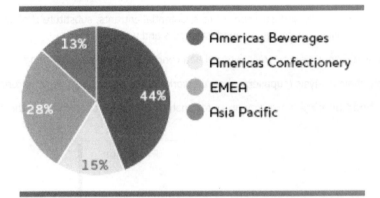

  ACTIVITY

application

You should now have read through the case study. Before going any further, think about your immediate first impressions in terms of

- What is your overall feeling about the case?
- What were the main issues discussed in the case?
- What are the contextual issues? eg the industry sector, timescales, areas of business

3.6 'Unpacking' the case study

Within this section we will look at what to do with the case study once you have received it and read it through for the first time. To 'unpack' the case study means to identify the main issues within it and to understand the core points. It is best broken into a number of stages.

Stage 1 - The initial read through

You will have completed this by this point.

Stage 2 - The active read through cycles

When reading through again, you should go through with a highlighter. If necessary, scan the case, photocopy it or download an extra copy for use at this initial stage. Your aim is to go through and pick out the key information with your first impressions in mind and any other key points that you may have missed on first reading the case. Begin to group these ideas into key themes, using diagrams, mind maps, tables or lists. Generally it does not matter the format you use at this stage so long as it makes sense to you. As you go through these cycles of active reading, you should consider the topics that are covered by the syllabus and your reading of the study text. Think about the activities you have completed as self study or within a classroom, are any of these relevant to the case study?

You should expect this stage to take a number of cycles. There are really no rules about how many times you should actively read through the case. Ultimately it will be until you do not see anything completely new. You should also try to leave short periods of time between these cycles so that you do not become 'blind' to the case. It is amazing how after a few days away from it, new issues become apparent.

Stage 3- The analysis

You should aim to complete the following analyses in order to put the case material into context:

- Organisational context (Type, size, legal form, sector)

- Internal analysis (5M's: Materials, Money, Men, Machines, Management; 7S's: Structure, Strategy, Systems, Shared values, Style, Staff, Skills)

- Customer analysis (identifying the value proposition, segments, needs analysis, consumer behavioural factors)

- Competitor analysis (industry competitors, potential entrants, substitute products, power, collaboration, competitor response profiles, strategies pursued, strengths and weaknesses)

- Stakeholder analysis (Internal, external and connected; Mendelow mapping)

- Supply chain analysis (supplier power, networks, trade agreements, raw materials sourcing, distribution channels)

You can also **head up pages** with key areas for analysis to help you sort through the case.

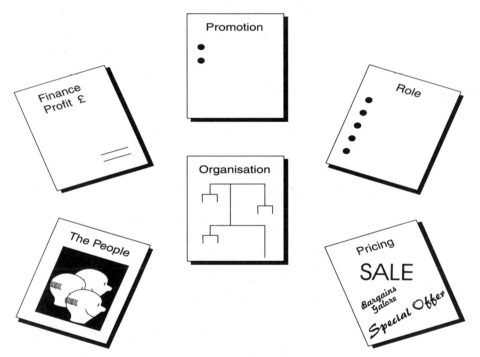

To help you to contextualise the case material you could use the syllabus content and the topics covered within the study text to provide a structure to these analyses. Work through the theories and identify whether there is any information about the scenario covered within the case study.

For example syllabus item 1.1 is shown in the following table where we use the syllabus as a checklist and use a few analytical tools such as the 5M's.

1.1 Evaluate the different characteristics of the internal marketing environment, and consider the challenges facing the organisation in developing the customer value proposition including:

- Resource capability
- Competency
- Internal politics
- Objectives
- Key internal drivers

Now taking each of these issues in turn we can identify whether there is anything within the case material which directly or indirectly addresses them.

1.1 Evaluate the different characteristics of the internal marketing environment, and consider the challenges facing the organisation in developing the customer value proposition including:

Resource capability (5M's analysis will help with this.)	**Materials** - sourced from a range of 40,000 suppliers, wide range of raw ingredients, price fluctuations minimised through long term contracts, futures and EU quota/duty programmes. Ethical sourcing and procurement implemented. **Money** - revenue spread through the core regions but a larger second half of the year. **Men** - linked to core goal to "*nurture the trust of colleagues and communities*". **Machines** - there is little information in the case about these issues except that operations increased in Americas for non-carbonated drinks. **Management** - profitability, responsibility to society and shareholder value are key priorities. Company organised into four key regions and then by product. Capabilities referred to within the case as '*best in class*' as a priority goal.
Competency	Focussed on regions where sustained competitive advantage possible within beverages. Excellent market positions within confectionery globally and beverages regionally in concentrated markets. Long established and recognised brands. Growing sugar free gum market with 70% of Cadbury gums being sugar free, providing first mover advantage. Large organisation with presumably considerable economies of scale and scope. Global reach and understanding of consumer markets. Actively competes on the basis of quality, taste and price of products.
Internal politics	plc status - recognised as a separate legal entity – board, shareholders and employees. Shareowner interests a key priority which may conflict with the interests of employees or longer term goals. The need to reinforce reputation with employees was identified as a key goal. Not known what the existing perceived reputation is. Human rights ethical trading policy is an effective recruitment and internal marketing tool. Varied internal stakeholder groups with a range of internal strategy groups such as the Cadbury Schweppes' Food Issues Strategy Group which could possibly lead to potential conflicts of interests between their findings and existing corporate goals and strategies.

Objectives	3 year goals and priorities outlined.
	Assumed objective to maximise profit and shareholder value.
	Confectionary expansion through organic growth and acquisition.
	Focus on business areas where there is sustained competitive advantage within beverages.
Key internal drivers	Need to manage the business profitably and responsibly.
	Need for shareholder value as plc.
	Growth in global confectionary and regional beverages through team development and core capabilities.

Even demonstrating just one syllabus item, you can see that a significant amount of information can be extracted from the case study which will require summarising.

Stage 4 - The summary

It is only at this point where you will understand the case sufficiently well enough to begin to compile your summary PESTEL and SWOT four key pages to take along to the exam.

Remember that although it is good practice to work with peers to jointly analyse the case, this part of the process should be completed alone, as only your own work will be accepted by the CIM.

You should also remember that you are assessed on the key issues of the case rather than the minor details. As in real-life there are likely to be anomalies and you will be expected to outline your assumptions where appropriate.

3.7 Cadbury Schweppes (CS) suggested PESTEL

 KEY CONCEPT

concept

The PEST, SLEPT or PESTLE model is the most popular framework for classifying factors in the macro or external environment. To remind you, the following factors are included.

- **Political factors** include government policy, political stability/instability in overseas markets, foreign trade policy and so on.

- **Economic factors** include business cycles (boom, recession, recovery), interest and foreign exchange rates, inflation, employment figures and energy costs. Such factors affect both the costs of doing business and the disposable income of consumers.

- **Socio-cultural factors** include demographics (age, location, socio-economic status and other structural factors in the population as a whole); lifestyle and fashion trends; consumption, shopping and media use; business and social customs; and consumer values and concerns (eg 'green' consumerism).

- **Technological factors** include new products (eg digital music), new processes (eg e-procurement and e-commerce); risk of product obsolescence; increasing global competition; and virtual teamworking and organisation.

- **Legal factors** include law and regulation on employment (eg health and safety, equal opportunities), marketing (eg advertising standards and restrictions), consumer rights, product safety/labelling and so on.

- **Environmental/ethical factors** include sustainability of energy/resource use, recyclable products/packaging, pollution control, ethical trading with suppliers, ethical investment and so on.

You are required to complete your PESTEL and SWOT analyses within **four pages** of typed **A4** size paper with text **no smaller** than **font size 11**. Please note that 'this is font size 11', our materials are written in size 8.5 and so you should not use our own SWOT and PESTEL as an indication of the size that you can use for the purposes of your exam. (Please note however that when tested, our PESTEL and SWOT was within 4 pages of A4 at size 11 so the level of content can be used as an indication of the level of detail which is possible).

The CIM information to candidates also explicitly states that:

"*The four sides of A4 provide candidates with scope for a reasonable breadth of analysis with numerous points under each heading and a reasonable depth of analysis of each point. Candidates should not include any further models or notes beyond the PESTEL and SWOT analyses as it may fall outside the scope of the syllabus. In addition, additional annotations may be perceived by the examiner to have been an attempt to 'best-guess' the questions and prepare model answers which could result in the candidate being penalised.*"

Note. You must not do any research outside the Case Study as this will be penalised by the Examiner. Additional information would only confuse the issues, so just use your own general knowledge and the information given. Certainly you must not bring 'facts' from any external search to bear on your answer in the exam. The world is as described by the examiner for the duration of the case.

3.7.1 Political factors

Global politics and overseas markets

- Need for an operational understanding of a diverse range of political persuasions (as a global organisation).

Foreign trade policy

- EU involvement has helped to regulate fluctuations in the key sugar market.

- Various national governments are co-operated with in terms of supply prices and quotas.

- A high reliance on West Africa and the Far East for supplies of critical ingredients may be risky due to the absence of governmental level trade agreements. Although it is not foreseen that there will be issues with supply, it is dependent on continued positive local trading agreements.

Involvement with political bodies

- Involvement with groups concerned with health related issues such as World Heath Organisation (on important consumer concerns). A signatory of the UN Global Compact and Declaration of Human Rights.

- Need to continue to be actively involved with such political bodies and NGO's in order to maintain positive attitudes amongst stakeholders and pressure groups.

Employment related issues

- International Labour Organisation conventions and OECD guidelines are adhered to and, as a result, require monitoring for changes and involvement where appropriate.

- CS Board commitment to international standards will influence internal corporate and functional strategies in terms of labour rights (HR), dignity at work, diversity and respect for opportunity (HR), fair remuneration (HR and finance), health and safety (operations). Each will have implications for the overall corporate strategy and outputs within the organisational system.

3.7.2 Economic factors

Consumer related issues

- Above inflation pricing of carbonated soft drinks has contributed to sector decline.

- Competitive pricing is a key element of the customer value proposition and an element of the brand strategy.

Operating costs

- The use of long-term contracts and forward contracts means that only a small proportion of raw materials are purchased at fluctuating prices. This policy assists with planning and budgeting.

- Linkages with the EU and national governments through quotas etc will also regulate materials costs.

Employment related issues

- International labour market trends will impact the ability to recruit staff. Opportunities exist for staffing within countries where labour is cheaper (whilst maintaining human rights requirements).

- In markets with growing populations, issues of labour mobility emerge and labour is more readily available.

3.7.3 Socio-cultural factors

Consumer buying behaviour

- CS has a variety of programmes to ensure consumer insight is built into strategy.

- Primarily products are impulse purchases which will vary considerably between cultures, consumer lifestyle and life stage.

- Switching behaviour to non-carbonated drinks within US markets (a key market for CS).

- Switching behaviour to diet drinks within US markets - CS has a 6/10 of the top non-cola diet drinks.

- The branded nature of the chocolate and gum markets is positive for CS.

Lifestyle issues

- Population growth within markets has contributed to sales growth, especially in developing markets which account for 30% of sales.

- Healthier alternatives being favoured by an increasing number of consumers such as non-carbonated drinks, sports and water based products within key markets.

- Preference for diet products is positive for CS given their increased sales yet there is public concern for levels of artificial ingredients - likely to be reviewed by the CS Food Issues Strategy Group.

Cultural elements

- Shopping behaviour is culturally dependent and therefore key distribution infrastructures used by CS may not be as relevant for the growing markets such as Egypt, Mexico etc.

- Brand and product perceptions vary considerably culturally even amongst relatively similar cultures, eg. differences between perceptions of the use and eating occasions of chocolate between the British and French.

3.7.4 Technological factors

New products

- New products are used as a competitive device. Product innovation has been used especially within developing markets by CS.

- Need for effective marketing information systems to manage the volume of information within CS.

3.7.5 Environmental/ ethical factors

Corporate social responsibility

- Extensive coverage of CSR via a CS CSR committee and positive ratings through external organisations.

- CS Food Issues Strategy Group's 12 point action plan to respond to consumer health concerns (obesity and poor lifestyles).

- An Ethical Sourcing Standards Programme involving employee and supplier training and engagement.

- Community Programmes - education, enterprise, health, welfare, environment.

Physical Environment

- CS EHS Steering Group - environmental impact of production processes, raw materials sourcing and consideration throughout the supply chain.

3.7.6 Legal factors

- Varied legal implications include employment, fair trading, competition and consumer laws and their international differences eg US is a key market where there are very strict competition laws.

- Legal implications of marketing in relation to children and with non-healthy products.

- Human rights and ethical trading practices are assisted by the HRET Policy in operation at CS.

- Regulations relating to product safety, labelling, ingredients usage etc are often very difficult to interpret and require extensive knowledge within CS on an ongoing basis due to their frequent changes.

3.8 Cadbury Schweppes (CS) suggested SWOT Analysis

KEY CONCEPT

concept

SWOT analysis is a commonly used technique to assess the current situation of the business.

The features of the environmental situation can usually be summarised into **strengths, weaknesses, opportunities and threats**. This process is called **SWOT analysis**. **Strengths** and **weaknesses** are features of the **organisation**; **opportunities** and **treats** are features of the **environment.** Effective SWOT analysis does not simply require a categorisation of information, but also requires some assessment of the relative importance of the various factors.

Strengths and weaknesses are features of the organisation itself and its product/service range.

(a) **Strengths** are features from which the company may be able to derive competitive advantage. They are also known as core competences.

(b) **Weaknesses** are disadvantages that may have to be remedied. For example a company's growth is being hampered because its people have weak customer handling skills. A training programme could be introduced to help its people develop strong skills.

Opportunities and threats are features of the environment, particularly the immediate competitive or task environment.

Cadbury Schweppes' SWOT Analysis

Strengths

- Long-established brands reinforced with the customer value proposition of quality, taste and price.

- Strong or leading market share within global confectionary (10% global share).

- Significant profit growth in the years from 2004 to 2005.

- Appreciation of the importance of employees to goal achievement and HR policies used to support.

- Secure supply agreements with no single supplier responsible for more than 10% of raw materials.

- Price fluctuations are minimised through long-term contracts and forward agreements.

- CSR practices Committee in 5 activity areas ensures comprehensive coverage of key social issues.

- Range of committees within CS and ability to access, lobby and work with NGO's, governments and pressure groups.

- Scale and scope of CS as a large MNC.

- Clear identification of CS core competencies.

Weaknesses

- Lack of presence within the growing water and sports based drinks markets.

- Complexities within the supply chain of 40,000 suppliers (although also on strengths for not being dependent on one supply source).

- Despite seasonality uplifts being spread as a result of global differences in weather, festivals and holidays - still a significantly larger second half of the year which impacts on financials, operational issues and production capacity.

Opportunities

- Goals imply ability to secure the beverage share - possibly investing in water/sports/diet categories.

- Projected continued growth in the new regional markets for confectionary.

- Extend licensor agreements into new markets.

- CSR opportunity to differentiate CS from competitors within an industry where there is heightened public awareness about fair trading and health issues associated with sugar and cocoa products.

- Utilise the effects of growing populations especially in markets where CS has market development opportunities such as Poland, Mexico etc.

Threats

- Growth of sports and water based drinks where there is no CS presence.

- Strength of own label and regional brands in fragmented sugar market despite major branded market share.

- Intense competition within the confectionary and soft drinks industries.

- Wrigleys brand strength and market share within the gum market may be difficult to penetrate.

- US beverages market contributes a proportionally greater profit - however this market is in decline partly as a result of inflationary pricing within the sector. Price pressure may occur in the future as a result, compounding the threat.

4 Tackling the specimen exam paper

4.1 The specimen paper

Part A

ALL TASKS ARE COMPULSORY (40% weighting)

Task One

Describe how the legal form, ownership and control of Cadbury Schweppes differs from that of a charity. (8 marks)

(Syllabus reference 1.2)

Task Two

Briefly explain the business cycle and give **TWO** reasons why it is important to Cadbury Schweppes. (8 marks)

(Syllabus 3.4)

Task Three

Cadbury Schweppes needs to consider the influences of many global pressure groups. Identify **TWO** different pressure groups that may be interested in Cadbury Schweppes' global operations and explain why.   (8 marks)

(Syllabus 2.3)

Task Four

Identify **TWO** key sources of qualitative data and **TWO** key sources of quantitative data that Cadbury Schweppes might use in order to forecast future supply and demand for its products, giving reasons for your choice.   (8 marks)

(Syllabus 3.10)

Task Five

Identify **TWO** connected stakeholders and **TWO** external stakeholders for Cadbury Schweppes, giving reasons for your choice.   (8 marks)

(Syllabus reference 2.1)

Part B

ALL TASKS ARE COMPULSORY (60% weighting)

Role

You are a Marketing Assistant for Cadbury Schweppes and have been asked by the Marketing Manager to prepare a short report for circulation to the Marketing Team. Based on your knowledge of this unit and your analysis of the case study material previously provided, address the following tasks. Include your SWOT and PESTEL analyses as appendices to your report.

Task One

Having analysed the competitive environment facing Cadbury Schweppes, identify the key success factors that have contributed to Cadbury Schweppes' profitability.   (20 marks)

(Syllabus reference 2.1, 2.6, 4.1, 4.2)

Task Two

Assess how information relating to social, cultural and demographic trends might inform Cadbury Schweppes' marketing mix (7Ps).   (20 marks)

(Syllabus reference 3.3, 4.1, 4.2)

Task Three

Recommend **TWO** areas of research that may inform Cadbury Schweppes' approach to corporate social responsibility (CSR) over the next **THREE** years, giving reasons for your choice. (20 marks)

(Syllabus reference 3.9, 3.1, 4.1, 4.2)

(Total 60 marks)

4.2 Suggested Answers Part A short answer questions

EXAM TIP concept

Throughout our suggested answers we have highlighted the key points using bold font.

Task One

Describe how the legal form, ownership and control of Cadbury Schweppes differs from that of a charity. (8 marks)

Cadbury Schweppes (CS) is a public limited company (plc). This means that it is a private sector **commercial organisation** (as opposed to public sector state controlled organisation). Charities are also classified as private sector organisations but they are referred to as **non-commercial**.

The legal status of CS as a public limited company means they are incorporated and the business should be regarded as a **separate legal entity** from it's owners. The key point from this is that the company's finances are separate from the personal finances of the owners. As a 'public' limited company, the **owners** of the business are those who **own shares**. Shareholders may be individuals or other companies. They are **not responsible** for the company's **debts** unless they have given guarantees (of a bank loan, for example). However, they may lose the money they have invested in the company if it fails. There is a clear distinction between **shareholders** and **directors** of limited companies.

- Shareholders are the owners, but have limited rights, as shareholders, over the day-to-day running of the company. They provide capital and receive a return (dividend).

- Directors are appointed to run the company on behalf of shareholders. In practice they have a great deal of **autonomy**.

Charities will differ considerably from a plc primarily because unlike commercial organisations, they do not exist to make a profit but **have altruistic goals**. A number of issues tend to be more difficult to manage within non-commercial organisations, these include: **obtaining funds** in competition with other non-commercial organisations; a **conflict** between the allocation of resources to the given cause and the costs of running the organisation; the **monitoring of effectiveness** against objectives. A charity such as the NSPCC for instance is frequently criticised for their expensive and controversially hard hitting marketing campaigns. Without these campaigns however, it could be argued that they are not in a position to raise sufficient funds to help children most in need.

Within an organisation such as CS, the **directors** will be ultimately **responsible** for ensuring that the organisation is efficient and effective on behalf of shareholders. Within a charity a Board of Trustees will play a similar role but they will have a **different set of stakeholders**, including non-salaried volunteers, donors and recipients of the charitable output.

Task Two

Briefly explain the business cycle and give **TWO** reasons why it is important to Cadbury Schweppes. (8 marks)

The business cycle is the continual **sequence** of **rapid growth** in national income, followed by a **slow down** in growth and then a fall in national income. A sustained fall in national income is an economic **recession**. After the recession comes growth again, and when this has reached a peak, the cycle turns into recession once more.

The understanding of business cycles can be crucial in many sectors, especially the **capital goods sector**, as investment in capital goods represents an expensive anticipation of future rewards.

There are a number of reasons why the business cycle is important to CS. Wide fluctuations in the levels of economic activity can damage the **overall economic well being** of society and particularly levels of **employment**. **Marketing mixes** and **HR issues** will in turn be directly impacted by the business cycle.

From a **marketing mix perspective**, price and promotional adjustments will need to be made. For CS, a period of **boom** is likely to mean that they experience high demand for their impulse related product. When consumers are relatively affluent, they are more likely to purchase *non essential* products such as chocolate. In periods of **recession**, spending power is reduced and customers will not be as likely to purchase non essentials unless prices are low or discounted. In these periods, retailer own brands and cheaper to produce 'value' variants with **low selling prices** tend to become popular, unless there is particularly strong **brand loyalty**.

From an **HR perspective**, CS is influenced considerably by the business cycle because recruitment may be suspended during recessionary periods this will have a significant effect also on their CSR and work within local communities where employment by CS had been high. In boom times, it will be relatively **more expensive** to employ the specialists they need in order to develop a highly effective team. How employees are treated during both boom and recessionary periods will have a direct effect on the **internal marketing initiatives** of CS and their ability to produce **high quality products** for consumers.

 EXAM TIP   concept

There are other points that you could make to address this question. For example there will be significant operational issues such as the need to manage stock control. In periods of recession, reduced levels of demand will mean that production plans need to be amended or CS will find themselves holding expensive surplus stock. The perishable nature of their products mean that they cannot maintain high levels of stock because a product will pass it's 'use by' dates.

Task Three

Cadbury Schweppes needs to consider the influences of many global pressure groups. Identify **TWO** different pressure groups that may be interested in Cadbury Schweppes' global operations and explain why. (8 marks)

Pressure groups are organisations with **concerns about specific causes**, business and trade interests or matters of public policy or social issues. There are many thousands of groups ranging from global umbrella groups to small local ones established for specific purposes.

Large multinational corporations like CS are often targeted by pressure groups which are opposed to their corporate practices or the promotion of their specific brands. Tesco for example is subject to a long-running pressure group campaign in the form of a website Tescopoly which is dedicated to raising concern amongst the general public about the retailers building projects and procurement practices. CS is likely to be subject to a vast number of pressure groups within it's regions. For example, vegetarian groups interested in it's ingredients, health related groups interested in tackling rising obesity levels and sugar dependency rates and environmental groups interested in production processes and packaging.

With regard to it's global business practices amongst others, pressure groups who are likely to be interested in CS are the **Fairtrade Foundation** and **Friends of the Earth**.

The **Fairtrade Foundation** are interested in the **procurement policies** of large MNCs. In particular in **commodity markets** such as sugar, cocoa, coffee and fruits. Given the large proportion of commodity ingredients that are included within CS products, and the proportion of the world cocoa supply they purchase, CSR policies are likely to be viewed closely by this organisation. The Fairtrade Foundation awards organisations with a Fairtrade logo for use on their products if they are seen to participate in ethical trading agreements with local suppliers. It is in the interests of CS through their CSR Committee to engage with such a powerful group and maintain their ethical sourcing standards programme.

Friends of the Earth will be interested in the **environmental impact** of CS production along with their **procurement policies** and farming and production practices throughout the supply chain. The CS EHS steering group should be aware of the **strength** of this pressure group and again **maintain contact** with them where necessary.

Task Four

Identify **TWO** key sources of qualitative data and **TWO** key sources of quantitative data that Cadbury Schweppes might use in order to forecast future supply and demand for its products, giving reasons for your choice.
(8 marks)

Forecasting supply and demand is critical so that **consumers' needs are met.** Accurate forecasts facilitate product availability at the required time in sufficient quantities (in an efficient and profitable manner for CS). **Secondary data** (data which has been collected for another purpose) and **primary data** (data collected for the purpose of gaining the specifically required information) are both used to assist forecasting.

Qualitative data provides **contextually rich information** and is able to address issues concerning 'why ?' questions and are not dependent on historical observations.

Quantitative data provides **numerical information** which can be used to project trends and provide statistically robust generalisations.

- **Qualitative supply information source – Interviews** with buyers within the **purchasing/procurement department** regarding their opinion about **potential supply 'issues'** that may threaten the availability of raw materials. This method will be useful because the respondents are experienced in dealing with suppliers and will provide high quality (short term) forecasting information.

- **Quantitative supply information source - Questionnaires** amongst raw materials **suppliers.** Suppliers could be sent a questionnaire to respond to which requests information about their **planned production** over the next three years. This information will enable CS to identify whether they need to source additional suppliers. Questionnaires are appropriate as there are over **40,000 suppliers** which would prevent qualitative method being employed due to cost and time limitations. Questionnaires are relatively inexpensive and fast to administer. A representative **sample** of suppliers could be considered as CS do not rely on key suppliers to any great extent.

- **Qualitative demand information source –** A series of **focus groups** could be conducted with different **consumer segments** in order to gather perceptions about **lifestyles, product attitudes and future product requirements**. Focus groups will provide detailed information to help identify **socio-cultural** impacts on demand.

- **Quantitative demand information source – Historical sales data** can be used in order to conduct **time series analysis and project future demand**. This will be useful in order to identify the complex global seasonality effects on sales patterns. The effects of promotional and distribution changes over time can also be included within the analysis.

 EXAM TIP

concept

WARNING!

In this question you could easily miss out the reference to the need to forecast future **supply** (we are very used to thinking about demand forecasting).

Task Five

Identify **TWO** connected stakeholders and **TWO** external stakeholders for Cadbury Schweppes, giving reasons for your choice. (8 marks)

(Syllabus reference 2.1)

Stakeholders are groups and individuals who have a **vested interest** in the performance and actions of the organisation. Stakeholders can be either internal (eg employees, managers), external connected (eg customers, suppliers, shareholders) or external to the organisation (eg pressure groups, communities, society).

Connected stakeholders for CS include both internal and external (but connected) groups. Internally, a key stakeholder group is **employees**. CS has a clear awareness of the need to nurture employees in order to achieve the corporate objectives. Labour rights, dignity at work and respect for opportunity are highlighted. The adherence to OECD guidelines and the International Labour Organisation conventions demonstrate this.

Suppliers are an external but **connected** stakeholder for CS. The HRET policy looking at ethical trading and use of long-term supplier contracts are evidence of their importance to CS.

External stakeholders of importance to CS include **local communities** (in areas where they have operations) and **governments**.

Local communities are important because they provide a **valuable labour supply** as well as being essential for maintaining a positive **corporate reputation** and image. Organisations who adversely effect the local communities are increasingly targeted by pressure groups and experience highly **damaging public relations** as word of mouth spreads. In the worst cases consumer boycotts of products have been experienced as a direct result of the effects on communities. CS' development of **community programmes** demonstrates their attempt build positive relationships with these stakeholders.

Various **governments** at **regional and national levels** and related **NGOs** are critical to the success of CS. The EU for example has proved to be essential in helping to regulate the price of sugar and other governments are influential in setting quotas and duties.

4.3 Suggested Answers Part B extended answer questions

ALL TASKS ARE COMPULSORY (60% weighting)

Role

You are a Marketing Assistant for Cadbury Schweppes and have been asked by the Marketing Manager to prepare a short report for circulation to the Marketing Team. Based on your knowledge of this unit and your analysis of the case study material previously provided, address the following tasks. Include your SWOT and PESTEL analyses as appendices to your report.

  EXAM TIP

format / application

You are asked at the beginning of the examination paper to assume the role of a Marketing Assistant for Cadbury Schweppes. Tasks are then outlined below this instruction. It would be very easy to **ignore the request of the role** and to just address the tasks in essay format. **Do this at your peril!** The CIM examination team have for many years stressed the importance of candidates remaining in their required roles in order to encourage '*application' of knowledge*'.

To integrate your role and respond to the request for a report - we suggest that you use a report format and provide sub sections within the report using titles clearly referring to each task.

Also, please remember to make up a name but not to use your own name on the report. The CIM do not allow candidates to identify themselves to examiners. Just to be safe you could add a highly improbably sounding name or use a favourite character name.

Internal report on Cadbury Schweppes(CS)

To: Marketing Team

From: Louby Lou (Marketing Assistant)

Date: xxxx xxxxx

Management Summary

This report identifies the key success factors that have contributed to our current level of profitability. These factors include our strategy, organisational size, structure and policies and our marketing philosophy. It then considers the socio-cultural trends that we have had to consider when planning our marketing mixes. Corporate social responsibility (CSR) has been an area which has been focussed on in recent years to good effect. We need to continue to monitor the effects of CSR and identify how we can use it to best effect in the future. The report suggests a programme of research amongst suppliers and local communities to assist this monitoring.

Key success factors contributing to profitability (Task 1)

We have benefited from a number of success factors and our specific strengths. Profitability increased significantly between 2004 and 2005 as a result of our strategy, organisational systems and development and marketing.

- **Strategy**

    The decision **to focus on our core competencies** and disinvest in the 160 countries where we previously sold beverages has contributed significantly to our profits. Concentrating on the US and Australian markets where sustained competitive advantage is possible has enabled us to avoid diluting our marketing efforts and **allocate resources more efficiently**.

- **Organisational size, structure and management**

    As a large **multinational** organisation we benefit from the **economies of scale** and scope and the financial resources available to us. This strength has helped by enabling investment expensive product development. We are also able to spread **the risks** associated with doing business between the various countries and regions in which we operate.

    As a well recognised global organisation we also benefit from the **credibility associated with our size** and perceived support that our trade customers require.

    The **structure** of CS means that we are able to **concentrate on geographic regions** and utilise cross product line teams within our EMEA and Asia Pacific business segments. The separate Americas Beverages and Confectionary business segments are increasingly focussed to enable **concentration on core activities**.

- **Systems and working practices**

    Supply chain risks are spread. Procurement systems are an essential advantage to CS. **Risks in supply of raw materials has been minimised** by the use of 40,000 suppliers and ensuring that we are not reliant on any one supplier for more than 10% of materials. The ability to **predict costs** more accurately and the ability to guarantee supply with the use of long term contracts and forward agreements is a critical success factor. Utilising a wide and varied distribution network also enables maximum opportunity for purchase by consumers and limits the risks of over reliance on key distributors.

    HR policies have been used to **support employees** in helping to achieve **corporate goals**. One core goal is identified as to '*nurture the trust of colleagues*' highlights the recognition by CS of the important role of staff. The HRET policy in operation is just one example of the commitment to staff appreciation. The CS Board also shows commitment to dignity at work, diversity, opportunities and fair remuneration.

    CS **manages stakeholder relationships** effectively. The needs of different stakeholder groups such as shareholders, trade customers, suppliers, consumers, governments, NGOs, pressure groups and employees are identified and stakeholders are engaged with via a range of committees and working groups such as the CS Food Issues Strategy Group, EHS Steering Group and CSR Committee. The integration of issues of relevance to stakeholder groups promotes positive relationships between CS and our stakeholders.

- **Marketing**

  The strength of our heritage brands is a critical success factor demonstrated by the level of market share. Key markets such as gum and chocolate are heavily branded which is capitalised by CS with brand USP's of quality, taste and a competitive price.

  Consumer **insights** and attention to issues of social importance are integrated into strategy and product development. Maintaining a wide **distribution network** also enables wider consumer segments to be reached.

  Corporate social responsibility is a '*top priority*' within CS and is heavily linked to the committees and groups mentioned previously. CSR and ethical business practice provide CS with a key opportunity to differentiate itself from competitors within an industry where there is heightened public awareness about issues specifically about fair trade, the natural environment, human rights, impacts on communities and health issues associated with sugar and cocoa based products.

Social, cultural and demographic trends which inform our marketing mix (7Ps). (Task 2)

A number of factors influence the consumer buying process, their behaviour and attitudes towards products and services. As products are required to meet customer needs, unless these factors are known to marketers it is not possible to create a customer value proposition to meet these needs.

Cultural factors exert the broadest and deepest influence on consumer behaviour. The culture in which we live determines our **values, beliefs and perceptions**. **Buying behaviour** is also affected by **subculture** and **social class**. Different social classes also display distinct brand preferences in lifestyle and product preferences (of which food and snacking habits is one of them).

A consumer's behaviour is also influenced by **social factors**. People are influenced in their buying by the groups they are members of, called **associate groups**, and by the groups whose behaviour they reject, called **disassociate groups**. Marketers, in planning their target market strategy, should try to identify the groups and the key individuals whose behaviours and lifestyles are followed.

A buyer's decisions and attitudes towards products and services are also influenced by **personal factors known also as demographics**. These include, age, gender life stage, occupation and economic levels of income.

- The **family life cycle model** proposes that as we move through different phases of our lives, we buy different products and services and change our priorities.

- **Occupation** also influences consumption patterns.

- A person's **lifestyle** also influences what is deemed important to purchase, where they search for information on those goods and how they make the purchase decision.

The consumer insights programmes we use to direct our commercial strategy. As a global business where cultural, social and demographic factors will vary considerably this is essential to reflect within our marketing mix.

i   Product

  Many aspects related to the product will be influenced by social, cultural and demographic factors. These include:

- **Brand perceptions** will be influenced by socio-cultural and demographic factors as different consumer segments will perceive the qualities and brand associations according to their own culturally bound beliefs, values and attitudes. For example, for consumers in lower socio economic groups may perceive CS products to be premium whilst higher socio economic groups may regard them as lower mainstream. This will impact

- **Product usage** will vary- for example culturally some groups may be more likely to snack on impulse whilst others plan consumption around mealtimes eg packed lunch contents etc. The implications of this will also inform the 'place' and distributive aspects of the marketing mix. Consumers may very according to whether they are using CS beverages as soft drinks (possibly children) or as mixers to alcoholic drinks. This will impact additional aspects such as the packaging and size of products. Whether CS products are shared, purchased for sole consumption or given as gifts may also be a function of socio-cultural issue as will the usage of the products to celebrate festivals and events.

- **Product attributes** and format –preferences for tastes and attributes of the product change. French consumers for example prefer high percentage cocoa chocolate (Bournville would be a minimal cocoa % for some tastes) whilst British consumers prefer milk based products like Cadbury Dairy Milk. Products aimed at younger demographic groups such as children are likely to be required in smaller sizes such as the Cadbury 'fun size' products. Healthier alternatives to carbonated sugary drinks are favoured by an increasing number of consumers but especially in the US where attitudes to healthier lifestyles is growth. Preference for diet products is positive for CS given their increased sales. In many societies a move towards healthier lifestyles will impact CS product range considerably.

ii Price

Demographic variables will influence price considerably (especially global differences). The extent that different consumer groups are prepared to pay for CS products will depend on what is expected in the price based on their cultural background. If confectionary is to be given as a gift, age and level of income may factors which determine how much consumers are willing and able to pay. A child for example buying a box of chocolates may perceive the price of CS products as high. An affluent professional on the other hand may perceive the products to be too inexpensive to give as a gift. Alternative variants and price levels will need to be adapted to the needs of the targeted consumer groups.

iii Place

Where consumers shop, how frequently they shop, whether they shop alone and other purchase occasions will inform the choice of distribution channels by CS. CS uses a wide distribution network based on consumer needs which demonstrates how varied shopping behaviour is. This behaviour can be as a consequence of lifestyle and the other socio cultural factors.

iv Promotion

Consumers respond differently to alternative promotional mechanisms. In-store sales promotions for example appeal differently to different consumer groups with some remaining brand loyal despite offers and others only purchasing products which are on promotion. Promotional messages need to be created to include a tone, appeal and proposition which is appropriate to the needs of the target market. Promoting diet drinks to consumers using the message that there is no sugar will not appeal to consumers who culturally are not concerned with high sugar contents in food.

v People

For FMCG products, such as confectionery, the people aspect of the marketing mix will be represented by CS employees such as the sales force. Culturally (within some countries) trade customers may expect a certain level of corporate hospitality to be part of the business negotiations. The training and expenses policies provided for the sales team will need to be planned according to this cultural information.

vi Process

How consumers prefer to obtain products within an FMCG setting mostly related to the 'place' distribution aspects of the marketing mix. There is a case to argue however that high internet shopping usage amongst some consumer groups could inform CS about whether to sell directly via the internet or not.

vii Physical evidence

For FMCG products the actual product, packaging, in store promotional materials, corporate website design and delivery vehicle livery will form the basis for the most obvious physical evidence for consumers. For the reasons discussed previously there will be vast differences in preferences for these. At a corporate level, stakeholders such as suppliers and trade customers will hold certain cultural expectations about aspects such as CS corporate headquarters and the look and feel of corporate documentation.

You may not be expected to include so many points for this task but you should aim for at least two thirds of them to gain the available marks.

Three year research plan to inform our approach to corporate social responsibility (Task 3)

As CSR has been identified as a key success factor which offers a good differentiating opportunity for us, further research would help to plan our CSR efforts.

We propose that two key areas of research are conducted over the next three years:

i   An investigation into the perception of CS' impact on the natural environment

ii   A review of ethical and fair trade initiatives

The two proposed areas have already been identified as important to CS and could integrate the work of a number of existing committees.

- **Research into the natural environment**

    This research project would involve two aspects.

    i   **Consumer omnibus tracking study** conducted at regular waves over three years to identify and track social concerns with the natural environment and perception of CS' environmental impact relative to competitors.

    ii   Environmental scanning – using **secondary sources** such as trade and national press, governmental reports, food industry trade body reports, internal findings from related projects. This would help to identify the overall societal view along with views of powerful stakeholder groups such a pressure groups, environmentally focussed NGOs and governments who would be in a position to impact CS' business practices.

    This research would assist the work of the CS EHS Steering Group. An understanding of the environmental impacts as perceived by consumers will be particularly helpful because it would help to create future marketing messages, identify additional areas of improvement to be made from the perspective of customers and to consider whether this will contribute to a sustainable competitive advantage of CS.

- **Research into ethical and fair trade initiatives**

    Although it is a distinct area of research, research into fair trade initiatives will complement the natural environment project because of the links between the natural environment, organic and sustainable farming and fair trade. The objectives of the research would be to identify the state of relations between CS and our suppliers, attitudes towards materials pricing and key stakeholder perceptions of CS' ethical sourcing behaviour. The research would benefit CS because it would assess any potential political problems with suppliers and connected stakeholders.

    This research would involve two main data collection methods:

    i   An annual survey amongst farmers and raw materials suppliers

    ii   Depth executive interviews with key stakeholders such as relevant NGO's and pressure groups such the Fair Trade Foundation.

You may have chosen alternative research areas including the local community or competitor CSR monitoring etc.

5 Additional question practice

There are a number of topics that you could practice prior to receiving the case study as part of your ongoing learning or early topic revision. We have pulled a number of questions from the previous CIM syllabus and have included these as practice resources. As you will not know the sector or context of the case until it arrives with you, these questions have been selected because they cover a variety of scenarios. Work through them and perhaps even consider how they would be answered differently with various business sectors in mind.

The questions are posed in section 5.1 and suggested answers in section 5.2 (question 5.1.1 will have a corresponding answer in 5.2.1). We would advise you to work through the questions for yourself before comparing your answers with ours.

5.1 Practice questions

5.1.1 Privatisation

(a) Explain the meaning of a privatised business.
(b) Using an example, compare the possible objectives of an organisation before and after privatisation.
(c) What are main drivers for change from a public sector organisation into a privatised organisation?

5.1.2 Organisation summary

For an organisation of your own choice, produce a concise mini case study to outline the following:

(i)   The organisation's legal form or status.
(ii)   Its mission statement
(iii) The nature of its internal environment.
(iv)   Its interrelationship with the external environment.
(v)   A brief justification of its **three** main drivers for change, ranked in order of importance.

5.1.3 Different objectives

You have recently changed organisations from one in the private sector to one in the voluntary sector. Using appropriate examples explain the differences you would expect to find in terms of the following:

(a) Objectives and mission statement
(b) Key stakeholders
(c) Organisational culture

5.1.4 Public, private and voluntary sector

(a) Using examples, distinguish between the objectives of a public, private and voluntary sector organisation.
(b) Examine **five** issues that may cause the objectives of a large private sector organisation to change over time.

5.1.5 Charity issues

You have started work for a charitable organisation that is concerned with care for the elderly on a local basis. Until recently, it relied solely on volunteers but now recognises the value of a more professional marketing approach. Prepare a report for the Board of Trustees that identifies the contribution that marketing could make to the future success of the Charity. The report should contain the following headings:

*   Information issues
*   Issues over client needs
*   Fundraising issues

5.1.6 Change

(a) Why is it important for the marketer to monitor change in the marketing environment?

(b) Provide a brief assessment of **two** of the following approaches, giving an application of each:

    (i)   Environment audits

    (ii)   Impact analysis

    (iii)   Opportunities and threats matrix

(c) Briefly state the significance of the product life cycle to forecasting.

5.1.7 Government marketing

You work for a government agency or department of your own choice and have been asked to contribute to training materials for new employees.

(a) Provide a definition and example of each of the following:

    (i)   Connected stakeholder

    (ii)   Pressure group

    (iii)   Market research

AND

(b) Concisely analyse **two** implications of each for the selected government agency or department.

5.1.8 Open systems and change

A company can be represented as an open system.

(a) Show how a company as an open system can respond to changing environmental conditions.
(b) Identify **two** pressure groups interested in your chosen company and discuss their potential impacts.

5.1.9 Mission and objectives

You are the marketing assistant for a national energy provider in a country of your choice. Your organisation has recently suffered bad press due to supply cuts and increased prices. In an attempt to re-position the organisation, your marketing manager has requested a report that:

(a) Explains the purpose of a 'mission statement'
(b) Identifies **three** external sources of influence on the objectives of the organisation.
(c) Recommends **three** promotional opportunities that could help change the image of your organisation in the country.

5.1.10 Responding to change

All marketing orientated businesses must, by definition, be open systems.

Demonstrate the truth of this statement by explaining how a road haulage (transportation of goods) company would respond to changing conditions in:

(a) Its competitive environment;
(b) Its macro environment.

5.1.11 Macro and micro: voluntary organisation

(a) Using an example, explain the difference between the macro and micro environment of a voluntary organisation.

(b) Selecting the macro environment, prepare a memorandum for your marketing manager summarising why an understanding of this environment is important from a marketing perspective.

5.1.12 Employees and intermediaries

(a)   Explain the role and importance of:

    (i)   Employees

    (ii)   Intermediaries

as stakeholders of a business.

(b)

    (i)   Taking a multinational manufacturer, examine the possible perceptions of **one** of the above stakeholder groups.

    (ii)   Suggest **two** ways in which such perceptions could be influenced by the marketer.

5.1.13 Micro environment and market structure

(a)   Concisely define the micro environment of an organisation of your choice.

(b)   Your product manager requires an analysis of the market structure. As a preliminary step they have asked you to:

    (i)   Suggest two alternative approaches to the analysis

    (ii)   Briefly outline the main features of each

    (iii)   Identify key sources of information to consult

5.1.14 Legal regulation and consumer protection

Prepare notes on **three** of the following aspects of the legislative environment, using examples where appropriate and relating to your own legal system.

    (i)   The beneficial impacts of legal regulation on business

    (ii)   The negative impacts of legal regulation on business

    (iii)   Government legislation to protect consumers

    (iv)   The case against using the law to resolve disputes between businesses

    (v)   The roles of the government in the legislative environment

5.1.15 Distribution dilemma

As a multinational producer of premium branded fashion clothing, you are concerned to learn that your goods are being sold through a national supermarket chain at prices 50% lower than their recommended retail price.

Your Marketing Manager has requested a briefing paper explaining:

(a)   **Three** arguments that the fashion company might put forward to stop this practice and ensure its products would only be available directly from its own appointed retailers.

(b)   **Three** counter-arguments that the supermarket might put forward to continue the practice.

5.1.16 Concept and theory

Explain what is meant by the following concept and theory, outlining how each might contribute to the marketer's understanding of the environment. Use an industry with which you are familiar to illustrate your answer.

(a)   Open systems
(b)   Porter's five forces analysis

5.1.17 Stakeholders, research and competition legislation

You are a marketing assistant in your country's largest logistics company. It is currently considering a diversification into delivery of valuables for the banking industry.

Produce a **report** for your marketing manager covering the following.

(a) Key stakeholders to be consulted and why
(b) Key external sources of information on the proposed diversification
(c) The possible impact of legislation.

5.1.18 Stakeholders and pressure groups

(a) Explain the nature of the interaction between a company in a sector such as travel and tourism and **three** of its key stakeholders.

(b) Outline the significance of **one** pressure group in this sector and discuss how the company might use this pressure to secure marketing advantage.

5.1.19 Industry environment

(a) Why is it important for a firm to monitor its industry environment?

(b) Identify the means or sources available to monitor its industry and competitors.

(c) List **four** good reasons for not colluding with competitors.

5.1.20 Change drivers and responses

(a) Organisations today have to meet external changes, how best can they do this? Give **three** examples.

(b) Assess the comparative strengths and weaknesses of **either** of the following organisations in meeting external environmental change:

    (i) A small local independent supermarket

    (ii) A multinational grocery retailer.

5.1.21 Pressure groups and the marketer

You work for a global fast food retailer that has recently produced a 'successful' line of high calorie packaged products aimed at the youth market. Your marketing manager, who is becoming increasingly concerned at public reaction to child obesity trends and environmental impacts, has asked you to send a memo to include:

(a) The significance and potential impacts of pressure groups who are acting as a focus for public concerns

(b) The role of the marketer in managing such pressure groups

5.1.22 College and stakeholders

(a) What is the nature of the interrelationship between a business college and its customer and employee stakeholders?

(b) What internal sources of information would help the business college understand the nature of this interrelationsip with customers and employees?

(c) Suggest **three** external sources of information on its potential customers and briefly explain the value of the information obtained.

5.1.23 Economic policies

Recent economic events have caused the managing director of a small quality jewellery company to question the government's official objective of continuous and sustainable economic growth. In your role of marketing assistant she has asked you to report on the following.

(a) What type of economic policies would be likely to produce continuous and sustainable economic growth?
(b) What factor may prevent the objective from being realised?
(c) What would be the implications of negative economic growth for the company?

5.1.24 Political environment

(a)   Explain the meaning of the term 'political environment'.

(b)   Give **five** key impacts that demonstrate how a government exerts influence on the economy.

(c)   Compare the marketing implications of a strong stable government with that of a weak and divided government.

5.1.25 Technological environment

For an organisation of your choice, comment on **three** of the following developments.

Define your organisation.

(a)   Teleconferencing

(b)   E-commerce

(c)   Teleworking

(d)   E-business to business

(e)   Navigational and communication aids, eg global position system (GPS)

5.1.26 Environmental sensitivity

You work in the marketing department of a vehicle manufacturer.

(a)   Explain the concerns of **three** of the organisation's stakeholder groups with how your company impacts on the natural environment.

(b)   Explain how the organisation might positively respond to these concerns about the natural environment.

(c)   How could the marketing department respond positively to these concerns?

5.1.27 Social and cultural environment

(a)   Using examples from your own country, distinguish between the social and cultural environment.

(b)   Using your understanding of the social or cultural environment, discuss ways in which you might market jewellery to the 35-50 age group.

5.1.28 PEST impacts

For an organisation of your choice, write a memorandum to the marketing manager summarising how any **three** of the following may have impacts for the marketing activities.

(a)   A newly elected government

(b)   The upturn point of the business/trade cycle

(c)   A new Internet bank enters the market

(d)   Digital (broadband) television sales rise rapidly in the household sector.

5.1.29 Environmental information systems

Briefly state the implications for effective marketing of **four** of the following elements of an environmental information system:

(a)   A sensing system

(b)   Market research

(c)   Online information from real time systems

(d)   Environmental audits

(e)   Trade sources

5.1.30 Public sector marketer

(a) Write brief notes on the relevance and application of the following concepts to a marketer working in the public sector:

(i) Marketing research

(ii) Marketing information system

(iii) Delphi technique

(b) Suggest **one** reason why the marketing objectives within the public sector might differ from the private sector and **one** reason why they might be similar.

5.2 Suggested answers

Only work through this section once you have attempted the questions for yourself!

5.2.1 Privatisation

(a) **Privatised business**

The term privatised business refers to an organisation that was previously state-owned, but has been transformed into one that is owned by a private shareholders. Sources of investment now come from private sources rather than the government. Similarly, any profits made are remitted to private shareholders rather than the government. In theory, privatised businesses become free of everyday government control, although in practice, many previously state owned monopolies are extensively regulated by government when they become privatised businesses.

(b) **Objectives of an organisation before and after privatisation**

Public and private sector organisations span a wide spectrum, so it is difficult to classify objectives neatly into those purely associated with public sector organisations and those purely associated with private sector organisations. It is also wrong to assume that objectives suddenly change when an organisation goes from public sector ownership to private sector ownership-in practice, there is a long process of preparing a state-owned organisation for privatisation, during which objectives gradually change.

Nevertheless, a number of general statements can be made about the differences in objectives of an organisation before and after privatisation. The following headings summarise these differences, with reference to British Airways:

Profit: private sector organisations exist to make profits for their shareholders, in contrast to state-owned organisations that aim to achieve a specified contribution to government revenues.

Risk: because of its backing from government, a public sector organisation may pursue highly risky objectives. As a state-owned company, British Airways could afford to invest in high-risk projects such as the purchase of Concorde aircraft, but as a private sector operator, it is more likely to purchase low risk, well proven aircraft.

Timescale of objectives: as a state-owned organisation, British Airways could afford to set long-term objectives. However, as a privatised company with shareholders expecting ever rising dividends, the company must ensure that it sets short-term objectives in order to meet shareholders short-term expectations.

Social objectives: public sector organisations have often been given explicit or implicit social objectives that aim to meet government social priorities rather than the need to make maximum profits. Before privatisation, British Airways had pressure put on it to pursue government objectives of developing new technology (for example, the requirement to purchase Concorde aircraft). It also served isolated rural communities in Scotland that would not otherwise have been profitable.

Quality of service objectives: as a state owned organisation, British Airways was driven by government set objectives for quality of service. However as a privatised company operating in a deregulated market, quality of service objectives are essentially forced upon the company by customers' expectations rather than government plans.

(c) **Main drivers for change from public to private sector organisation**

Converting state-owned organisations into private sector organisations was very popular in many countries during the 1990s, especially in the United Kingdom, many EU countries, and also other more developed economies of Australasia and South-East Asia. Although many people have come to question the merits of privatisation, a number of key drivers behind the move can be identified:

Improved service to the public: there is a widespread feeling that government controlled organisations are not sufficiently responsive to public needs, and that they provide goods and services which they prefer to produce, rather than what consumers prefer to buy. An important driver for privatisation has therefore been the desire to provide more goods and services through the discipline of market based organisations. However, privatisation does not in itself create a more competitive marketplace. In many cases of privatisation, a public sector monopoly was replaced with a private sector monopoly and many of the old problems of lack of choice remained.

Improved efficiency: many public sector organisations had become notorious for poor working practices and over staffing. This was often the result of a government planning mentality in which the needs of a customer came behind the need to keep industrial peace within the workforce. Privatisation has often changed the mindset of management, so it's operational efficiencies can be achieved and passed on as low prices and / or better-quality goods and services.

Reduction in public sector borrowing: the principal source of finance for state owned organisations is the government, and as such, investment in these organisations has to compete for funds with other government services, such as education, health and defence. It has been argued by many supporters of privatisation that in the private sector, organisations would be free to raise their own capital from any source, rather than being restricted by government funds and rationing.

Ideology. Many politicians believe that it is right to roll back the extent and influence of the state in people's lives. Privatising state owned manufacturing and service industries has been seen by many as a relatively easy way of achieving this ideological objective

5.2.2 Organisations summary

This question is answered in the context of the online search company Google.

- **The organisation's legal form or status**

  Google is an incorporated company, based in America, with subsidiaries based in other legal jurisdictions. In America, separate legal identity, which distinguishes the company from its owners is recognised by Incorporation ('Inc'). Subsidiaries in Britain are incorporated with limited liability ('Ltd').

- **Mission Statement**

  Google has a stated mission to 'organise knowledge', which is manifested through its basic search engine, and additional specialised search facilities, for example Google Scholar. The mission statement expresses the essential purpose of the organisation, without describing the detailed tactics by which the mission will be achieved.

- **Internal environment**

  The internal environment refers to aspects such as organisation structure, culture, staffing and management. Google is a relatively new company, and has grown very rapidly during its short existence. The sense of growth and excitement is a major feature of the organisational climate. Because of the diverse nature of challenges faced by Google, the organisation structure, culture and management style are intentionally flexible, with frequent formation of new work groups focused responding to on new business opportunities and challenges.

- **The organisation as an open system**

  As noted above, the internal environment reflects the very turbulent nature of the company's external environment, by striving for agility and adaptability. The company faces competitive challenges on a number of fronts: software companies such as Microsoft are increasingly challenging Google's search engine competence. It is therefore important that Google can rapidly form teams (often virtual teams linked by ICT technology) to assess new opportunities and threats. (As an example, Google spotted an opportunity for offering telephony services, and formed a team of market and technical experts to address this opportunity.)

At the same time, Google itself develops outputs which create change in the external environment: changing the way marketing organisations position themselves on the web; creating virtual communities; developing new methods of global research and information-gathering.

- **Drivers of change**

  In order of importance, three important drivers of change for Google are as follows.

  1   **Challenges to Google's competitive advantage** in areas of its core competence. The company has grown on the strength of its search engine capabilities, and is now the clear leader in this market. However, although Google is now a large and well-resourced company, it faces a challenge from Microsoft: even better resourced, and with potential to become a key player in the market for search services. On the other hand, Microsoft's domination of operating systems has stimulated further innovation by Google.

  2   **Increasing regulatory pressure.** A few years ago, Google was a relatively small, market challenger: today, it dominates online search services, and has attracted the attention of regulatory agencies that see market domination as being against the public interest. Regulators pose an opportunity as well as a challenge for the company. The dominance of Microsoft has been challenged by domestic and international regulators, and some would argue that this has made life easier for Google. On the hand, Google itself is likely to be subject to increasing scrutiny, which will influence the manner in which it rolls out new services, and acquires competitors.

  3   **Higher Internet speeds.** Broadband access has spread rapidly, and offers new opportunities for things that can be done online. Search databases are likely to become increasingly sophisticated, for example not simply looking for keywords, but types of movies or tracks out of songs. Google may see opportunities to move into aspects of services that it has not previously provided, for example online video services.

5.2.3 Different objectives

Differences between private and voluntary sectors

(a)   **Objectives and mission statement**

  (i)   Objectives are more likely to be quantifiable for private sector organisations. Many voluntary sector objectives are more subjective and refer to general benefits rather that profit objectives.

  (ii)   Voluntary sector objectives must recognise the wider constituency of stakeholders involved in such organisations, and not just shareholders.

  (iii) Similarly, the mission statement of a voluntary sector organisation must reflect the core benefits to its stakeholder groups, and not focus on competitive advantage and profitability.

  (iv)   Because of the wider stakeholder group, accountability for objectives may be more difficult in the voluntary sector organisation.

  It must however be noted that many voluntary sector organisations are run along business lines and the differences compared with a private sector organisation may not be too great (eg the retail chains of same charities set many objectives which are similar in nature to those of commercial retail chains).

(b)   **Key stakeholders**

  In principle, the range of stakeholders is similar for private sector and voluntary organisations. However, their relative importance can differ markedly, and some types of stakeholder may not exist at all.

  (i)   Shareholders are important stakeholders in private sector organisations, but generally absent from voluntary organisations. The latter are more likely to obtain their capital from grants and donations rather than profit-seeking shareholders.

  (ii)   Community groups of one form or another (eg the disabled, local neighbourhood groups, pressure groups) are usually a driving stakeholder group for voluntary organisations. For private sector organisations they may still be very important, but not core to the business.

  (iii) The role of financial institutions may be less in voluntary sector organisations, although it must be remembered that these groups often depend on banks for loans.

(iv) Employees as a stakeholder group within private sector organisations may be replaced with volunteers who provide their time free of charge.

(c) **Organisational culture**

There is considerable difference of culture within private sector organisations, as well as between this group of organisations and the voluntary sector. Nevertheless, some general differences between the two groups can be identified.

(i) A culture of 'the customer is always right' which is prevalent in the private sector must be moderated in the voluntary sector to recognise that the 'customer' may need 'training' to adopt a particular view.

(ii) The culture of a voluntary organisation may focus more around staff than consumers, especially where staff are unpaid volunteers.

(iii) Honesty, integrity and ethics may be more important issues in the culture of a voluntary organisation than opportunism and maximisation of profits.

(iv) The culture of a voluntary organisation may take longer to adapt to a changed environment (although there are many private sector organisations where this is also true).

5.2.4 Public, private and voluntary sectors

(a) **Objectives of public, private and voluntary sector organisations**

It can be difficult to strictly distinguish between these three types of organisations, because there is a lot of overlapping at the edges. Many public sector organisations, for example, have been reconstituted as 'QANGOs' with objectives that may seem more familiar to the private sector than the public sector. Also, many voluntary organisations have commercial trading arms that have objectives more typical of the private sector than the voluntary sector. Having made this caveat, we can distinguish between these three types of organisations' objectives.

Public sector organisations typically have objectives that emphasise public benefit, as well as financial targets. Health authorities often have objectives to raise awareness of health issues, for example with regard to the dangers of smoking or eating excessive amounts of fats. In these circumstances, financial objectives may act as a constraint rather than the primary objective. The health promotion authority may seek to maximise awareness of the issue, within the constraints of a centrally allocated budget. In many situations, public sector organisations' objectives can be difficult to quantify, and even more difficult to measure the extent to which they have been achieved. For example, it can be difficult for the health promotion authority to accurately measure how many people have seen its messages, understood them, and subsequently gone on to change their behaviour.

Private sector organisations tend to focus more on quantifiable financial objectives. Ultimately, private-sector organisations are interested in achieving an adequate return to their shareholders. In achieving this, organisations set a range of objectives, both short-term and long-term. These typically relate to sales, new product developments, customer satisfaction etc. Although companies may prefer quantifiable objectives, they should not overlook the fact that objectives may sometimes be difficult to quantify, but may nevertheless be very important (for example, brand image may be vital to a sports goods manufacturer, but may be much more difficult to measure than sales). Another difference between public and private sector objectives is that the private sector organisation can generally measure its results, because they are much more internal to the organisation. While the public sector organisation may focus its objectives on external public benefits, most private sector organisations focus on direct benefits to the organisation, for example sales, profits and market share.

Voluntary sector organisations' objectives reflect the specific nature of the organisation. Like many public sector organisations, objectives are likely to focus on external benefits, for example helping to relieve poverty in Africa, or to preserve a wildlife habitat closer to home. Financial objectives in themselves are likely to be of less importance than pursuing these external objectives. It was noted earlier that despite having very unquantifiable social objectives, some aspects of voluntary organisations might have quite clear financial objectives. Many charities such as the British Heart Foundation and Oxfam run chains of shops with clear financial objectives. Profits from these activities are used to support the charity's wider social objectives.

(b) **Five causes of change in objectives over time**

Within a large private sector organisation, the following factors may cause objectives to change over time:

- Ownership of the organisation may change. Companies differ in their long-term orientation, and some owners of the company may be happy to gradually build up the business over time, and would focus on long-term objectives rather than short-term ones. By contrast, other owners, such as private equity firms, may acquire the business with a view to a short-term turnaround and sale. The objectives of the company are therefore much more likely to be short term.

- Government changes may have the effect of forcing a company to change its objectives. For example, legislation concerning companies' pension funds may require it to lower its objective of returning funds to shareholders, and instead allocate more money to its pension fund.

- Public attitudes to large organisations may cause a change in objectives. There is increasing concern with the idea of corporate social responsibility, and many organisations now realise that an important objective, alongside making adequate profit, should be to address the needs and concerns of its key stakeholders.

- The level of competition in the markets the company serves may force the company to change its objectives over time. If the market becomes progressively more saturated, it may have to lower its profits objectives.

- In the short term, objectives may need to be revised in response to changes in the level of national economic activity. For a consumer goods manufacturer, a fall in household disposable income may lead to the lowering of sales and profit objectives.

5.2.5 Charity issues

REPORT: HOW MARKETING DISCIPLINES COULD BENEFIT CARE FOR THE AGED

Prepared by Your Name, Marketing Assistant, for the Board of Trustees, and submitted on [date]. This report highlights the potential contribution that a professional marketing approach could make to the future success of the Care for the Aged charity in three key areas: information, client needs and fundraising.

1   Information issues

Information is fundamental to both service provision and fundraising. Marketing disciplines could improve the charity's performance in both areas as follows.

- There is potential for systematic marketing research and information systems to improve our management of the environment and stakeholders of the charity. We need to consider not just current but future information needs. There may be potential to use databases to develop relationship marketing to donors and volunteers, to secure repeat contributions. There may be potential to use marketing research to enhance our ability to 'compete' with other fund-raising organisations. We could use data to segment and target direct mailings – and so on.

- Marketing focuses on anticipating the needs of customers. A charity needs a good understanding of who its 'customers' are: the beneficiaries of our services (and how we could service them better); our donors (and how we might locate and target additional sources of funds); and our volunteer helpers (and where additional help can be found).

- Another important information issue is knowing how well (and cost-efficiently) we are performing our chartered tasks. How many of our appointments with clients did we make on time? What is their level of satisfaction with the service that we provide? How cost-effective is our service provision compared to private-sector 'competitors' or charity benchmarks? How motivated are our volunteers? Marketing disciplines include the gathering and analysis of feedback for control and improvement.

2   Issues over client needs

A charity requires a 'marketing orientation' just as much as a commercial business. In other words, we need to see our purpose as anticipating and satisfying our various stakeholder groups – particularly our clients – in order to fulfil our charter (and donor's expectations). Professional marketing can contribute insights in this area, in the following ways.

- We must prioritise our limited resources to clients who are in greatest need, out of social responsibility. This may involve complex decisions about the relative importance of needs, the availability of alternative care/services and the economic feasibility of helping intensive-need aged.

- Market research is needed to establish what the needs of clients (and prospective clients) really are, and what gaps there are in current service provision. Are transport, meals-on-wheels, visiting or respite care facilities most valued, for example? Are our clients primarily the aged or their families and carers?

- There is a need for demand management; given the ageing population in the UK, we need to anticipate growing demand and manage community and client expectations.

- There may be potential to segment our client base: for example, on the basis of services uses, frequency of use, severity of disability, location, shut-in/mobile and so on. This would enable us to target and prioritise efforts more cost-effectively, and mobilise volunteers with specialist expertise or local affiliations.

- Above all, there is a need to foster a customer care orientation among all staff, volunteers and service providers. We need to train them to listen to clients, treat them with respect and dignity, and support them through life challenges and changes, as befits our mission.

3   Fundraising issues

Like most charities, our organisation obtains funding from a number of sources.

- We receive a government grant from the local authority, some of which is given out of its discretionary budgets, and some of which is provided specifically for aged care services. Marketing can help us identify competitors for direct government funding, and policy objectives, to enable us to tailor grant proposals appropriately.

- We rely on donations from members of the public, through volunteer collections, payroll giving schemes and so on. Marketing can help us improve our communication programme with potential donors and widen our reach and 'competitiveness'. As a local charity, we could extend our local fundraising initiatives (eg to events). We could also be more creative in soliciting local sponsorships (eg from businesses in the 'grey' market such as cinemas). We might also engage in public relations (eg articles in local papers on 'third age' issues), develop our website for funding appeals, and develop our database for relational direct mail companies (leveraging current donor loyalty). None of these need be prohibitively costly options.

- We obtain some income from trading, mostly through the sale of donated goods at our high-street outlet. Marketing can help us improve the contribution of our trading activities, by additional promotional activity, more attractive store display, training of volunteers in sales services and pricing, and local advertising.

5.2.6 Change

(a)   The marketing environment comprises all of those people, organisations and forces that can have a direct or indirect impact on the fortunes of an organisation. These forces are continually changing and therefore their impacts on an organisation are likely to be variable. Some of the effects can be quite lagged, so if an organisation has a good understanding of its marketing environment as it is today, it will be able to predict the likely impacts on its business in the future. These impacts can include changes in fashion, tastes or changes in the level of demand in the economy and changes in production possibilities. An organisation which has a better understanding of its marketing environment than its competitors, and is able to act on its understanding, will gain a competitive advantage.

(b)   (i)   An **environmental audit** is essentially a set of procedures by which an organisation explicitly asks questions about the environments in which marketing operates. In the case of the macro-environment, the audit would independently verify or challenge any assumptions that the company had been making, for instance about the likely rate of economic growth or the speed of change in the technological environment. In the case of the micro-environment, the person undertaking an audit of the distribution environment could proceed by asking retailers themselves about how they perceive the company's products and future trends in retailing for that type of produce.

An environmental audit begins with the appointment of an independent person to undertake the audit. This could be a consultant from outside the organisation, or somebody from another position within the firm, either sideways or above the function being audited. A self-audit could be undertaken, but at the risk of a loss of objectivity.

It should be noted that an environmental audit is not itself a framework for decisions. The availability of good quality, timely information is crucial to undertaking an environmental audit.

(ii) **Impact analysis** proceeds by constructing a series of influence diagrams, so that a better understanding of the relationships between environmental forces and their impacts on the organisation can be obtained. If the price a company has to pay for raw materials is a critical factor, then the forces that influence the price of raw materials will be of interest to it. By monitoring these, it will have an earlier warning about price rises than if it were to wait until its supplier told it of the price increase.

A number of **specific influence diagrams** may be used to improve the understanding of how forces in the environment may influence particular aspects of an organisation. To gain a broader view, **impact grids** can be constructed. Specific environmental forces or events are identified and their impact on particular aspects of the business is assessed. Weighting can be carried out (1 equals no effect, to 10 equals a substantial or critical impact).

As with environmental audits, impact analysis cannot make decisions for a company: it can only identify factors which should be taken into account. The technique is only as good as the information used. Furthermore the nature of impacts may change over time, for example as a result of technological innovations.

(iii) In order for an environmental audit to have a useful input into the marketing planning process, a wide range of information and opinions needs to be summarised in a meaningful way. This is particularly true where a variety of analytic techniques have been used. The information collated from such analyses needs to be simplified and summarised for planning purposes.

An environmental **threat and opportunity matrix** provides a summary of the environmental factors that are most critical to the company. This provides a useful report to stimulate debate among senior management about the future of aspects of the business. It is often suggested that factors should be weighted according to their importance and then rated for their impact on the organisation.

Opportunities should be assessed for their attractiveness and success probability. Attractiveness can be assessed in terms of potential market size, growth rates, profit margins, competitiveness and distribution channels; other factors may be technological requirements, degree of government interference, environmental concerns and energy requirements. Set against the measure of attractiveness is the probability of success. This depends on the company's strengths and competitive advantage and on such issues as access to capital to finance new developments and technological and productive expertise.

Assessing such factors can be quite a subjective and speculative task. The matrix should not therefore be relied on as a definitive guide to decision-making, but rather an aid which presents information concisely.

(c) The **product life cycle** reminds us that most products go through some form of cycle in which early slow sales are followed by rapidly expanding sales, followed by a levelling off and eventually by a falling off in sales volumes. Forecasting needs to understand how the life cycle of a product is likely to evolve during the forecasting period. It is not sufficient to simply extrapolate forwards recent trends, because the product may be about to enter a different part of the product life cycle in which the rate of growth is significantly different to that which occurred during the previous period.

5.2.7 Government marketing

Ofcom

Training material

Induction Session 3: Stakeholders

1   What are stakeholders?

Stakeholders are groups who have a legitimate stake or 'interest' in an organisation and its activities.

Connected stakeholders are stakeholders who are external to the organisation (ie not its employees) but are bound to the organisation by contractual or relational interdependencies. Examples include customers, suppliers, funding bodies and (in the case of an industry regulator) government (which would be an 'external' stakeholder for most private sector organisations). In our case, there is a special category of connected stakeholder: the telecom providers whose activities we regulate.

Pressure groups are groups which represent the interests of a particular section in society, or a particular cause, and seek to influence decision-makers in order to bring about a change agenda. The pressure applied can vary, depending upon the nature of the issue, and the resources of the group. Examples include Greenpeace (in the area of environmental protection) or Amnesty International (in the area of social justice).

Market research is a systematic process of gathering information about a particular market. Typical issues to be researched can include: the size of the market; growth trends; identifiable segments within the market; consumer preferences and how they change over time. Market research can combine quantitative approaches (such as statistical data monitoring) with more qualitative approaches (such as focus group interviews).

2   Implications for Ofcom

Connected stakeholders. As the UK telecommunications regulator, Ofcom has social and legal responsibilities in relation to a range of connected stakeholders, including the equipment manufacturers and service providers in the industry, consumer groups, suppliers, trade unions and government.

- Connected stakeholders, by their nature, have a high degree of *interest* in the organisation's activities, and although they have varying degree of *influence* (suppliers and industry players obviously less than government, say) Ofcom has social responsibility obligations to take their needs and concerns into account, but also to be ethical, fair, impartial and fully compliant in its dealings.

- As a public sector organisation, there is also a high degree of public accountability for our actions towards connected stakeholders. For example, the EU Public Procurement Directives affect our relationships with suppliers (compulsory competitive tendering to ensure fairness and so on), while the Freedom of Information Act obliges us to be transparent in information held on file.

Pressure groups. The nature of pressure groups is that they exercise power in the area of their interest, whether by appeals to the media, or by lobbying government, or (in more extreme cases) by organising popular demonstrations or even direct action. Mobile phone companies have faced pressure from local community groups opposed to the siting of new phone masts.

- It must be remembered that pressure groups have the power to directly influence our activities (eg by influencing government policy), and may also damage (or enhance) our image and credibility in the eyes of the public (our ultimate external stakeholder).

- Pressure groups require careful stakeholder communication and management, often on a proactive 'issues management' basis (rather than waiting for crises or conflicts to arise). This may be accomplished by public relations activity direct to the pressure group 'public', or via the media.

Market research. As a regulator, Ofcom must back its regulatory decisions with a good understanding of the markets that it regulates.

- It must have market knowledge (and systems for market intelligence gathering) just as good as the companies that it regulates, who may disagree with the regulator's diagnosis of industry dynamics, pricing and so on.

- It must have up-to-date information, not only about a market as it is today, but as it is likely to develop in the future.

5.2.8 Open systems and change

(a)   Open systems

Open systems imply that it is difficult or impossible to control what is within the system and what is outside it. A company as an open system implies that the organisation faces challenges from new competitors, new market segments appearing and disappearing, and changes in suppliers who are able and willing to supply to the organisation, among other things.

Using a systems perspective the following are typical ways in which an organisation can respond to environmental change:

(i) The organisation may expand or contract in order to adapt to changed conditions. It may achieve this through outsourcing, sub-contracting and the use of short-term contracts for its staff.

(ii) As new competitors emerge the organisation may seek to work with these, as far as competition laws allow, in areas such as the development of industry-wide technical standards.

(iii) Long-term agreements with suppliers to collaborate on market research and new product development may provide a stronger base for responding to environmental change.

(iv) Government regulatory agencies can be crucial to success for many organisations and therefore it can be important to develop a strategy to accommodate the requirements of such agencies.

(v) New pressure groups may emerge and a strategic decision needs to be made on how to handle them, from outright condemnation of the group, to close working together on research and development.

(b) **Pressure group impacts**

Two pressure groups interested in the activities of the Esso oil company are the StopEsso campaign and Greenpeace. Both have campaigned against the company's hostility to measures designed to reduce emissions of greenhouse gases.

The following are possible impacts on Esso.

(i) Some buyers of petrol may agree with the pressure groups and may happily go to another petrol station because the cost to themselves may be quite minimal.

(ii) The pressure groups may do more long lasting harm to the brand reputation of Esso, which might make it more difficult for the company to enter new markets, for example.

(iii) The groups may appeal to government and press for legislation which is against the long-term interests of the company.

(iv) In the short-term, extreme members of the two pressure groups may take violent direct action against the company's assets and personnel.

5.2.9 Mission and objectives

The following question is answered in the context of a UK energy provider.

(a) **Mission statement**

A mission statement is a means of reminding everybody within the organisation of its essential purpose. *Drucker* identified a number of basic questions which form the basis of a corporate mission statement:

- What is our business?
- Who is the customer?
- What is value to the customer?
- What will our business be?
- What should our business be?

By forcing management to focus on the essential nature of the business which they are in and the nature of customer needs which they seek to satisfy, a narrow, short-sighted view of its business is avoided.

(b) **External sources of influence**

(i) **Government regulatory bodies**: Energy markets rarely exhibit the characteristics of intense competition, because scale monopolies favour a dominant supplier. The UK is no exception to this, and therefore the energy supply market is highly regulated in order to avoid exploitation of household and business users of energy. In the UK, the regulator Ofgem has considerable power to determine companies' prices and service levels. There is an assumption that gas and electricity suppliers should be allowed to earn a reasonable level of profits in order to encourage future investment, but not excessive profits. It follows that pricing and profit objectives will be highly constrained by the demands of the regulator.

(ii) **Competitors**: Although the gas and electricity market in the UK is highly regulated, there is nevertheless competition between suppliers, especially in the market for large industrial customers, who are deemed by regulators to need less protection. Price and profit objectives will be constrained by prices charged by competitors. The company may also be forced to improve its quality of service objectives, in response to higher standards offered by competitors.

(iii) **Environmental pressure groups**: We are all becoming more familiar with arguments about global warming, and for contribution of traditional fossil fuel-based sources of energy to global warming. The UK Government has implemented its Kyoto Protocol requirement for an increase in the proportion of energy derived from renewable sources, and this will be reflected in individual companies' own objectives. By being seen to have proactively 'green' objectives, UK energy companies may prevent further regulation by the Government, and may give an individual company a positioning advantage in the eyes of private consumers, for whom gas and electricity is otherwise a generic product.

(c) **Promotional opportunities to change organisational image**

(i) **Invest in renewable sources of energy**: Like most large energy suppliers in the UK, this company has invested in new, relatively environmentally friendly sources of energy, such as wind turbines and solar panels. Although this was done partly to meet Government requirements that a larger proportion of energy be sourced from renewable sources, the development nevertheless gives a wonderful public relations opportunity. Even though they account for a minute proportion of the company's total energy output, wind turbines provide a graphic illustration to consumers, to government regulators and to politicians that the company is taking global warming seriously. However, it should be noted that such investments may also bring bad public relations side effects; for example, many residents living near wind turbines have formed protest groups to campaign against visual and noise intrusion.

(ii) **Sponsor a television programme associated with ecological concerns**: The image of energy companies held in most people's minds is probably based on power stations emitting pollution. The company needs to change people's top of mind associations, so that the immediate connection they make with the company name is concern for the environment. Sponsoring a television programme about nature conservation will provide exposure linked to an environmentally beneficial activity. However, the company must make sure that this image is at least backed up by some reality of environmental concern, for example a programme of investments in renewable energy sources. The public and pressure groups may see through 'spin' that is not backed up by real efforts on the company's part.

(iii) **Create awareness of improvements to existing technology**: It is likely that for several years, or even decades to come, supply of energy by this company is going to be dominated by traditional fossil fuels. We must not overlook the great improvements that have been made in the efficient use of fossil fuels, and the great new opportunities for cleaning emissions, and reducing the amount of carbon dioxide emitted from power stations. Although the subject may seem boring, we must get the message across to news editors that the company can make a big contribution by improving its existing technology, as much as by introducing new alternative forms of energy. The company should regularly brief journalists and newspaper editors about developments, and look for innovative ways of making old technology sound interesting, for example by sponsoring educational materials used in schools and colleges.

5.2.10 Responding to change

(a) **Response to changes in the competitive environment**

The competitive environment of a road haulage operator comprises an open system. It can be difficult to define just who are the competitors of a road haulage operator. The following 'levels' of competition can be defined in terms of the threat posed.

- Direct competitors are other road haulage operators in the same locality. These provide a similar product to the same market as that served by the company.

- The company also faces competition from other operators located further away, including those based in low-cost countries but who provide services to UK-based customers, following EU deregulation of service sectors.

- Road haulage companies might also be able to identify more remote forms of competition, such as rail and airline services. Rail services may be competitive for some high-volume, low-value goods, while air transport may be competitive for some high-value, low-volume goods.

The response will depend upon the nature of the change in the road haulage competitive environment. If the main threat were to come from other local operators competing for the same customers, the company could differentiate itself by offering a slightly different service, for example specialising in particular types of goods transport (such as specialised electronics equipment movement). It could augment its additional services, by managing its customers' warehouses, or offering home delivery services direct to its customers' customers.

If the competitive threat were to came from overseas operators competing on the basis of lower operating costs, alternative responses are possible. Firstly, it could seek to reduce costs to a level comparable to the overseas competitors. While it may not be able to match the low labour costs of some new EU member state operators, it may be able to offset this with increased efficiency. It could also emphasise the benefits of having a locally-based operator who better understands and is able to work in partnership with local customers when compared to a foreign operator.

It is the third kind of competition – the more indirect competitors, such as air and rail – which a road haulage operators will find it most difficult to respond to. The basis of the competitive threat may be changing cost structures that an individual road haulage operator working in isolation cannot match. For example, if government gave railway companies large subsidies to encourage more goods to be carried by rail, it would be difficult for a road haulage operator to match the subsidised costs. The only response would be to stress the added value benefits of continuing to use road haulage. If the road haulage operator felt that the competitor had an unfair advantage, it could join a lobby group to campaign for a 'level playing field' for road haulage operators.

(b) **Response to changes in the macro-environment**

The macro-environment comprises all those forces and pressures that may not affect the road haulage company immediately, but which are likely to lead to changes eventually in a company's operating, or micro-environment. Key elements of likely change in a road haulage operator's macro-environment, and ways in which it might respond are explored below.

Legal environment: Road haulage companies have been faced with increasing levels of national and EU-wide legislation, governing such factors as road safety, driving hours limits, minimum wages, and vehicle design. The smart road haulage operator will seek to identify the direction of legislative change and be ready to respond before new legislation actually comes into effect. For example, there maybe discussion about introducing new regulations which will allow larger lorries to operate. The smart operator will not wait until the law comes into effect before ordering new heavier lorries. By being first with the heavier lorries, it may be able to gain a competitive advantage.

Economic environment: Road haulage companies business cycles are sensitive to the business cycle. If economies go into recession, the volume of goods transported between businesses and between businesses and consumers falls. A sound understanding of the current position in the business cycle will help a road haulage operator to determine the size of its fleet. If the operator believes that the economy is about to turn down, it may defer vehicle replacements.

Environmental and ecological environment: Environmental groups have voiced increasing concern about the damage caused to the natural environment by heavy lorries. The anti-social, unhealthy and environmentally damaging effects of atmospheric and noise pollution have been reflected in legislation intended to reduce the environmental damage caused by lorries. A smart operator will seek to limit the effects of legislative changes, and may profit economically and politically by being seen to be an environmentally responsible operator. By carefully planning its operations, the company may be able to cut down the amount of empty mileage driven by its trucks, reducing costs and cultivating a sound environmental record.

These are just three inter-related aspects of the macro environment that the road haulage operator could be expected to respond to.

5.2.11 Macro- and micro-: voluntary organisation

(a) Macro-environment and micro-environments of a voluntary organisation

The macro-environment refers to general pressures in an organisation's environment. There are a number of factors which typically affect a voluntary organisation.

- Political/legal – what is government policy regarding the role of the voluntary sector?

- Economic – do changes in wealth and irregularity result in changes in demand for the organisation's services?

- Social – what esteem or stigma attaches to voluntary sector organisations?

- Technological – what are the impacts of the Internet on service delivery for a voluntary organisation (eg online counselling and advice sites)?

By contrast, the micro-environment of a voluntary organisation includes those individuals and organisations with which the voluntary body deals, or is accountable to in some way (its external stakeholders). Those typically include:

- Users – eg users of a play centre.
- Members of the governing body.
- Local authorities – who may give grants.
- Financial institutions – who may lend money.
- Government regulatory agencies – eg the Health and Safety Executive.

(b) MEMORANDUM

To: Marketing Manager

Subject: Importance of the Macro-environment to this organisation

The macro-environment concerns forces and pressures that may not affect us immediately, but could nevertheless have an impact on our organisation in the medium to long-term. We must watch carefully today for trends which could emerge to affect us in the future.

From a marketing perspective, these are some of the most important factors that we must monitor.

Political/legal environment: We must identify changes in government thinking, which could eventually feed through to policies and legislation. We also need to keep a close eye on legislative proposals which might affect our operations, especially those relating to health and safety and employment.

Economic environment: We depend on government agencies and users for our funding, so we must detect any early signs of wavering for our support. Are private sector organisations emerging which could take away some of our users?

Social/demographic environment: If we appeal to narrowly defined age groups, we must monitor trends in age cohorts. Elderly groups are likely to grow in size.

Technological environment: What new opportunities are opening for us to deliver our resources? What IT developments are there which will allow us to make better use of our website?

5.2.12 Employees and intermediaries

(a) (i)   Employees as stakeholders

Employees expect their employer to be responsible for more than simply paying their wages. As a stakeholder, employees would look at an employer to act responsibly in terms of fair recruitment policies; training which is appropriate to long-term career development; and monitoring, control and reward systems which are fair. For most people, their job is a major part of their lives and they look to an employer to protect their personal state in their employment.

(ii) Intermediaries as stakeholders

Intermediaries handle goods and services for a company, mediating between them and the final consumer. Some intermediaries have become very dependant upon one manufacturer and can be regarded as stakeholders in that manufacturer's business. The actions of the manufacturer are likely to impact on the intermediary. Such issues as continuity of contract, prompt payment and a good returns policy are likely to affect an intermediary as a stakeholder.

(b)   **(i)**   **Perceptions of a Ford car employee**

Ford is a large multinational manufacturer. Different employees and groups of employees are likely to have different perceptions of their role as stakeholders in Ford. However, some general issues of perceptions can be identified:

(1)   Employees are likely to have differing perceptions on the role of Ford as a fair, equal opportunities employer. Although many people regard Ford as a good employer in this respect, there have been well publicised instances when the company appeared to be acting against disadvantaged groups.

(2)   Faced with the planned closure of their plant, Ford may appear a poor employer.

(3)   For many employees, Ford has provided continuity of employment on terms and conditions which are better than they could obtain locally, especially in the case of many assembly plants in less developed economies.

(4)   Ford has a good record of investing in the training of its employees.

   (ii)   **Influence of the marketer on employees' perspectives**

(1)   In respect of equal **opportunities policies,** the marketer should ensure that advertising depicts a **full range of ethnic groups** in a positive manner. The company received bad publicity in the mid-1990s when it airbrushed out black faces in an advert.

(2)   In respect of **employees' training,** the marketer can have an input in a bid to include a **customer orientation** in all employees' training. A production line mechanic should be made aware that he is not just building a car, but contributing to a happy experience in the eyes of the final customer.

5.2.13 Micro environment and market structure

(a)   The micro environment of the Ford car company

This comprises the individuals and organisations that impinge on the company's activities. They can be defined under the following headings.

- Customers (individuals, corporate entities)
- Suppliers (parts suppliers)
- Employees
- Local community groups and pressure groups
- Competitors
- Government agencies

(b)   Approaches to market structure analysis

Two approaches are identified and discussed here, with respect to the Ford car company.

(i)   **Sector analysis**

This is a relatively straightforward and descriptive approach which is based on breaking the car market down into a number of sectors and analysing the relationship between supply and demand within each of these sectors. The car market is quite diverse in terms of products and the needs which these seek to satisfy. A typical sector analysis may focus on small hatchbacks, family cars, larger executive cars and multi purpose vehicles.

Analysis on the supply side would look at existing capacity, barriers to entry/exit and the likely trend of capacity in the future.

On the demand side, analysis would focus on the size of the market (by country/region), recent and likely future trends and the composition of buyers (eg private buyers versus company buyers).

A sector analysis would identify the market share of the principal suppliers and the profitability of each sector.

(ii) Porter's Five Forces analysis

This is a more analytical approach and can be applied at the level of individual subsectors of the car market, or the car sector as a whole. Porter suggested that market structure could be analysed with reference to five phenomena.

- The power of buyers (eg fleet car buyers)
- The power of suppliers (especially the large multinationals)
- The threat of new entrants (from electronics companies)
- The threat of substitute products (more public transport)
- The intensity of rivalry between firms

Market structure is defined in terms of these five elements and the intensity of competition emerges as a result of the interaction of these forces.

(iii) Sources of information for market structure analysis

- Specialist research organisations, eg Keynote, Mintel
- Industry association bodies, eg Society of Motor Traders
- Office for National Statistics, eg Business Monitor services
- Financial Times sector surveys, also online archive at www.ft.com

5.2.14 Legal regulation and consumer protection

(i) Beneficial impact of legal regulation on business

Businesses generally like certainty, and the presence of a stable and transparent legal framework increases the certainties in their environment.

Companies can invest in new product development and in the development of intellectual property, knowing that the legal framework will provide protection for their investment.

Legal frameworks generally provide the basis for fair and competitive markets. Without this framework of legal regulation, small companies may have difficulties facing up to larger and dominant predators.

Legal regulation often specifies the obligations of business organisations to government, but they can also specify the rights of government towards business organisations.

A robust legal framework is essential for a business organisation to be able to enforce its contracts with customers, suppliers and intermediaries.

(ii) Negative impacts of legal regulation on business

Complying with regulations costs money which could be better spent in other business activities.

For small companies, the need to keep abreast of changes in regulations takes up a disproportionate amount of management time compared to larger organisations that can afford to employ specialists to understand and implement new regulations.

Excessive regulation can create a 'Can't do' rather than a 'can do' mentality, thereby stifling innovation by business.

It can be argued that parties to a contract entered into the contract freely, and it is no business of legal regulation to intervene by specifying minimum conditions. For example, if an employee is prepared to work for less than the minimum wage rate, why should the law prevents the company giving employment to somebody who wants the job?

Legal regulation is observed by legitimate companies, but often does not prevent 'cowboy' companies who operate outside the law, and can bring a whole industry sector into disrepute before such companies are eventually prevented from operating.

(iii) Government legislation to protect consumers

Most developed economies have seen a large increase in the amount of legislation designed to protect the interests of consumers, reflecting the change in balance of power within economies, from producers to consumers.

In the UK, consumers have traditionally relied on common law principles to protect themselves against companies. Increasingly, this is being supplemented with legislation, for example the Consumer Protection Act, Consumer Credit Act and Trade Descriptions Act.

As well as new regulations, the UK, like many other countries, has seen an increase in governmental bodies charged with overseeing and enforcing the regulations (for example, Trading Standards departments and the Office of Fair Trading).

In addition to legislation that protects individual consumers' rights against companies, there has been an increase in regulation at a macro-level to preserve the competitiveness of markets, and thereby indirectly protecting the rights of consumers to buy the best available goods at the best possible price.

Some would argue that an increasing level of consumer legislation is fuelling a litigious society, and unrealistically raises expectations of consumers.

(iv)   The case against using the law to resolve disputes between businesses

In the UK, like most countries, legal services are expensive, and therefore businesses should seek to save costs by using alternatives to law. The high cost of fighting a case which is subsequently lost may leave a company out of pocket.

The law is also very time-consuming, and may distract management attention from more pressing business problems in the business environment.

A protracted legal dispute between businesses may entrench divisions between companies who might at some time in future otherwise be valuable co- operators (for example, a manufacturer who pursues an intermediary through the legal system may find it difficult to supply that intermediary again in the future if the business environment changes).

At a more general level, there is often pressure to introduce new legislation that will help to resolve recurring types of disputes between businesses. This often affects issues of fair competition, for example regulations to make it easier for mobile phone customers to switch supplier. Companies generally prefer the flexibility of regulations agreed among their trade association, rather than that rigid regulations imposed on them by government.

(v)   Roles of the government in the legislative environment

Initiator of law – the government brings forward Bills which become Acts of Parliament, and thereby create the bases for law.

Protection of government processes – government needs legislation to protect its sources of revenue, and to ensure that its expenditure is correctly applied.

As guardian of competitive markets – governments create and use the law in order to preserve the competitiveness of markets, for example through the Office of Fair Trading.

As an instrument of social justice – governments often use legislation to protect the relatively weak and vulnerable from more dominant predators. For example, regulations on advertising are designed to protect young children from exploitation by advertisers.

To promote innovation in the economy – government uses legislation on patents and copyright to promote investment in innovation, mindful that investors will be more likely to invest if their inventions are subsequently protected by a patent or copyright.

5.2.15 Distribution dilemma

(a)   Reasons why a fashion clothing manufacturer should stop a supermarket undercutting recommended prices

(i)   Brand position: For many products, consumers find it difficult to compare the quality of one brand against another. It may, for example, only be possible to tell whether a shirt is of high quality or not after washing it several times. In these circumstances, price may be an indicator of quality, with many consumers assuming that a higher price indicates higher quality. A higher price may also indicate exclusiveness, which may be a valuable and sought attribute in its own right. If the price of an item of clothing is so low that anybody can afford it, it would lose its sense of exclusiveness. When a supermarket offers prices at 50 per cent below the recommended price, it erodes this company's brand position, and confuses consumers who may no longer regard the company's products as exclusive and high quality.

(ii)   Expectations of other retailers: The company had to accept a lower margin from the supermarket, in order to sell a very high-volume of clothes. This is normal business practice, and the company could justify the lower margin per item on the bases of a higher volume. However, if the supermarket then charges much lower prices, it may simply take business away from the specialist clothing retailers, from whom the company earns a higher margin. Furthermore, these specialist retailers may see their sales falling, and may either stop selling the company's products, all may come back and demand a better wholesale price, which will affect this company's margins.

(iii)   Customer service levels: Supermarkets have a tendency to 'pile it high and sell it cheap'. Of course, many customers are happy with this approach, and it works well for simple products where consumer knowledge is high and there is only a minimal requirement for after-sales service. Such an approach may harm this company's products because consumers often need advice, for example about fitting to the customer's own figure. There is also a problem that supermarkets often only sell the most popular sizes (eg women's sizes 10-14), and therefore do not cater for very small or very large sizes. Supermarkets often do not have facilities for customers to try on the company's clothes, which results in a higher return rate than in a specialist retailer where advice and a fitting service would be available.

(b)   Reasons why a fashion manufacturer should continue supplying to a price-cutting supermarkets

(i)   Legislation: In the UK, as in many other countries, it is illegal for a manufacturer to insist on the price at which wholesalers and retailers sell its products (except in a few clearly-defined cases, and this does not apply to fashion clothing). Legislators, and recent case history, have made clear that both direct and indirect methods of maintaining price controls are illegal, so merely withholding suppliers from the supermarket, or charging a higher price, could amount to unlawful price-fixing. A charge of price fixing could result in a fine on the company, and take up a lot of management time in the process. It could also bring the company bad publicity.

(ii)   Consumer preferences: Supermarkets are taking a growing proportion of consumers' total expenditure. In the UK, it has recently been estimated that the retailer Tesco accounts for about 12 per cent of all consumer expenditure, for example. People often prefer the convenience of buying household goods and clothes along with their weekly shopping. If the company tries to make sales to supermarkets more difficult, it would be in danger of going against a trend and becoming relatively isolated if it relies on smaller independent shops, which are accounting for a diminishing proportion of total retail sales.

(iii)   Segmentation strategy: The company could still serve both the supermarkets and the specialist retailers, and keep both happy. It may develop a basic range of products for supply through supermarkets at low prices, low margins, but with high- volumes. The company could then develop a more upmarket range, sold through specialist retailers, at higher margins, high prices, and lower volumes. The family buyer looking for cheap children's clothes may be happy with the relatively basic offer at the supermarket, while the discerning, fashion conscious individual who enjoys comparison shopping in the High Street, will be happy with the extended range offered through smaller specialist retailers. Also, the small specialist retailers themselves will not be so conscious of supermarkets undermining sales of this company's products.

5.2.16 Concept and theory

(a)   **Open systems**

A **system** can be defined as a set of inter-related components, so that change in one component leads to change in other components. In order for a system to survive, there must be self-correcting mechanisms which prevent the system from destroying itself. For example, a thermostat on a gas boiler prevents damage from the boiler getting too hot.

Closed systems occur where all components can be identified and, in effect, a boundary can be put around the limits of the system. By contrast, **open systems** have no boundaries, meaning that it can be difficult to tell what is part of the system and what is not. Economic systems tend to be open in nature.

For a **car manufacturer** seeking to forecast demand for cars on the basis of the strength of the economic environment, it can be difficult to identify the variables within the system that will affect it. For a UK manufacturer, to what extent should the economic systems of overseas countries by incorporated into a systems model? What factors will influence exchange rates? How will terrorist activities affect people's spending patterns? What will the effects be on world GDP in general and on UK GDP in particular? These are all examples of influences on economic systems which can be difficult to identify and to quantify.

The marketer will try to close the system as far as possible by incorporating peripheral elements. In this way, the predictive ability of a system improves. But it can be difficult to identify some of the more obscure peripheral elements, and to predict their effects on the system in general and the company's demand in particular.

(b) **Porter's five forces analysis**

The usefulness of this analytic framework to marketers will be illustrated with reference to traditional UK 'High Street' bookshops. The Five Forces framework provides a useful framework for assessing the factors that affect the level of competition within a market. These are the five forces:

(i) **Threat of substitutes**. Traditional bestsellers are threatened by substitute ways of buying books, especially online bookstores, and supermarkets selling selected book titles. Books themselves have substitutes – electronic books, as well as other forms of entertainment / education.

(ii) **Threat of new entrants**. It is relatively easy for a new bookshop to be set up, especially if it targets narrow niches. Also, UK retailers are threatened by the incursion of book chains from overseas (eg Borders).

(iii) **The power of buyers**. Buyers' power is strong where there are few buyers relative to sellers. Large book retailers are able to drive hard bargains with publishers in order to get the maximum promotional support and the lowest wholesale prices.

(iv) **The power of sellers**. Sellers' power is strong where there are few sellers relative to buyers. In the case of top book titles, publishers may be in a very strong position in relation to retailers, who must buy the book for their shelves at any cost.

(v) **Intensity of rivalry**. Finally, markets vary in the ferocity of competition between rivals – UK bookshops have became increasingly competitive, as witnessed by increasing levels of promotion, special offers and price discounting.

5.2.17 Stakeholders, research and competition legislation

Report on diversification strategy

Produced by John Smith (Marketing Assistant) for Charles Parker, Marketing Manager, Number 1 Logistics Ltd.

Date 7th December 200X

This report discusses a number of issues that are important considerations for our proposed diversification into the delivery of valuables for the banking industry.

(a) Key stakeholders

Our proposed diversification will create new stakeholder groups for us, and raise new issues with our existing stakeholders.

- Employees. Our employees have been used to delivering low value parcels. Will they need additional training to deal with the bank's valuables? Dealing with valuables which are attractive to thieves, staff may be concerned for their personal security, so we must address this issue.

- Suppliers. As we enter this new area of business, we may need our suppliers to adjust what they supply to us. Our insurers, for example will need to be advised of the greater risk that they will now bear as we carry high value consignments.

- Local resident groups. This new work may involve our depots opening for longer hours. We must try to minimise impacts on residents living near our depots.

(b)   Key external sources of information

I would recommend consulting the following sources to guide our proposed diversification.

- Specialist trade research. We should check whether any of the specialist companies such as Keynote and Economist Intelligence Unit have produced a report on this subject.

- Business press. We should do a search of FT.COM to see if it gives us any leads.

- Trade bodies representing the banking and logistics bodies may be able to provide us with some key trends data, or even a specially commissioned survey.

(c)   Possible impact of legislation

Legislation is continually evolving, and we need to understand the possible impacts of legislation for our proposed diversification.

- Employment legislation. We need to ensure that we do not fall foul of the law on working hours, especially working time directives as this diversification is likely to require new patterns of working.

- Health & Safety legislation. The law requires us to provide a safe work environment for our staff, so we must ensure that we provide adequate security for them when they are handling valuables.

- Land use planning legislation. We must ensure that our planning permission permits us to use our depot in the evening, something that will be needed for our proposed diversification.

The most significant legislative threat is posed by our market dominance in our home country. A diversification programme could attract the attention of the competition authorities and we could be subject to a Competition Commission investigation. If we were found to be exploiting our position, we could be fined or forced to divest our activities.

5.2.18 Stakeholders and pressure groups

(a)   Interaction between a tourism company and its key stakeholders

Three important stakeholders for travel and tourism companies are: local communities in holiday destinations, employees, and suppliers. The nature of the interaction between a company and each of these groups can be complex and is discussed below.

(1)   Local community groups

For many local community groups, tourism makes a vital contribution to the local economy. The spending of tourists helps to create employment, and indirectly may reduce many social problems associated with poverty. Many local groups therefore welcome initiatives from tour companies to develop new facilities in their area. However, excessive development of tourism in a destination may cause resentment from local groups. They may find themselves competing with tourists for residential property that becomes increasingly expensive. Some natural resources, especially water may become scarce because of the high seasonal demands from tourists.

Tourism companies must work with local community groups. Not only can such groups indirectly affect regulation of the tourism sector, they have a more direct effect through supplying labour to the companies in the sector. Tourism companies must make their sector seem an attractive place for local people to work, offering good wages and sustainable careers. This is likely to be particularly important in highly developed tourism sectors, where there are many competing sources of employment.

(2)   Employees

The tourism business tends to be a people focused business, and obtaining adequate numbers of well-trained and reliable staff can be a key to success. In well-developed economies, tourism companies must compete with other sectors to obtain the best staff. In less developed economies, tourism companies may have more choice in their recruitment. However, they must avoid charges of exploitation, which may come about by offering very insecure forms of employment (for example, laying off staff at short notice if demand is low), and paying low wages. However, in many destinations, wages may be regarded as low by Western standards, but they may nevertheless represent prestigious jobs within their local community. Tourism companies should consider what training they provide for their employees. A well-trained workforce will not only provide employees with transferable skills, but will result in better quality of service to the company's customers. However, investments in transferable skills may be lost if employees move to a competitor company, so a company must ensure that it has an appropriate strategy to retain good staff.

(3) Suppliers

Tour operators essentially bring together the activities of a large number of suppliers, especially airlines, hotels and road transport operators. Close working relationships are crucial if package holidays are to come together in the eyes of customers. There has been a lot of discussion about the nature of relationships between these suppliers, and the extent to which they should be long-term or short-term in nature. Many tour operators have long-term supply agreements with hotels and airlines, but there is a trend towards more short-term opportunistic purchasing of capacity by some newer competitors in the sector. In all cases, suppliers will need reassurance that the tour operator is a credible organisation to deal with, and that they will be paid for the services supplied promptly.

There has been a trend towards integration within supply chains, and many suppliers have been acquired by tour operators, for example the German tourism business TUI owns travel agents, tour operators, airlines and hotels. This integration has occurred at the same time as many consumers prefer to buy different elements of a package holiday separately, rather than as a package.

(b) Significance of pressure groups

The travel and tourism sector has been identified as a significant contributor to climate change, caused by emissions from aircraft. Groups such as Friends of the Earth have campaigned against the damage caused by increasing volumes of air travel, and among other things, have campaigned for tax to be levied on aircraft fuel (it is currently exempt from taxation).

The significance of Friends of the Earth to travel and tourism companies is that it has frequently captured the public imagination, which politicians have subsequently picked up on. Eventually, this is likely to result in new legislation. Friends of the Earth has already raised awareness of global warming, and the contribution of aircraft, and politicians have begun to think about how tax could be levied on aviation fuel. This would have serious implications for the tourism sector, because fuel costs account for a high proportion of the costs of operating an aircraft. If tax was levied on aircraft fuel at the same rate as it is typically levied on petrol used by cars, airfares could be expected to double. Not only would this affect airlines, it would affect most businesses that depend upon large numbers of visitors arriving by air.

Tourism companies can take a number of approaches to try and use this pressure to their advantage. Airlines operating modern, fuel-efficient aircraft can promote this fact in their publicity, and appeal to environmentally concerned individuals who have qualms about booking the cheap flight.

Domestic tourism companies who do not rely excessively on customers arriving by air may see pressure for higher aircraft fuel tax as an opportunity to encourage more people to stay at home, rather than flying overseas for a holiday or short break. A British hotel chain, for example, could stress the environmental benefits of staying at one of its upgraded spa resorts, which would offer many of the advantages of a short break in Spain, but without causing environmental damage.

5.2.19 Industry environment

(a) A number of areas of concern can be identified.

(i) **Need to monitor trends in customer preferences**. By spotting emerging trends, the firm can switch its resources to products with a growing demand, and away from those which are going out of fashion.

(ii) **Need to monitor competitors**. New sources of competition can emerge to threaten the firm, both from within the industry sector and from beyond.

(iii) **Need to monitor suppliers' activities**. New competitive sources of supply may emerge (eg from lower cost Far Eastern products). Suppliers may develop new technologies which the firm can incorporate into its own production methods.

(iv)   **Need to monitor government attitudes to the sector**. Policy statements may lead to new legislation which affects the industry. The firm can seek to amend new legislation where this is harmful to the industry. Where legislation is actually passed, the firm can prepare for its implementation ahead of its competitors.

(b)   **Means and sources of information**

Sales personnel. These are close to industry trends and the firm should arrange and collect, analyse and disseminate intelligence gathered by sales personnel.

Industry associations. Most industry sectors have a trade association which disseminates intelligence through newsletters and seminars.

Retained consultants. The firm may pay a consultant to keep a watching brief over developments in the industry sector. A consultant may be able to do this more effectively and efficiently than relying solely on the firm's own personnel.

Media cuttings. The media (newspaper, TV, radio, internet) can be regularly trawled for emerging trends. A firm may engage a specialist agency to do this.

Analysis of the firm's own data. Routine analysis of sales figures, disaggregated by product type and market segment, may give a clue about emerging trends with the industry.

(c)   **Reasons for not colluding with competitors**

(i)   The firm may face a fine from a regulatory agency if it is found to be in breach of legislation prohibiting anti-competitive behaviour.

(ii)   An investigation may itself waste valuable management time, so it is advisable to avoid suspicion of collusion.

(iii)   Collusion with other companies implies restricting some aspect of a company's marketing plan. It may in the long term be more profitable for the company to pursue its marketing plan single-mindedly.

(iv)   Collusion can be unstable where one of the colluders gains a cost advantage over the others.

5.2.20 Change drivers and responses

(a)   **Meeting external challenges**

Organisations can respond to external environmental change effectively if they adopt the following principles.

(i)   Organisations should have a good system of environmental scanning so that they can pick up at an early stage environmental changes. Greater warning will allow an organisation more time to prepare its response. As an example, many organisations subscribe to press cuttings services which provide details of environmental change as they affect their sector.

(ii)   Organisations can go one step further by developing models of how change in their macro-environment impacts on their sector. For example, tour operators have developed models to predict the effects on holiday bookings of changes in the level of interest rates and consumer confidence. This allows them to adjust their capacity so that it is in line with demand.

(iii)   Organisations need internal flexibility if they are to be able to respond to external change. There are many examples of large bureaucratic organisations, such as Marks & Spencer and Sainsbury's that have been too slow to change. Examples of methods used by organisations to improve their response times include the use of outsourcing, hiring a greater proportion of staff on short-term contracts, and introducing a culture of openness to change within the organisation.

(b)   **Comparative strengths and weaknesses for change**

(i)   *A small local independent supermarket*

A small local independent supermarket is close to its customers and a strength is its ability to pick up environmental trends from its customers. This type of business is typically not very bureaucratic in its structures and processes and should have fewer internal barriers to change compared with its larger rivals.

A weakness of the small retailer is that although it may be good at spotting change, it may have only limited resources and be unable to implement many of its ideas for responding to environmental change (eg many small retailers have not been able to capitalise on the trend to online shopping for this reason). A further weakness is that the small retailer may be good at understanding the changing needs of its immediate micro-environment, but may lack the resources to engage in extensive scanning of its macro- environment.

(ii)   *A multi-national grocery retailer*

The strengths of the small retailer noted above tend to be the weaknesses of the larger multi -national retailer and vice-versa. The multi-national retailer would tend to be more distant from its customers, but is more likely to be able to afford more extensive research into its macro-environment. Many large retailers have found their internal structures and processes a barrier to rapid response to external environmental change.

5.2.21 Pressure groups and the marketer

To: Marketing Manager

From: Marketing Assistant

Report on potential impacts of pressure groups

Pesticides are an emotional issue with many individuals who readily join and identify with the aims of pressure groups that seek to minimise their use. Furthermore, many individuals are suspicious of the actions of multinational companies, so it should not be surprising that a multinational company seeking to develop large chemical plants in possibly environmentally sensitive seaport locations, could attract the attentions of pressure groups. The following lists, in order of their importance, the most likely pressure groups which may affect this company's operations.

Greenpeace: This is an international pressure group that has active branches in many of the countries where this company operates. It has campaigned on a wide range of ecological issues, and has an active campaign against the use of pesticides. It is engaged in many high-profile 'stunts' which have attracted the attention of the media. This is important, because the public, and through them, politicians, are more likely to believe statements made by a not-for-profit pressure group, rather than an apparently greedy self--seeking multinational chemical company. In the case of the dismantling of the Brent Spar oil platform, the tactics of Greenpeace won the day, even though most scientists agreed that the proposals of the Shell oil company were ecologically much more favourable. Greenpeace has the ability not only to limit our production possibilities, but it could also very seriously affect the company's image. This company has tried to promote an ecologically friendly image for itself in its advertising, but high-profile campaigns by Greenpeace could undo the efforts of our advertising campaign.

Stop XXXChemiCo campaign: This is a campaigning group specifically set up to curb the actions of our company. This is a phenomenon that has affected many large multinational companies operating in the petro-chemicals market, including Esso, Shell, and Monsanto. Similar groups have organised successful boycotts of a company's products, for example the stop Esso campaign diverted significant volumes of sales away from Esso petrol stations in favour of its competitors, as many quite ordinary consumers took note of the pressure group's claims and sympathised with its allegations of poor ecological practices by Esso. As well as organising boycotts, such company-specific pressure groups run websites, make adverse contributions to chat rooms and can launch E mail campaigns against the company. Admittedly, many company-specific pressure groups do not amount to much, but as can be seen from the stop Esso campaign, we should be very concerned about this group using any of these tactics against us and thereby causing a fall in sales in the short term, and possibly long-term harm to our company's image.

Maverick groups: These groups are very difficult to classify, and often comprise quite small numbers of individuals who have broken away from mainstream groups such as Greenpeace. They may have no patience with the more diplomatic and considered actions of the mainstream group, and may instead resort to direct action and violence against the company. Such groups may not even be specifically concerned with ecological issues, but may be campaigning more generally against the apparent evils of capitalism that this company would appear to represent. It can be very difficult to identify who makes up these groups, and even more difficult to negotiate with them. Their activities are likely to comprise guerrilla tactics, which are difficult to anticipate. Fortunately, many of our customers will sympathise with us and would not condone the activities of these breakaway groups. So although such groups may be a nuisance to us and adds to our short-term costs, they may not necessarily harm our corporate image in the long term.

Local pressure groups: In many of the locations where we operate, we face local, community-based pressure groups. These groups' concerns are primarily with local issues, such as the pollution affecting their houses, and the smells which our plans unit. These groups tend to be particularly strong in western developed countries, where they know that they can influence the planning system. Persistent local campaigns have often led to restrictions being imposed on the operation of our plans, for example restricting night-time operations, or requiring expensive modifications to our filtration equipment. Such local pressure groups are unlikely to greatly affect our long-term image, but may have significance local impacts on our operating costs.

Methods of handling relationships with these pressure groups:

The first action to take should be to try and engage in dialogue with the pressure groups that we face. This means trying to genuinely understand their concerns, and to show that we are concerned. Very often pressure groups gain support because their members are quite ignorance of what we are actually doing as a company. We should hold regular briefings with pressure groups such as Greenpeace and local community groups in order to explain what great leaps in technology we have developed and to point out some of the good points about pesticides, such as a significant reduction in toxic contents that has occurred over previous years. This approach is obviously going to be less effective when we are dealing with maverick groups who we may not even be able to identify very easily.

Secondly, we should go on the offensive in our promotional efforts. We should not let ourselves be seen as the 'bad guy 'and our advertising could emphasise many of the big contributions that we have made to society, for example eradicating pests in Third World countries which have allowed local populations to be well fed, rather than allowing the pests to eat their food first.

Thirdly, we should make conscious efforts to design our production processes and our products so that they are as ecologically sensitive as possible. Let's make sure that we give pressure groups nothing that they can legitimately complain about.

Finally, we must recognise that some maverick groups will never enter into discussion and may resort to direct action and violence. In these cases, we must install adequate security procedures to prevent an attack on our staff, our facilities and our brands.

5.2.22 College and stakeholders

(a)   Inter-relationship between a business college and its employee and customer stakeholders

Stakeholders of an organisation are individuals or other organisations that have effects in, or are affected by the organisation. There need not necessarily be any financial or contractual relationship between the two. The relationship can be two-way. The following inter-relationships occur between a college and its customer and employee stakeholders.

Customers: It can sometimes be difficult to define just who the customers of a business college are. They could include: students themselves; parents or employers who pay their fees; or government, who may have a direct interest through grants given to the college, or indirectly through its interest in developing a skilled workforce. A college has a duty to provide an appropriate standard of education to these customer groups and to do so with integrity and a high standard of ethical behaviour. It should do so without unfair discrimination against disadvantaged groups. Customer groups have a responsibility to the college to take their share of their responsibility for learning and paying their fees.

Employees: The most important resource of most colleges is their employees, so their availability and continuing contribution to the college can be crucial. As an employer, the college has a duty to pay employees' salaries and to comply with all relevant health and safety legislation. Beyond this, employees as stakeholders will be concerned that the college promotes good employment practices, for example with respect to training and development and fair procedures for promoting or laying off staff. The employer will expect employees to act in good faith for the benefit of the college.

(b) **Internal sources of information about customer and employee stakeholder groups**

A Management Information System should record the following:

Customer:
   Student demographic details.

   Detail of courses previously completed.

   Geodemographic details based on residence.

   How the student learned about their course.

   Details of fee paying organisation (eg size of organisations, location, industry sector).

Employees:
   Demographic details, including information to monitor discrimination based on gender, race and disability.

-   Skills level at time of starting employment.

-   Subsequent training and development.

In addition, management may learn more internally about both stakeholder groups through a process of 'Management by Walking About', and by organising small focus groups of current students and employees.

(c) **Sources of external information on potential customers**

(1) Commercial list broker, eg Christian Brann.

  Value to the College: Database list brokers offer files of customers who conform to specific criteria, eg age, location and educational achievement. Lists may be easily obtained, for a fee. However, they may not be sufficiently well developed to incorporate information on individuals' educational aspirations.

(2) Directories of local businesses, eg Chamber of Trade Directories.

  Value to the College: Trade directories will indicate organisations within different trade sectors within the local area. The college could target organisations in high growth sectors, or sectors with historically high training requirements. This is a relatively cheap source of information.

(3) Students attending local schools.

  Value to the College: It is relatively easy to acquire a mailing list of students attending local schools, who may historically show a high tendency to subsequently enrol at the college. Students undertaking specified courses of study could be singled out. Although the Data Protection Act limits the ability of schools to pass on students' details, this is generally a very cost effective method of gaining access to a significant target market.

5.2.23 Economic policies

(a) **These are some key points for continuous and sustainable economic growth on which governments should focus.**

- The government should maintain a stable level of prices by removing inflationary forces from the economy. This will help create stability and reduce uncertainty.

- To help towards this, government should carefully control its level of borrowing. Growth that is brought about solely by government spending is not generally sustainable.

- Underlying productivity is crucial to long-term growth and government fiscal policy should reward innovation. Deregulation is also likely to lead to productivity improvements.

- Through its interest rate policy and foreign currency dealings, the government should seek to maintain a steady rate of exchange for the currency. This will help importers and exporters in planning for their businesses.

(b) **Factors preventing continuous and sustainable economic growth**

- For a trading nation, a downturn in the world economy may harm plans for growth.

- Rigidities in the domestic economy (eg restrictive trades union practices) may prevent the improvements in productivity which underlie growth.

- Currency speculators can cause short-term diversions from the government's aim of pursuing a stable exchange rate.

- Politicians may bow to public pressure to increase public spending, thereby increasing inflationary pressure within the economy.

(c) **Implications of negative economic growth**

- Jewellery is a luxury, and the company would expect its sales to go down as a result of negative economic growth.

- The company may have invested in the expectation of economic growth leading to increased sales. The company's marketing objectives may not now be achieved.

- Negative economic growth may lead to a period of price deflation, which may include falling prices for jewellery, with greater price competition.

- The company might seek a niche market unaffected by the recession and might look towards international markets, eg through Internet trading.

5.2.24 Political environment

(a) **The political environment**

This term refers in its broadest sense to the activities of politicians and the actions they implement through their officers. The political environment can be seen at a number of levels – local, national and supra-national.

At a national level, governments are responsible for passing legislation which impacts on business activities. Politicians are also instrumental in influencing the economic environment of a country.

At a supra-national level, the activities of the European Union are increasingly having an impact on UK marketers.

(b) **Five key impacts of a government on the economy**

(i) Government is responsible for fiscal policy, which determines the amount of taxation taken from companies and households.

(ii) Through legislation (eg on minimum wages), governments can affect the costs of business organisations and hence their international competitiveness.

(iii) Government influences exchange rates and hence influences and balance of payments.

(iv) Governments influence interest rates and hence the cost of firms' borrowing.

(v) Through its competition policy, a government can affect the structure and competitiveness of an economy.

(c) **Marketing implications of strong and weak governments**

Strong and stable government

This political environment gives business what it needs most – some degree of certainty about the future. If it can be sure that there will be no sudden change in government policy, a firm would be more willing to invest in productive capacity which will yield long-term benefits.

A strong and stable government is more likely to be associated with openness and transparency, with less resort to bribery and corruption. Against this, a very strong and self-minded government may be difficult for the marketer to lobby when seeking change in government policy.

Weak and divided government

This type of government is likely to change its policies opportunistically at short notice. This makes marketing planning by firms very difficult to achieve.

A divided government may give no clear signals about how the economy will be handled, making market forecasting very difficult.

Confidence in a weak government by overseas investors may lead to a fall in the value of the country's currency, making life difficult for the marketer of imported goods.

A weak and divided government may be more open to lobbying by business interests.

5.2.25 Technological environment

The following recent technological developments are discussed in the context of a manufacturer of mid-range furniture, which it sells through intermediaries, and also directly to the public.

Teleconferencing

The traditional conference implies a number of people coming together to confer – to exchange ideas, to develop strategies and action plans. Inevitably, this may mean a lot of disruption to the individuals concerned, in terms of the time that it takes to travel to a meeting point that is acceptable to all participants. If the people who need to confer come from around the world, the travel costs (air fares, accommodation, and the cost of employees' time) may be considerable. Teleconferencing overcomes many of these costs as instead of conferring face-to-face, individuals do so through the medium of the telephone, and/or computer. Basic systems only allow dialogue, but more sophisticated systems allow participants to see the facial expressions and body language of their colleagues. Reasonably sophisticated teleconferencing systems allow individuals to present slides and charts to their colleagues, as if they were in a face-to-face conference.

For a manufacturer of furniture, teleconferencing may be useful for bringing together regional sales staff on a regular basis to discuss strategy and tactics. Instead of having their monthly meeting at the central location, a couple of hours could be set aside each month when everybody would be near to teleconferencing facilities. Teleconferencing could also be used with suppliers, designers and intermediaries to improve the supply chain by bringing together chain partners in a simultaneous discussion of supply-chain issues.

Teleconferencing may significantly reduce costs for the furniture manufacturer, and may allow greater flexibility in organising conferences at short notice. However, even the best teleconferencing facilities cannot allow for the development of social networks between the disciplines, in a way that is relatively easy with face-to-face conferences.

E-commerce

There are many definitions of e-commerce; the one which will be used here is by Chaffey who defines e-commerce as '...... *transactions of goods or services for which payment occurs over the Internet or other wide area networks'.*

E-commerce is essentially about transferring the supply chain functions that were previously conducted through the medium of face-to-face contact, telephone and mail, to computer-based media. For a furniture manufacturer, e-commerce can be used in sourcing suppliers of raw materials and components. This can take a number of forms, for example the manufacturer may use the Internet to set up supply auctions for its materials. Alternatively, it may source materials on other companies' websites. Most likely, it would have developed close working relationships with its suppliers, so that's it can rapidly re-order raw materials and components when it needs them. In a well-developed e-commerce system, it will also be able to pay its suppliers when payments become due.

As well as dealing with its suppliers, the furniture manufacturer is likely to use e-commerce in its dealings with intermediaries and final consumers. Just as the manufacturer may order raw materials from its suppliers, the company's intermediaries may order replacement stock from the company using Internet-based ordering systems. Sometimes, the intermediary's systems may be directly linked to the manufacturer's, so that when one item of furniture is sold by the intermediary, an order is automatically placed with the manufacturer for a stock replacement.

The manufacturer may also use its e-commerce system to promote its furniture to the final consumer, take orders, and payments, and then handle delivery advice and after-sales service.

E-commerce systems can result in significant gains in efficiency for the furniture manufacturer, and the speed of the system can make it much more effective at fulfilling orders. However, if the manufacturer produces a large number of bespoke items, a basic e-commerce systems may not be very good at handling such diversity.

Teleworking

This is again a term which has been interpreted slightly differently by different people. The essential feature of teleworking is employees working relatively independently through the medium of the telephone. They may be geographically remote from their employer, but receive instructions, and produce their work through the medium of the telephone.

Teleworking is particularly relevant to information intensive businesses, such as telephone directory enquiries. For a furniture manufacturer, its role may be slightly less, but it may nevertheless be important for some sales functions. For its sales to final consumers, a furniture manufacturer may maintain one central telephone number for sales enquiries. Instead of maintaining the central call centre at its head office, it may choose to route these calls to individuals whom may be quite distant from the company's operations. Teleworking may take place in individuals' own homes, which may suit people who need to be close to home. Mothers with young children may choose to work around the needs of their children and could avoid the need to travel each day to a central office. The company may also reduce the overhead costs of having to maintain the central call centre.

For the furniture manufacturer, teleworking allows for flexible management, by allowing it to bring in part-time teleworkers at times when it expects peak demand (for example, following a television advertisement for the company's products). The company may also be able to reduce its overhead costs by using teleworkers. However, control may be more difficult, and the individuals concerned may not feel part of the manufacturer's team, if they work independently at home. To counter this, many companies using large numbers of teleworkers arrange for frequent face-to-face meetings of their teleworkers.

E business-to-business

This is an aspect of e-commerce which focuses on transactions between companies in a supply chain, and can be seen as a more focused and specialised aspect of e-commerce which was discussed earlier. Business-to-business is essentially about the dealings the company has with its suppliers, and with the intermediaries who handle its products. Together, these make-up a supply chain. It is important for a furniture manufacturer that its supply-chain works as efficiently and effectively as possible. Furniture tends to be very cyclical in terms of consumers' preferences for styles and fashions. It is important that when a new fashion trend emerges, the furniture manufacturer is able to source component materials as quickly as possible in order that it can manufacture the right items of furniture, and get them into the right places in plenty of time before the fashion changes. If the supply chain is too slow, it may end up with completed items of furniture having to be sold at discount prices because they are no longer considered by buyers to be fashionable.

Business-to-business e-commerce systems imply shared procedures between all members of the supply chain for speeding up the process of order, delivery, and payment. Some older systems used proprietary EDI systems (electronic data interchange). However, newer business-to-business e-commerce use open platform Internet based systems. This has an advantage in allowing large numbers of suppliers and intermediaries to share a common technology base, unlike some EDI systems which required specialised hardware to be purchased and installed by each member of the supply chain.

Electronic business-to-business systems have managed to reduce costs and improve efficiency for many supply chains. However, there are many cases where programming faults have caused serious problems for members of the chain. In these circumstances, the company may have to rely on back-up systems based upon traditional telephone and mail communication.

Navigational and communication aids

A wide range of navigational and communication aids are becoming available to companies. These are particularly important for transport and distribution functions, and allow orders to be efficiently routed, and to be tracked and traced while they are moving between different points in a supply chain.

For a furniture manufacturer, the use of navigational and communication aids can be used to schedule delivery vehicles more efficiently. Many companies have been using vehicle scheduling programmes for some time. More modern systems using global positioning systems allow these to become more interactive, for example by taking account of current roadworks or blockages in the road network.

An important benefits of modern GPS systems is the ability to track consignments, whether these are moving from suppliers to the furniture manufacturer, or from the manufacturer to intermediaries and customers. This is particularly important when the company uses just-in-time production methods, and it needs accurate estimates of when a consignment will arrive at its factory. Similarly, many customers may urgently require delivery of the company's products, and a GPS system will allow them to judge when their consignments are likely to arrive.

At a much more local level, navigational aids are increasingly allowing materials to move around factories automatically. Components can be programmed to arrive at an assembly area without human intervention, thereby improving cost-efficiency, and reliability in production.

5.2.26 Environmental sensitivity

(a)   Stakeholders' concerns about the natural environment

This answer will consider the likely concerns for the natural – or ecological - environment of the following three stakeholder groups: local resident groups; government agencies; and customers.

Local resident groups are likely to have an immediate concern with discharges from the vehicle manufacturers' plant into their local natural environment. There may be concerns about atmospheric pollution, leading to illnesses such as asthma. Local residents' groups may also be concerned about damage caused by air pollution to buildings and property. Discharges to watercourses may be a major concern, especially if local drinking water is drawn from watercourses into which the manufacturing plant discharges.

Local regulatory agencies ostensibly look after the interests of local groups, as well as the broader national interest. Local environmental health officers will seek to apply national and European-wide directives concerning the emission of pollution to the natural environment.

Customers may not be immediately concerned by harmful emissions to the natural environment, or use of scarce resources, so long as their car performs well and can be bought at a low price. However, car manufacturers are increasingly concerned with their image, and many customers may be put off a car brand if it has come to be associated with ecologically damaging practices. With little difference between many popular family cars, a company's record on preserving the natural environment may be a deciding factor when a customer comes to choose between one brand of car and another.

(b)   Ways in which the organisation might positively respond to concerns about the natural environment

The first way in which a vehicle manufacturer could respond to concerns is by removing the cause of stakeholders concerns. So, the company could examine all of its discharges and examine whether there is a better way of handling its waste materials. If it is depleting natural resources, it should look into alternative materials which are not as damaging to the natural ecology. Very often, ecologically sound solutions may not cost the company any more money. Many companies have found that using recycled materials is just as cost-effective as using new resources.

Very often, stakeholder groups are ignorance about the true extent of damage to the natural environment. They may not be aware of the vehicle manufacturer's efforts at, for example, using recycled materials or cutting emissions from its factories. The company should engage with its stakeholder groups to explain fully the steps that it has taken to protect the natural environment

Sometimes, it is just not cost-effective for a vehicle manufacturer to be proactive in developing production techniques that are our less harmful to the natural environment. This is particularly true for high-volume, low-value cars that compete on the basis of low price. If another company chose to use more harmful production methods, it may nevertheless gain market share among customers who are more concerned with low-price rather than ecological friendliness. The company may nevertheless support moves to change legislation that will put all of its competitors on a level playing field by requiring them all to act in an ecologically sensitive manner.

(c)   How the marketing department of a vehicle manufacturer could respond to these concerns

The marketing department could respond positively in any of the following ways:

(1)   The company is probably doing many good things that are ecologically sound. It may have innovated in many apparently boring production methods, and a task for the marketing department is to present these to the media as exciting new developments.

(2)   If the company is to present itself as an ecologically friendly manufacturer, it must ensure that its actions back up the claims which it makes in its promotional material. It could do more harm than good for the company if its ecological claims were subsequently found to be false. Many customers may no longer trust the brand. The marketing department must not promise what operations people cannot deliver.

(3)   The marketing department could initiate new product development that capitalises on many customers' concerns for the natural environment. It could highlight ecological sensitivity as a key selling point, possibly replacing safety and performance, which have become accepted as standard between competing cars, and therefore no longer an important differentiator.

(4)   In developing new ecologically friendly vehicles, the marketing department should identify the key market segments that will be attracted by such a positioning. It should seek to fully understand these groups' motivations and develop new variants of its cars in order to address the needs of these groups.

5.2.27 Social and cultural environment

Social and cultural environment

The concepts of the social environment and the cultural environment are closely related, but can be distinguished from each other. The Social Environment comprises the people and institutions that surround an individual and have an influence on their behaviour and attitudes. For any particular individual, their social environment is likely to include friends, family, work colleagues and members of social organisations to which they belong. Through the social environment, an individual acquires identity and learns about acceptable forms of behaviour.

The cultural environment comprises more embedded element within a society. Culture comprises the set of learnt beliefs, attitudes and behaviours that are passed on from one generation to another. The cultural environment tends to be more enduring than the social environment, so it is possible to distinguish, for example, a Western culture based upon progress and material values with a culture dominant in many less developed countries which emphasises family values and religious sacrifices.

It is difficult to generalise about culture, as many countries show evidence of distinct sub-cultures who develop their own social environment.

Social and cultural influences on the marketing of jewellery to the 35-50 age group.

Throughout the ages, jewellery has represented a cultural and social statement by individuals. Ancient tribes have worn hand-carved items of jewellery, which although it may look quite different from modern Western jewellery, satisfied many similar social and cultural needs.

The first important task in marketing jewellery is to understand the set of cultural and social values held by buyers of jewellery in a particular market at a particular time. This answer will consider how analysis of the social environment can improve the marketing of jewellery in the United Kingdom.

Jewellery makes a statement about an individual, in much the same way as an individual's choice of clothing. An individual may wish to be seen as a trend-setting, conservative, chic, etc. This need may derive from an individual's personality make-up, but is reinforced by social pressures on the individual. An individual may wish to be accepted by a group and to identify with them. Jewellery is one means by which this can be achieved , for example by wearing a type of jewellery that is currently fashionable with the group that the individual seeks to identify with.

Sources of identity may derive from the people that an individual works with, their family, friends and other acquaintances. Further reinforcement may come from the portrayal of individuals on the media. Many young people have been known to identify with particular pop stars, and have copied the jewellery worn by the pop stars as a means of trying to identify with them.

For a company marketing jewellery, it is important to understand the social role models that individuals seek to emulate. Qualitative focus group research may seek to understand what designs of jewellery are currently considered fashionable by target groups. By understanding at an early stage what is becoming fashionable, the jewellery buyer can source products so that they are available in the shops when the effects of social pressure have worked through.

Promotion of jewellery has often stressed the social acceptability of wearing good-quality, and fashionable jewellery. The advertising slogan 'Diamonds are a girl's best friend', is a simple one, but stresses the social impact of jewellery. Many adverts for jewellery show the wearer in favourable social situations, where admiration of the jewellery is transferred to admiration for the individual.

5.2.28 PEST impacts

MEMORANDUM

From: Marketing Assistant

To: Marketing Manager, Post Office Counters Ltd

Date: 7th December, 200X

Subject: Impacts of external events on the marketing activities of Post Office Counters Ltd

(a)   A newly elected government

As a state owned organisation, Post Office Counters Ltd is subject to the changing attitudes of the politicians, the ultimate masters. The mail delivery business has been subject to political debate in the UK and Europe in recent years, with many advocating greater liberalisation of the market. The EU has passed Directives which require some opening up of the market to greater competition, although there is discretion for member state governments to specify the speed at which their markets are opened up. Greater competition will change the way our business is run; in pricing services should we offer bigger discounts for our business customers, and charge higher prices for our personal customers?

We currently have a Government that is nominally socialist in nature, and who we would therefore expect intervention by government, to limit deregulation However, the current Government has already made moves to implement EU deregulation policy, especially in the case of high-value mail, and bulk business mail.

An incoming Conservative government would be expected to speed up the process of deregulation; because of a much stronger ideological belief in the power of markets to improve benefits to consumers. However, during the previous period of Conservative government, little effort was made to deregulate or privatise the Post Office, possibly the task was considered too large-scale, and there were more pressing areas of the economy for deregulation.

Another possibility is that an incoming government could be a coalition government of Labour, Conservative and Liberal parties. In this situation, it is likely coalition members would fail to agree on a new policy, so our business may be able to carry on in its existing form. We would however, need to become more market-orientated in order to meet the challenges raised by deregulation already enforced. However, in this scenario, there would be less pressure to become more competitive in pricing and developing new products and services, especially in the low-volume, personal sector.

(b)   The upturn point of the business/trade cycle

Volumes of mail handled by the Post Office tend be cyclical and related to the current point in the business cycle. During periods of economic prosperity, households make more purchases. Some of these will inevitably involve mail order, and the Post Office will pick up a share of this higher volume of business. As an example, consumers may purchase more music CDs and home electrical items through Internet based suppliers. During a period of recession, consumers typically cut back their expenditure, so the number of items requiring delivery could be expected to fall. This will affect our level of activity, and our level of profits.

A prosperous economy is also likely to involve businesses sending more direct marketing flyers through the mail. Even though the goods may be purchased and collected from a high-street store, the promotional material will add to our volume of business.

It is always difficult to tell the turning point in the business cycle at the time when it is actually happens. An upturn may be just a temporary blip, or it could be the start of a much more long-term improvement in business conditions. Nevertheless, we need to closely monitor trends, and we need to be ready to act when we see signs of an imminent sustained increase in the level of activity in the economy. At this point, we should begin to increase our capacity (for example, recruiting more staff, enlarging our depots and leasing extra delivery vehicles). This way, we will be able to capitalise on any increase in business, without having to turn it away to a competitors because we do not have the capacity to handle it. Of course, if we get our forecasts wrong, we would have invested in additional capacity which will be under-utilised.

(c) A new Internet bank enters the market

The Post Office is affected by the activities of banks in a number of ways.

Firstly, the Post Office carries a lot of mail for established 'high street' banks. This include statements of account, new cheque books, and routine correspondence and promotional items from the bank. The further development of Internet banking is likely to reduce the volume of printed material that banks need to distribute through the Post Office, or one of our competitors. Each time a bank uses e-mail rather than printed material to promote its services, the level of business from the banking sector to the postal delivery sector reduces.

Secondly, Post Office Counters Ltd offers a banking service at some of its branches and will doubtlessly lose customers to the Internet sector. Worse still, these customers may no longer come through our doors, so our opportunities for selling them other services such as insurance may be reduced.

Thirdly, many Post Offices now include a cash machine withdrawal facility for anybody who has a bank ATM card. Internet banking will never provide users with cash that they can withdraw directly from their computers. A visit to a bank or a cash machine is necessary in order to obtain cash. Cash is, for the foreseeable future, likely to remain popular for many low-value transactions. We should expect to gain some business from the new Internet bank in the form of its customers who use our cash machines, for which we collect a fee.

(d) Digital broadband television sales rise rapidly in the household sector

Digital broadband televisions offer users a range of features for reviewing and buying goods and services. This poses a number of challenges and opportunities for us.

(i) We can offer services to our customers through this new interactive media, for example a parcel tracking service could be offered.

(ii) Digital broadband represents a new promotional medium for us, but we will need to assess its cost effectiveness, and address the challenge of how to get customers to see our messages.

(iii) As sales of the hardware increase, we could capitalise on the delivery opportunities that this presents us with.

(iv) We are a trusted brand with outlets on most high streets. We might consider offering support services for consumers who have bought digital televisions, for example breakdown insurance, and finance facilities to facilitate purchase of higher specification models.

(v) The greatest challenge is to avoid our current customers buying related services entirely online and not coming through our front door, where we might have opportunities for selling other services. However, if our current customers migrate to broadband services, we might be able to reduce the costs of operating our branch network by selectively closing branches.

5.2.29 Environmental information systems

(a) Implications of a sensing system

In the context of an environmental information system, a sensing system allows a company to pick up trends before they become major issues. The element of the environment which is being sensed could range from ecological issues (for example, the level of pollution being emitted by a company's factory) through to social issues (for example, attitudes towards global capitalism and the symbolic meaning attached to the company's brand). An effective sensing system must use as many senses as possible if it is to be effective. This can include reading through a wide range of publications, listening to customers, and trying to decode the subtext of what they are saying.

(b) Market research

Market research is generally understood to be a structured and formalised process of collecting characteristics about a market, for example in terms of buyers' preferences and willingness to pay for actual or hypothesised products. Good market research can be crucial to the success of a product. However, it can be quite difficult to interpret what customers say in response to structured questions. There have been many high-profile failures of new products where consumers have said one thing and their subsequent behaviour has been quite different. The failure of 'new' Coca-Cola is a good example. Market research, as an element of an environmental information system, needs to be linked to other forms of market sensing and environmental scanning.

(c) Online information from real time systems

A real-time online system implies that it is continually updated, in contrast to many web pages which are updated only periodically. A good example of online real-time systems is provided by airlines that use such systems to collect trends on bookings for particular flights, and adjust the prices of each flight to reflect the current strength of demand. This is a good example of a situation where customer feedback is directly built into the company's marketing – the more people who book a flight, or enquire about it, the higher the price. This is carried out in real time, so that as specified sales targets on each flight are met, the price rises to the next band. The company gains greater revenue than if it had relied on charging an average price for all of its seats. In doing so, the company will gain maximum revenue when demand is strongest, and can afford to offer very low prices at quiet times, on the basis that some revenue is good, as long as it is greater than the company's fixed costs.

(d) Environmental audits

Audits independently monitor the integrity of a company's systems. The most well established audits relate to the finances of a company, and involve examining the extent to which the company's finances have been prudently and honestly managed. The same principles apply to an environmental audit. Ideally, this should be undertaken by an independent body. It would ask basic questions about the company's policies with regard to the environment, and the extent to which it meets its objectives. Like a financial audit, there can be disagreements on what constitutes good practice, so there may be discussion about whether a company's policy towards conservation of natural resources, is a good one or not. If it is shown during an environmental audit that a company is recycling a lot of its waste paper, is this necessarily a good thing, bearing in mind that there is currently the surplus of recycled paper, which has been expensively gathered and reprocessed? Would it be better to burn the paper to create electricity?

(e) Trade sources

In many business sectors, this is the most important source of information about new developments in the marketplace. Trade sources include customers, suppliers, and intermediaries. An intermediary, for example, may have been approached by a new entrant to the market which is planning to launch a competitive product. If the company's sales personnel have a good relationship with its intermediaries, they may be able to get news of the potential market entrants from them. They may also be kept informed of further developments in the competitor's market entry strategy. To be effective, the company needs a strategy for capturing this information, so that little bits of information can become corporate knowledge. This can be achieved through structured reporting systems, or informally through meetings of sales personnel and key decision makers within the organisation.

5.2.30 Public sector marketer

Relevance to the public sector marketer

(a) (i) Marketing research

Public sector organisations are increasingly facing marketing-mediated, rather than planned environments. This means that a wide range of research techniques for learning about their marketing environment are becoming increasingly relevant. Typical applications include:

- User satisfaction surveys.
- Studies to identify the most convenient location for new facilities (eg new branch libraries).
- Ad hoc studies to assess users' reactions to new service formats.

(ii) Marketing Information System

As public sector organisations become more market oriented, they require ever increasing amounts of information in order to keep in touch with their marketing environment. A Marketing Information System (MIS) integrates multiple sources of data. For a public sector organisation, this might typically include:

- Information on current and previous users of a service.
- A demographic database, probably linked to census data.
- A database of companies operating in the area covered by the organisation.

As with Marketing Information Systems in the private sector, these need to be linked to other databases, within the public sector organisation, especially financial, operational and personal databases.

(iii)   Delphi technique

This is a process of gaining consensus among a group of experts during a series of interactions of a discussion topic. The technique has reference to public sector organisations through the following applications:

- Meetings of stakeholders in a new recreational facility to gain an understanding of the best use that can be made of the proposed new facility.

- Discussion of the effects of changing attitudes to healthy eating, with a view to developing a promotion campaign.

- Meetings of stakeholders in a public library to develop a policy with regard to future IT provision, when future developments in IT are uncertain.

(b)   Public sector marketing objection

Difference with private sector: Private sector organisations usually work toward a profit objective. However, public sector organisations do not generally have shareholders and therefore profit objectives are not directly relevant. Public sector organisations are more likely to base their objectives on financial contribution to the organisation, or wider public interest objectives (eg to increase health awareness levels).

Similarly with private sector: Many quality of service objectives are similar between sectors, for example both may set an objective for 90% of users/customers of their service to be 'happy' or 'very happy'.

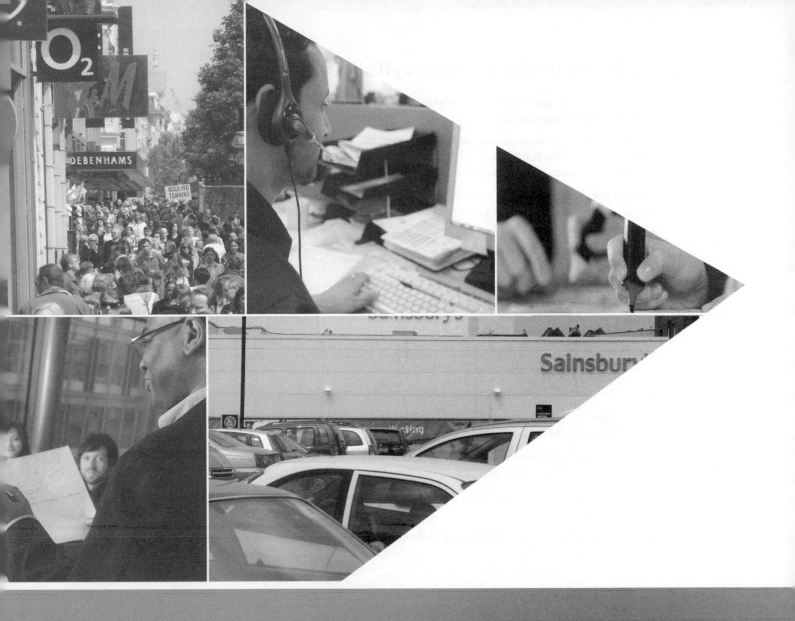

Section 4

Marketing information and research

Topic list

1   Unit overview and syllabus
2   The assignment brief
3   How to prepare for your assignment
4   Tackling the assignment

1 Unit overview and syllabus

This unit focuses on the importance of marketing information in gaining a more in-depth understanding of both the market in which the organisation operates and the customers it seeks to serve.

It aims to provide an understanding of how marketing information supports marketing decisions within the organisation and how information contributes to the overall marketing process. The unit explores different research methodologies and encourages consideration of complementary approaches to collecting a range of market and customer information.

The unit also considers the role of databases in information management, the nature and scope of the research industry, and of various research methodologies linked to the collection of primary and secondary data.

By the end of the unit, students should be able to demonstrate a thorough knowledge and understanding in the ways of collecting and manipulating information to support and justify key marketing decisions.

1.1 Overarching learning outcomes

By the end of this unit, students should be able to:

- Identify appropriate information and marketing research requirements for marketing decision making

- Evaluate the importance of customer databases and their contribution to providing detailed market information to support marketing decisions

- Review the processes involved in establishing an effective database

- Explain the nature and scope of the research industry and discuss the importance of working in line with the industry's code of conduct

- Explain the process for selecting a marketing research supplier, in domestic and international markets, developing the criteria to support that selection

- Explain the process for collecting marketing and customer information, utilising appropriate primary and secondary sources

- Appraise the appropriateness of different qualitative and quantitative research methodologies to meet different research situations

1.2 The syllabus

The syllabus is outlined below along with details of the chapters where the individual elements are covered within our corresponding study text.

SECTION 1 – The importance of marketing information (weighting 20%)

1.1 Discuss the need for information in marketing management and its role in the overall marketing process:

- Information on customers
- Information on competitors and other organisations
- Information on the marketing environment
- Descriptive v comparative v diagnostic role of information

1.2 Evaluate the impact of information technology on the marketing function and discuss the challenges facing organisations in collecting valid, reliable and measurable information to support the decision making process:

- Growth in information sources (The Information Explosion)
- The Internet/Intranet
- Consumer generated media eg, on-line communities/blogs
- Customer databases
- Internal reporting system, scanning/inventory control etc
- Validity and reliability of different information sources

1.3 Explain the concept of a marketing decision support system and its role in supporting marketing decisions:

- Definition
- Components (data storage, reports and displays, analysis and modelling)
- Types of information held
- Manner in which it can assist decision making

1.4 Review the key elements and formats when reporting or presenting marketing information to decision makers:

- Understanding the audience/audience thinking sequence
- Physical and On-line Research Report Format
- Oral presentation format
- Using tables and graphs

SECTION 2 – The role of databases in information management (weighting 20%)

2.1 Demonstrate an understanding of the role, application and benefits of customer databases in relation to customer relationship management (CRM):

- Types of customer data (behavioural data, volunteered data, attributed data)
- Role in profiling customers
- Role in marketing intelligence testing campaigns/forecasting
- Role in determining life-time value
- Role in personalising offerings and communications
- Role in building relationships

2.2 Identify and explain the different stages in the process of setting up a database:

- The importance of evaluating software and what is needed to ensure it works properly
- Evaluating software
- Identifying needs of users of a database
- Processing data (formatting, validation, de-duplication)

2.3   Explain the principles of data warehousing, data marts and data mining:

- Understanding how databases can be used to select, explore and model large amounts of data to identify relationships and patterns of behaviour

2.4   Explain the relationship between database marketing and marketing research and explain the legal aspects of data collection and usage, including the Data Protection Legislation:

- Data protection legislation
- List brokers
- Profilers and their offerings (eg, Acorn, Mosaic etc)
- Issues involved in merging marketing research and customer database information (transparency, aggregation of data, using customer databases for marketing research purposes)

SECTION 3 – The nature of marketing research (weighting 25%)

3.1   Discuss the nature and structure of the market research industry:

- Marketing Research Departments v Marketing Research Agencies
- Types of Marketing Research Agency
- Scale of Industry
- Professional Bodies and Associations in the Marketing Research Industry

3.2   Explain the stages of the market research process:

- Identification of problems and opportunities
- Formulation of research needs/the research brief
- Selection of research provider/the proposal
- Creation of research design
- Collection of secondary data
- Collection of primary data
- Analysis of data
- Preparation and presentation of research findings and recommendations

3.3   Evaluate a range of procedures and criteria used for selecting a market research supplier in domestic and international markets:

- Short-listing criteria
- The research proposal
- Supplier assessments (Pitch)
- Selection criteria

3.4   Explain how best to liaise with the research agency on a day to day basis to leverage best levels of service, support and implementation and high quality information to support the business case development:

- Monitoring working arrangements using quality and service standards

3.5   Explain the stages involved in order to develop a full research proposal to fulfil the brief which support the information needs of different marketing projects:

- Content of proposal covering background, objectives, approach and method, reporting and presentation procedures, timing, personal CVs, related experience, contract details

3.6   Evaluate the ethical and social responsibilities inherent in the market research task:

- Need for goodwill, trust, professionalism, confidentiality

- Codes of marketing and social research practice (eg, Market Research Society code of conduct)

- Responsibilities to respondents (Use of information/protection of vulnerable groups such as children, etc)

- Responsibilities to clients (transparency, data reporting, etc)

SECTION 4 – Research methodologies (weighting 35%)

4.1   Evaluate the uses, benefits and limitations of secondary data:

- Benefits

- Limitations

- Sources of secondary data

- Internet search strategies

- Integrating secondary data with primary data

4.2   Evaluate the various procedures used for observing behaviour:

- Categories of observation (natural v contrived, visible v hidden, structured v unstructured, mechanised v human, participant v non-participant)

- Audits and scanner based research

- Television viewing measurement

- Internet monitoring

- Mystery shopping

4.3   Identify and evaluate the various techniques for collecting qualitative data:

- Types of research most suited to qualitative research

- Individual depth interviews

- Group discussions (including basic guidelines on group moderation, stimulus material and projective techniques)

- Using the Internet for qualitative research (online group discussions, chat rooms, blogs)

- Overview of approach to the analysis of qualitative research

4.4   Identify and evaluate the various techniques for collecting quantitative data:

- Face to face survey methods

- Telephone interviews

- Postal surveys

- Online surveys

- Omnibus surveys

- Forum voting (pressing voting buttons)

4.5   Identify and evaluate the various techniques for undertaking experimentation:

- Hall tests

- Placement tests

- Simulated test markets

4.6   Design a basic questionnaire and discussion guide to meet a project's research objectives:

- Discussion guide format

- The questionnaire design process

- Question and response formats
- Scaling techniques (Likert and semantic differential)
- Sequence and wording
- Design layout and appearance
- Questionnaire generating software

4.7 Explain and evaluate different **basic** sampling approaches designed to maximize the benefit of market research activities:

- The sampling process
- Difference between probability and non-probability samples
- Knowledge of convenience, judgement and quota samples
- Determining sample size
- Sampling and non-sampling error
- Panels

2 The assignment brief

You will be assessed by assignment for this unit. The nature of marketing research easily lends itself to the assignment route for assessment because it is more realistic to be able to spend time reflecting on a research proposal. Generally, in our experience students tend to struggle with the topics involved within marketing research within exams however with assignments they tend to perform better and find assignments very useful especially when they are related to their own organisations.

For your assignment you are encouraged to use your own organisation to base your answers on. Of course if you are not currently working then you can:

(a)   Find a host company who would be willing to let you use them (often charities and small local organisations are interested in any offer of free 'consultancy' work carried out as part of student projects.

(b)   Consider whether a previous company you have worked with would be suitable.

(c)   Discuss with your tutor the use of a case study company.

 EXAM TIP   concept

Remember you are being assessed on your ability to prepare a programme of research and not whether you are working for a suitable type of organisation. Often the most interesting research proposals are written for the most unusual organisations so don't feel that because you may not work for a 'cutting edge' marketing orientated company you are disadvantaged in any way.

2.1 Format of the assignment

You assignment will have three compulsory tasks.

- **Task One** - Research Proposal in response to a brief based on your choice of organisation. (**50%** of the marks).

- **Task Two** – This will change for every assessment but will examine practical aspects of the syllabus such as designing a questionnaire, fieldwork guidelines, focus group discussion guides etc (**25%** of the marks).

- **Task Three** – This task will also change to ensure good syllabus coverage. It will require you to apply knowledge of research methods and purpose etc to the context of the organisation you refer to in task one (**25%** of the marks).

2.2 The specimen assignment

Task One Research Planning for Decision Making (50% weighting)

In your role as Research Executive for a Marketing Research Agency, you have been asked to produce a research proposal for an organisation of your choice. Before developing their products or services further, the chosen organisation is keen to identify current awareness and understanding of, and attitudes towards the product or service being developed, relative to the competition in one of its key markets.

You have been asked to develop an appropriately structured research proposal that covers the following objectives:

- To examine knowledge of the chosen organisation/brand in this key market, relative to its competitors
- To explore attitudes towards the chosen organisation and its products/services, relative to its competitors
- To understand how members of this key market choose their supplier.

The research proposal must also include:

- Background information on the chosen organisation and rationale for the research
- Appropriate objectives
- Justification for the method/approach adopted.

Research Proposal maximum 12 pages

(Syllabus References 3.2, 3.3, 3.4, 4.1, 4.2, 4.3, 4.4, 4.5, 5.2)

Assessment / Marking Criteria	Marking Scheme- % Mark available
Appropriate structure	10%
Relevance of contents in each section	10%
Background on organisation and rationale for research	15%
Clarity and appropriateness of objectives:	25%
- knowledge of the organisation/brand in the key market, relative to its competitors	
- exploration of attitudes towards the organisation and the products/services, relative to its competitors	
- demonstration of understanding of how members of the key market choose their supplier	
Justification for the method/approach adopted	30%
Presentation, format and style of research proposal	10%

 EXAM TIP format

We have shown the Assessment and Marking criteria within one table so that you can see how the two are similar. In the assignment you will be given these separately so look to see where marks are awarded for each assessment criteria.

Task Two Questionnaire Design and Field Force Instructions (25% weighting)

Using the information from the research proposal in Task A, you are required to produce a questionnaire and a set of guidelines for the Marketing Research Agency's field force to administer the questionnaire.

The questionnaire should be suitable for quantitative research and should assist in satisfying some of the objectives and information targets of the proposal in Task 1.

(a)   The questionnaire must:

- Address the objectives

- Use appropriate question and response formats

- Use appropriate wording

- Include appropriate sequencing of questions

- Be presented using an appropriate approach to design and layout.

(b)   The set of field force guidelines must explain how the questionnaire should be administered in order to ensure that:

- The research is undertaken with appropriate respondents

- Response rates are maximised

- The accuracy of the collected data is maximised

- Professional codes of conduct for carrying out marketing research are adhered to.

Questionnaire maximum 8 pages

Word count for field guidelines 1,000 words, excluding relevant appendices

(Syllabus References 5.1)

Assessment / Marking Criteria	Marking Scheme- % Mark available
Questionnaire	-
Extent to which objectives are addressed	12%
Use of appropriate question and response formats	16%
Use of appropriate wording	8%
Sequence of questions	8%
Design, layout and appearance	8%
Field Force Guidelines	-
Recommendations for respondent selection	12%
Recommendations for increasing response rates	12%
Recommendations for improved accuracy	12%
Awareness of Professional Code of Conduct issues	12%

Task Three Information for Marketing Decisions (25% weighting)

Your Marketing Manager is interested in gaining a better understanding of the role, applications and benefits of customer databases in relation to customer relationship management (CRM). For your organisation, or one of your choice, produce a report for your Marketing Manager that addresses the following tasks:

- Provide a brief background to the organisation, its customer base and product/service range (if not previously described)

- Explain the meaning and nature of customer databases

- Describe the benefits of developing and maintaining customer databases, in the context of customer relationship management (CRM) and their value to the chosen organisation

- Analyse the potential limitations and weaknesses of information held in customer databases

- Outline the ethical issues that the organisation should be aware of when holding data on customers.

This task should utilise a range of perspectives and illustrate points made using the organisation selected as a basis of suitable examples.

Word count 1,500 words, excluding relevant appendices.

(Syllabus References 1.1, 2.1, 2.4)

Assessment / Marking Criteria	Marking Scheme- % Mark available
Explanation of the meaning and nature of customer databases	10%
Description of the benefits of developing and maintaining customer databases, in the context of customer relationship management (CRM) and their value to the chosen organisation	30%
Analysis of the potential limitations and weaknesses of information held in customer databases	15%
Outline of the ethical issues that the organisation should be aware of when holding data on customers	15%
Structure of argument and examples used *(marking criteria - not shown as assessment criteria)*	20%
Presentation, format and style of report *(marking criteria - not shown as assessment criteria)*	10%

Appendix

Brief background to the organisation, its customer base and product/service range if not previously described (two sides of A4 maximum, no marks allocated).

3 How to prepare for your assignment

3.1 Before you receive your assignment

There are a number of preparatory tasks that you can complete before you are given your assignment.

(i) Read the study text and complete the activities

(ii) Compile a company background (remember, this will also help you in Unit 4 Stakeholder Marketing so it is well worth spending time producing a good overview)

(iii) Think about real research projects that would be useful within your organisation

(iv) Familiarise yourself with the CIM guidelines for the unit

We will assume that you are completing your reading as you study. You can find out about writing your company background in section 1 of the workbook and also in later in this section we show an example.

 EXAM TIP   add text + icon (lc)

It is worth spending time considering whether there are areas of research that your organisation really does need. Many students in the past have benefitted by using research proposals and reports 'live' within their workplace. This also helps with the writing of the assignment because it is more real and the actual research practicalities are more closely considered.

We will now look at the key aspects of the CIM guidelines.

3.2 The CIM Guidance

The following notes pick out the key points that you **MUST** adhere to from the CIM's instruction for candidates. It also gives you tips about how to succeed by using these notes to your advantage.

3.2.1 Context

- The assignment should be **based on your own organisation** or an organisation you are familiar with. You should discuss the organisation you plan to use with your tutor.

- Write a brief **overview of the organisation** chosen, including legal classification, product or service offered, target market and structure. This should be included in the **appendix** (please see section 1 of this workbook for further information about writing your company background). No marks will be allocated to the background and it will not count against word count limits.

- Do not include **sensitive data** from the chosen organisation or create an anonymous name for the organisation so that it cannot be identified from your work.

- Each assignment must be completed **individually**, not as part of a group.

3.2.2 Working with your tutor

- You are entitled to a minimum of **15 minutes individual tutorial** time for this unit.

- You are able to discuss with your tutor your **choice of organisation and any questions** about the assignment.

- You are allowed to gain **feedback on one written assignment draft**. Do not ask your tutor to look at your improved draft because they are not permitted by the CIM to coach you or provide any more feedback.

- Your tutor will **not** be able to tell you the grade a piece of work is likely to achieve.

3.2.3 Word count

Word counts always cause students concern. At the beginning it seems like a daunting task to be able to actually write the required number of words. Amazingly, by the time you have completed your first draft the problem is very likely to have transformed into a major word reduction exercise. Writing succinctly and clearly is far more difficult to achieve than endless pages of 'waffle'.

- You must remain within **+10%** of the specified word count. This means that if you have a word count of 1000 words you must not write more than 1100 words. In this unit you may be given a **page limit**, in which case you should stick to the number of pages requested.

- You must **state** the number of words on the **front page** of your assignment.

- Headings, index, references, bibliographies, appendices and tables **do not count towards** your word limit.

- **Diagrams and tables** are encouraged however if **all or most** of your work is presented in this format then they **will be counted** towards your word limit.

3.2.4 Plagiarism

Copying someone else's work or quoting from another source without referencing the source will be regarded as plagiarism. To avoid being suspected of plagiarism, ensure that you Harvard reference all sources as described in section 1 of this workbook.

Candidates found guilty of plagiarism may be:

- Disqualified from CIM membership
- Refused award of the unit or qualification
- Refused the right to retake the unit.

Remember to submit electronic copies of your work in the procedure specified by your tutor so that it may be passed through anti-plagiarism software by the CIM.

3.2.5 Assessment criteria, Mark schemes and Grade Descriptors

- **Assessment criteria and marking scheme**

    The assessment criteria is useful because it outlines what the examiner is looking for when assessing you. It is linked to the marking scheme which you will also be privy to. You should pay careful attention to these because they will give you a good indication of the level of content that is required in each section of your work.

It is highly advisable to use the assessment criteria as a basis for the structure of any reports that you are asked to complete as tasks. For example with the task 3 outlined in the specimen paper, you could use the following headings within your report to ensure that the examiner can easily find where to award you marks for each part of the marking scheme.

1 Management overview
2 An overview of the meaning and nature of databases
3 Benefits of customer databases
4 Potential limitations and weaknesses of information held in customer databases
5 Ethical issues to be aware of when holding data on customers
6 Summary

The headings follow conventional report style but are also linked to the specific points requested in the assignment brief. You will not leave the examiner searching for your points when they sit with the marking scheme and need to consider where to award your marks.

- **Grade descriptors**

    Grade descriptors are also available on the CIM website. You should look through these because they outline what candidates need to demonstrate in order to achieve the various grades.

4 Tackling the assignment

4.1 Tackling the Exemplar Project

To address the specimen paper, we will provide an example company and use this to demonstrate key assignment writing tips. We do not provide a completed project because it will not add any more value to your studies. We cover task one in a little more detail than two and three because the format for task one will remain the same for each assessment round. The only aspect that will change will be the specified area for research. In the specimen assignment task one requests an attitude and awareness study, this could for example have been a customer satisfaction study or internal piece of research instead.

Your first task should be to work on your company background to include in the appendix. This will enable you to think clearly about the research that will be appropriate within the guidelines of the task one set.

4.2 Specimen organisational background (Appendix 1)

The following overview, for the purposes of demonstration the case study organisation and its situation are essentially fictional.

The Student House Company (SHC)

The Student House Company (SCH) is a UK based partnership specialising in premium property for students at leading universities.

Origins

The company began informally in 1981when twin brothers Steve and Paul Newby purchased a house to share (and rent out spare rooms) whilst at university. The house was purchased using inheritance. Following their graduation, the brothers rented the house initially friends and then later to a series of unknown student tenants. Over the next five years, ten additional houses were purchased in the surrounding area as long term investments.

In 2001 the brothers decided to change careers and enter into the property business in a more formal capacity and established a formal partnership in the name of The Student House Company. (The original houses purchase in Manchester were not integrated into SHC but continue to be owned by the brothers and managed by a renting agency on their behalf.) A report by The Joseph Rowntree Foundation (2000) identified that the expansion in the UK HE sector had not been matched by increases in university provided accommodation leading to a 60% increase in the need for private housing In the sector. In order to differentiate their offering from existing private landlord, SHC identified a need for premium housing. A former 30 bedroom hotel in Bloomsbury, Central London was purchased and converted it into luxury student accommodation.

Corporate aim and customer proposition

The company aim from 2000 remains as:

"*To provide luxurious accommodation for the discerning student who is willing to pay a premium to maintain a comfortable lifestyle whilst at university*"

The product proposition for SHC is:

- High quality standard of rooms all with en suite and internet facilities
- Modern communal lounges and quiet study areas
- Fully serviced daily cleaning service and live in property manager

Rent paid by students at SHC is typically 50% higher than the average rent for student properties within the area.

Property portfolio

By 2005 SCH had rapidly expanded with a portfolio including similar properties in other major university towns. Locations were selected according to the following criteria:

- Size of student population with high socio-economic demographics
- Number of colleges/universities in close proximity to the property

The current portfolio of properties is shown in the following table:

Location	Properties
London	Property 1 – 30 rooms
	Property 2 – 40 rooms
	Property 3 – 45 rooms
Bath	Property 1 – 20 rooms
	Property 2 – 35 rooms
Manchester	Property 1 – 30 rooms
	Property 2 – 20 rooms
Cambridge	Property 1 – 20 rooms
	Property 2 – 30 rooms
Oxford	Property 1 – 35 rooms
	Property 2 – 35 rooms

Target market

Target consumers are students from affluent backgrounds with the desire for and propensity to live in premium accommodation. Parents are an important stakeholder group because they are central to the decision making process when students select their accommodation. In many instances parents pay rent directly on behalf of SHC's resident students.

Over 80% of tenants come from a privately educated background (60% of those boarded at boarding school). There is also a high proportion of overseas student tenants especially within the London, Oxford and Cambridge properties where on average 70% of students are foreign to the UK. Students from the US and China are key overseas markets for SHC.

The competitive market

The market has become increasingly competitive with large property developers entering the student accommodation market. Although individual private landlords (40%) and university halls of residents (25%) still possess the largest market shares, larger commercially branded properties account for 15% of student housing with the remainder living at home with parents or owning their own properties.

Key competitors are large property developers who have built large (average 100 rooms) halls of residence style accommodation. These properties have rooms which are functional in nature and are considered to be 'mid range' appealing to the mainstream student market.

- **Student Home** owns eight large properties in university towns including all SHC locations. The rent charged by Student Home is typically 40% less than SHC but this reflects the functional style of accommodation provided and shared bathrooms. It is 10% more expensive than the average rent.

- **Study House** own similar properties in five university towns (again all in SHC locations). Rent charged is 20% less than SHC because of their provision of en suite bathrooms within individual rooms.

The market is becoming increasingly competitive with new market entrants anticipated in the next two years.

4.3 Tackling Task One

The task requires that you adopt the role of Research Executive for a Marketing Research Agency, you have been asked to produce a research proposal for an organisation of your choice.

 EXAM TIP format

In our case the client will be SHC.

The next element of the task outlines the scenario which is

"*Before developing their products or services further, the chosen organisation is keen to identify current awareness and understanding of, and attitudes towards the product or service being developed, relative to the competition in one of its key markets.*"

 EXAM TIP concept

For SHC this will involve identifying awareness, understanding and attitudes towards their student housing compared to the competitors which will include individual private tenants, commercial tenants, university accommodation and family accommodation.

In the next part of the task outline you have been asked to develop an appropriately structured research proposal that covers the following objectives:

- To examine knowledge of the chosen organisation/brand in this key market, relative to its competitors
- To explore attitudes towards the chosen organisation and its products/services, relative to its competitors
- To understand how members of this key market choose their supplier.

Hints are given about the structure of the proposal as the task outlines that your work must also include:

- Background information on the chosen organisation and rationale for the research
- Appropriate objectives
- Justification for the method/approach adopted.

 EXAM TIP concept

To attempt this question, your starting place will be the structure of a research proposal. Go to chapter five of the study text to remind yourself about the detail of the research proposal which should contain the following sections:

(a) **Background** and **rationale**. This sets out your understanding of the 'client' company, its products and services and its market place, an understanding of why the research is required and what decisions need to be made. In the case of SHC we can add some of the details from the company background and also need to consider why they would need to conduct research. The task brief' asks for an awareness and attitude study which is required before the organisation develops it's product any further. In the case of SHC this research could assist them in deciding whether the 'premium' status of the accommodation is considered worth the additional rent within their target market. It may also assist in developing future expansion plans or improvements to properties.

(b)   **Objectives**. These should be based on the brief, although they are stated in a highly generic manner and will require clarifying for the organisation (SHC in this case). We will discuss specific objectives as related to SHC later.

(c)   **Approach and Method**. How the agency proposes to carry out the research, what methods will be used, where the sample will be taken from. This section needs the most detail. Proposals that are weak fail miserably because they lack sufficient detail in this section.

(d)   **Reports**. How the final information will be presented and whether interim reports will be made.

(e)   **Timing**: how long the research will take and how it will be broken down into separate stages if appropriate.

(f)   **Fees and expenses**: this is self-explanatory but remember you should be as realistic as possible.

(g)   **Personal CVs** of the main agency personnel who will be involved in the project.

(h)   **Relevant experience/references:** the agency will wish to assure the client that it is capable of carrying out the research, so it will include information about similar projects undertaken in the past, and possibly reference details (previous clients who are willing to testify to the competency of the agency).

(i)   **Contractual details** will set out the agency's terms of trade and clarify matters about ownership of the data collected.

You will not gain direct marks for the sections g, h and i however you could include a token reference to these because it will show that you appreciate the full purpose and requirements of a proposal and gain some marks for format and presentation. On this point you should also note that the proposal is essentially a sales document for a research agency. As such, they tend to be highly professionally presented with good quality title pages, and nice layout etc. You will benefit by making your proposal look as professional and 'real' as possible.

4.4 Common problem areas with research proposals and things to remember

With the research proposal structure in mind we will now look at areas where students tend to have problems and give you some tips to help you to avoid these issues.

4.4.1 Responding to the research brief

The task one 'brief' is the basis of your assignment. The proposal you write must address that brief. One of the things the examiners will be looking at is whether the research you set out in the proposal does actually address the requirements set out in the brief.

It may be that the brief is not as clear as you hoped. This will be because you are not given an actual real life brief in the same way that an agency is given one. You are provided with a highly generic brief which can be responded to with a client organisation of your choice in mind.

You need to show the marker that you realise this by clarifying the relevant sections. The background section of the proposal is therefore very important. Make sure that you communicate clearly what the client's 'business' problem is, what the research problem is, and how the research objectives relate to this. These three things are linked, and you need to show that you understand that. You will need to show that the research you propose will deliver the information needed to meet them research objectives and so allow the client to address the problem. A good starting point would be to write your company background (as discussed in Section 1 of this workbook and written for SHC) first so that you can use this as a basis for the organisation you are using in the role of the client within your assignment.

When you are preparing your proposal, don't forget to keep referring back to the research brief. It is very easy to forget exactly what has been requested in brief – what the research must achieve – and to go off at a tangent, perhaps even including irrelevant suggestions.

4.4.2 An integrated proposal

Remember that all aspects of the research process – from brief, research objectives, research design, sampling, data collection, analysis and final reporting – are interconnected. You cannot decide on the type of data (quantitative or qualitative) or on the method of data collection (interview or observation; face to face or online) without knowing what problem the client wants to solve, how this has been translated into research objectives and what budget and time constraints the client has set for the research work. How to justify your overall research design will be covered in a moment.

4.4.3 Objectives

The research objectives that you set out in your proposal should be similar to those contained within the brief. Do not add in research objectives that have no relevance or link to the client's problem. There may be information that you think would be nice to know but the research should focus on what the client needs to know.

  EXAM TIP

concept

Remember that research questions help to identify specific questions that will need to be answered in order to address the objective.

For SHC we may construct objectives and research questions as outlined in the following table in response to the brief.

Assignment task brief	Research proposal objective and research questions
To examine knowledge of the chosen organisation/brand in this key market, relative to its competitors	Objective 1 To examine knowledge of SHC amongst 'high net worth' students compared to alternative university accommodation options. RQ 1.1 Are high net worth students aware of SHC? RQ 1.2 Are they aware of competitors? RQ 1.3 Are high net worth students more aware than other segments of SHC?
To explore attitudes towards the chosen organisation and its products/services, relative to its competitors	Objective 2 To explore attitudes towards SHC amongst 'high net worth' students compared to key competitors and alternative accommodation options RQ 2.1 What do students think about SHC? RQ 2.2 Is the standard of accommodation seen as worthy of the premium price? RQ 2.3 What is the perception of competitors?

Assignment task brief	Research proposal objective and research questions
To understand how members of this key market choose their supplier	**Objective 3** To identify how 'high net worth' students choose their university accommodation. RQ 3.1 What features of accommodation are important? RQ 3.2 Is the property itself or other residents primary issues? RQ 3.3 Who are the key influencers when making property decisions? RQ 3.4 What do students dislike about the accommodation?

Remember that your research questions are not directly fieldwork questions but they will help you to construct your fieldwork questions.

Justifying your approach and method

You must show that you are aware of the strengths and limitations of your overall chosen research design. In other words, you must present a rationale or justification that sets out why your chosen method is suitable for your given research problem (and the research objectives that flow from it). The approach and methods section of the proposal is all important. Be clear if you are using different waves of research for example you may have identified the need to include:

- Phase 1- Secondary research
- Phase 2 – Primary research – Qualitative phase
- Phase 3 – Primary research Quantitative phase

If it is essential that you are clear about these phases and for each that you include:

- Justification about why it is relevant and will help address the research questions

- Details sample respondents used within each phase (population of interest, the sampling frame sampling method used and why it is appropriate, sample size and how the size was determined)

- The data collection methods to be employed and why they are suitable

To help you develop your overall research design, using a table like the one following will help you to be clear about how each of the methods addresses specific research objectives.

Objective	Research Question	Population of interest	Research method
Objective 1 To examine knowledge of SHC amongst target market students compared to alternative university accommodation options.	1.1 Are high net worth students aware of SHC?	Current target market students	Phase 3 Quantitative student online survey
	RQ 1.2 Are they aware of competitors?	Current target market students	Phase 3 Quantitative student online survey
	RQ 1.3 Are high net worth students more aware than other segments of SHC?	All students	Phase 3 Quantitative student online survey

Objective	Research Question	Population of interest	Research method
Objective 2 To explore attitudes towards SHC amongst 'high net worth' students compared to key competitors and alternative accommodation options	RQ 2.1 What do students think about SHC?	Current target market students	Phase 3 Quantitative student online survey
	RQ 2.2 Is the standard of accommodation seen as worthy of the premium price?	Current target market students	Phase 2 Focus group
	RQ 2.3 What is the perception of competitors?	Current target market students	Phase 2 Focus group
Objective 3 To identify how 'high net worth' students choose their university accommodation	RQ 3.1 What features of accommodation are important?	Current target market students	Phase 3Quantitative student online survey
	RQ 3.2 Who are the key influencers when making property decisions?	All high net worth students	Phase 1 Secondary research Phase 2 Focus group
	RQ 3.3 What additional aspects of accommodation do students seek that is not available from SHC?	Current target market students	Phase 2 Focus group
	RQ 3.4 What do students dislike about the accommodation?	Current target market students	Phase 2 Focus group

  EXAM TIP

format

Do not use this table within your actual proposal, it is for you to use to ensure that you are clear about your research design during your planning.

To make absolutely sure that you have justified your methods you could also for the purposed of your planning also use a table similar to the one following:

Research phase	Justification (as applied to SHC)
1 Secondary research	**Why the phase?** (eg existing information utilised on student accommodation to validate phases 2 and 3.) **What are the advantages of using this phase?** (Inexpensive and fast) **Which objectives will be addressed?** (Objective 2 and to inform other areas of research) **What data will be collected?** (Trends, news report, university statistics) **How will data be collected?** (online, purchased from information providers) **Where/who will data be collected from?** (internal and external sources) **How much data will be collected?** (limited amounts) **Any limitations anticipated with this data?** (will not cover any research objectives in their entirety)

2 Qualitative focus group	**Why the phase?** (contextual information about attitudes to accommodation as focus groups enable detailed investigations and to discover depth of attitudes)
	What are the advantages of using this phase? (ability to identify depth of attitude, relatively easy to administer with student groups)
	Which objectives will be addressed? (Part objective 2 and 3)
	What data will be collected? (discussion group topic guide based on the research questions for objectives 2 and 3)
	How will data be collected? (10 focus groups)
	Sample population? (current residents, non resident students within the target market)
	Sampling method? (current residents invited on a quota sample – with proportionate representatives from each SHC property. Non SHC residents will be selected from a student database purchased which is pre-screened to select the demographic student profile which more closely matches the target market)
	Sample size? (10 groups with 6-8 respondents per group)
	Any limitations anticipated with this data? (will not cover any research objectives in their entirety)
	Practical issues to consider? (need to offer an incentive to participants – appropriate example would be a charitable donation or meal for two. This should appeal to a large proportion of respondents and encourage their participation. Respondents will be recruited via short screening telephone interviewers).
3 Quantitative online survey	**Why the phase?** (Ability to identify awareness levels amongst large groups of students)
	What are the advantages of using this phase? (online surveys are fast and inexpensive. The large propensity for students using the internet and their familiarity with responding to research in this way)
	Which objectives will be addressed? (Part objectives 1, 2 and 3)
	What data will be collected? (online survey addressing attitude and awareness issues)
	How will data be collected? (online surey)
	Sample population? (all university students)
	Sampling frame? (purchased student database pre-screened to select the demographic student profile which more closely matches the target market)
	Sampling method? (quota sample to enable respondents in the required subgroups to be proportionately represented eg higher socio economic groups, SHC selected university towns)
	Sample size? (based on cost and time limitations- 300 students)
	Any limitations anticipated with this data? (response rates may be low as it is a self completion piece of work)
	Practical issues to consider? (respondents should be 18+ and already attending university. Incentives could be a donation to charity for every completed survey submission. Ability to use screen shots and photography online but this is more expensive)

4.4.4 Data collection methods

Secondary data

It may be useful to use secondary data, and to include a secondary research element, in the assignment • You may quote some sources of secondary data in the brief to illustrate the research problem and its context.

It is often appropriate to show that you have done some secondary research to get a better understanding of the research problem and its context. You would include the findings from this secondary research in the background section of the proposal.

  EXAM TIP concept

Secondary research may be an integral part of the overall research plan. However, remember that the main purpose of the assignment is to show your knowledge of overall research design and a range of methods. Make certain that any inclusion of secondary research supports and enhances the primary research element; it must not overshadow it.

Qualitative research

If you are including both quantitative and qualitative research within your proposal, make sure that you cover the qualitative research in as much depth as the quantitative research. In some proposals that are weak the qualitative research element appears as an 'after thought' and is given scant coverage and/or explanation.

Specifically, if you include focus groups, make sure you cover recruitment in enough detail within your proposal. You need to think carefully about who your population of interest is, how you are going to find a sample of them and exactly what combination of people you want within the groups. You need to think about whether these people will get on with each other. For example, it is no good inviting high net worth students and those struggling with debt to the same group or this could lead to an inflammatory atmosphere and the value of the research may be lost.

It is also a good idea to include a table to make it clear who the respondents are within each group and where they are to take place if they are spread geographically. For example:

Location	Group respondents
London	2 groups
	1 SHC residents
	1 mixed residents and non residents
Bath	2 groups
	1 SHC residents
	1 mixed residents and non residents
Manchester	2 groups
	1 SHC residents
	1 non residents
Cambridge	2 groups
	1 SHC residents
	1 non residents
Oxford	2 groups
	1 SHC residents
	1 mixed residents and non residents

You would need to then justify your split for the group and elaborate further within your subsection about focus groups.

Quantitative research

Quantitative research tends to be handled better by students however make sure that you are very clear about:

- The range of methods that you could select
- A good justification why you have chosen the method you have
- Extensive detail and justification related to your sampling desisions
- The practical issues related to the process of the research design.

4.4.5 Sampling

Sampling is one of the most important parts of the research process and creating and executing an appropriate sampling plan is central to the success of a research project. Make sure in preparing the proposal that you identify the links between the client's problem, the research objectives, the population of interest, the sample and the approach you are going to take to sampling. You must also explain the suitability of your sampling approach to the method of data collection you plan to use. Finally, you must point out the advantages and the limitations of your sampling plan, including the potential impact it will have on data quality (in terms of reliability and validity). It is therefore important that in planning your proposal you take time to understand the ideas behind sampling, the different sampling techniques available and their strengths and weaknesses, uses and limitations, and the procedures involved in executing a sampling plan.

Ensure that you are absolutely clear in your proposal for each phase of research:

- What is your population of interest? eg SHC residents

- Have you defined it clearly, precisely and accurately? eg. current residents living in all property locations

- What is your sampling frame eg a list of tenants

- What sampling methods you have chosen and why? eg Simple random sampling because it is easy to use with the well defined sampling frame. It also is a probability sampling method.

- What is the size of your sample and how did you decide on the size? eg 200

If your proposal features a qualitative research project, whilst statistical representativeness and random/ probability sampling are generally not applicable, you still need to consider the issue of representativeness: what is the relationship between your sample (your respondents or research participants) and the wider population of interest? Describe and explain this relationship. Set out your sampling plan. Describe the advantages and limitations of all key aspects of your plan including sampling method and sample size. Make the link between the sampling plan and the aims of the research. Make the link back to the client's problem and the research objectives and forward to the sort of analysis that you plan to do.

While it is useful to try to understand the theory and approach to working out the ideal sample size for a research project, you will not be tested on this. It is important, however, to be aware of the general principles. It is more important that in your proposal that you identify the sample size you plan to use and you explain and justify why that sample size is appropriate for the aims of the research. You need to make the link back to the client's problem and the research objectives and on to the sort of analysis that you plan to do. You also need to show that you are aware of and understand the relationship between cost and sample size.

Also, it is good practice to show in a summary table how you have organised your groups in terms of the participants and/or their location as it is easy to become confused by the number of groups and where they are to take part with whom when simply written into a paragraph. You may for example have

4.4.6 Practical aspects of your research

Think about what stimulus material you might need for your research and who should be supplying it (you or the client). Think about the implications of using stimulus material in terms of timing of the research, length of the discussion or interview, cost and so on.

Codes of conduct

When completing your assignment, it is important that you explicitly show that you are aware of the rules laid down in both the MRS *Code of Conduct* and the Data Protection Act 1998. Take care to ensure that the methods of data collection and processing you choose take into account the rights of respondents.

Costs and timings

You must include a section in your proposal on timings and costs. These can be in the form of tables or grids. Try to make both the timings and the costs as reasonable as possible based on the information you have at your disposal. They do not need to be highly accurate but you do need to show that in presenting a breakdown of them that you understand what is involved in conducting the research.

4.4.7 Appropriate appendix items for a research proposal

Typically students try to put lots of excess information into an appendix as a means to overcome the word count limit. To do this is a dangerous strategy because often key information is overlooked by the examiner and the overall flow of the proposal is jeopardised. The golden rules for appendices are:

- Number the appendix and only include things that you have/will refer to in the main report/proposal. Nobody will read an item in an appendix if you have not explicitly directed them to it.

- Essential information that you require your audience to read because it is key to the point you are trying to make should be in the main report or proposal.

- Don't use the appendix as a means to prove that you have gathered lots of information- you are expected to do this anyway. You will not gain favour with an examiner for your lack of ability to synthesise the information if you put too much into an appendix.

4.5 Tackling Task Two

Questionnaire Design and Field Force Instructions (25% weighting)

Using the information from the research proposal in Task A, you are required to produce a questionnaire and a set of guidelines for the Marketing Research Agency's field force to administer the questionnaire.

The questionnaire should be suitable for quantitative research and should assist in satisfying some of the objectives and information targets of the proposal in Task 1.

(a)   The questionnaire must:

-     Address the objectives

-     Use appropriate question and response formats

-     Use appropriate wording

-     Include appropriate sequencing of questions

-     Be presented using an appropriate approach to design and layout.

(b)   The set of field force guidelines must explain how the questionnaire should be administered in order to ensure that:

-     The research is undertaken with appropriate respondents

-     Response rates are maximised

-     The accuracy of the collected data is maximised

-     Professional codes of conduct for carrying out marketing research are adhered to.

Questionnaire maximum 8 pages

Word count for field guidelines 1,000 words, excluding relevant appendices

(Syllabus References 5.1)

Part A

To attempt this question you need to think very practically about questionnaire design and fieldwork data collection methods generally. Use the following steps to help construct your fieldwork questions:

Step 1   Clarifying what is required:

- What do the questions need to explore or measure? Put another way, what information does the research aim to gather? (Refer to your research objectives and research questions)

- What method of data collection is to be used? (eg online survey, self completion questionnaire etc)

- Who will answer the questions (that is, who is the target sample)?

Step 2   Deciding on the most suitable types of question and response format (remember to keep this varied)

Step 3   Wording the questions (remember the tips outlined in the study text and use a variety of question and response formats to provide variety and encourage a greater response)

Step 4   Writing instructions for the interviewer and/or respondent

Step 5   Putting the questions into an effective and logical order (sequence)

Step 6   Designing the layout (keep it clear, structured and use lots of space)

Step 7   Testing out a draft version (it is worth testing this on someone not familiar with your studies)

Step 8   Revising the draft and compile a final professional looking version.

Remember that the best fieldwork methods are presented very clearly and professionally. You are able to submit a paper draft of a questionnaire that has been completed using questionnaire software.

Part B

This part of the task requires you to think very practically about your research. Remember for this task who your audience is for the guidelines- fieldwork interviewers will require everything that is expected of them to be made explicitly clear. This means stating exactly where, when, how, for how long etc they will need to stand in a specified place (eg in the case of in-street interviewing).

The best approach to this task is to think 'if I were a fieldworker, would I know **exactly** what to do?'

You must also explain WHY you are writing a specific instruction and the best way to do this would be to stick to the headings provided in the task.

4.6 Tackling Task Three

Task Three Information for Marketing Decisions (25% weighting)

Your Marketing Manager is interested in gaining a better understanding of the role, applications and benefits of customer databases in relation to customer relationship management (CRM). For your organisation, or one of your choice, produce a report for your Marketing Manager that addresses the following tasks:

- Provide a brief background to the organisation, its customer base and product/service range (if not previously described)

- Explain the meaning and nature of customer databases

- Describe the benefits of developing and maintaining customer databases, in the context of customer relationship management (CRM) and their value to the chosen organisation

- Analyse the potential limitations and weaknesses of information held in customer databases

- Outline the ethical issues that the organisation should be aware of when holding data on customers.

This task should utilise a range of perspectives and illustrate points made using the organisation selected as a basis of suitable examples.

Word count 1,500 words, excluding relevant appendices.

(Syllabus References 1.1, 2.1, 2.4)

 ## EXAM TIP   format

This question requires that you stick to a report format. Again, try to use headings within the report which represent the bullet points outlined in the task brief. For example:

1   Executive summary
2   The meaning and nature of customer databases
3   Benefits of developing and maintaining customer databases
4   Databases and customer relationship management (CRM)
5   The value of CRM to SHC
6   Potential limitations and weaknesses of information held in customer databases
7   Ethical issues that SHC should be aware of when holding data on customers.
8   Summary and conclusion

Step 1   To start to address the task for you should initially define customer databases:

 ## KEY CONCEPT   concept

Customer databases can contain a wide variety of information about the customer such as **contact details**, **transaction history**, **personal details** and **preferences** and so on. Information may come from a variety of sources besides transaction processing systems, including specialist geodemographic data and lifestyle information.

Step 2   Think about the nature of databases within your own organisation. For SHC it would be likely that at the very least a database would hold information about tenants, duration of residency, university attended, possibly the courses that students are studying, home residence, and payment details and history.

Step 3   Work consistently through the sections of the report in a similar manner outlining the theory before applying it to your own organisation. For example the study text outlines the benefits of customer databases.

 ## KEY CONCEPT   concept

Databases can provide **valuable information** to marketing management.

(a)   Computer databases make it easier to collect and store more **data/information**.

(b)   Computer software allows the data to be **extracted** from the file and **processed** to provide whatever information management needs.

(c)   In some cases businesses may have access to the databases of **external organisations**. Reuters, for example, provides an on-line information system about money market interest rates and foreign exchange rates to firms involved in money market and foreign exchange dealings, and to the treasury departments of a large number of companies.

Other benefits of database systems might include:

(a) Increased **sales and/or market share** (due to enhanced lead follow-up, cross-selling, customer contact)
(b) Increased **customer retention** (through better targeting)
(c) Better use of **resources** (targeting, less duplication of information handling)

Databases enable marketing managers to improve their **decision making**

We can also consider the uses of databases for marketers which include:

- **Understanding customers** and their preferences
- Managing **customer service** (helplines, complaints)
- Understanding the **market** (new products, channels etc)
- Understanding **competitors** (market share, prices)
- Managing **sales operations**
- Managing **marketing campaigns**
- **Communicating** with customers

These tangible elements can then be applied to your organisation. Outline whether it is feasible that these benefits are possible within the organisation and if so how.

By taking this methodical approach, you will find that you are integrating knowledge and application elements of the marking scheme.

 EXAM TIP
format

Remember to keep referring to the assessment criteria and marking scheme to use this as a guide to the amount of information the examiner is looking for within each section of the report.

Section 5

Stakeholder marketing

Topic list

1 Unit overview and syllabus

The following is the complete syllabus, reproduced with the kind permission of the CIM, with our explanatory notes where relevant.

1.1 Unit characteristics

The focus of this unit is to recognise the nature and scope of an organisation's diverse range of stakeholders (of which customers are part) and their relative importance to the marketing process and the market oriented organisation.

The unit considers how to manage stakeholder relationships effectively, in terms of utilising a marketing mix that influences and satisfies stakeholder needs in line with the organisation's business and marketing objectives.

There is particular emphasis on developing approaches to communicating effectively with stakeholders based upon their relative importance and interest in the organisation, co-ordinated for maximum influence and effect.

On completion, students should be able to demonstrate a thorough understanding of the importance and status of different stakeholder groups and the priorities for managing an effective marketing and communications mix to aid relationship development.

 EXAM TIP application

Note the third paragraph, which closely reflects the examiners' objectives in setting assignments. Two key tasks in any project brief are likely to be:

- Determining the 'relative importance and interest in the organisation' of different stakeholder groups. This may take the form of a stakeholder audit, stakeholder mapping (eg using the Mendelow power/interest matrix and other variants) and/or an analysis of the power and interest of one or more stakeholder groups.

- Developing 'approaches to communicating effectively with stakeholders', which (a) reflect the priority given to different stakeholder groups and (b) are 'co-ordinated for maximum influence and effect'. This may take the form of a co-ordinated marketing and/or marketing communications plan, say, or a set of recommendations for stakeholder relationship management.

1.2 Overarching learning outcomes

By the end of this unit, students should be able to:

- Assess the relative importance of organisational stakeholders on the marketing function, and the impact they have on the organisation's marketing activities

- Explain the importance of relationship marketing in the context of the organisation's stakeholders in achieving stakeholder interest, involvement, commitment and loyalty

- Explain how the marketing mix can be effectively co-ordinated to support internal and external stakeholder relationships

- Explain how to co-ordinate the communications mix to communicate effectively with the organisation's stakeholders in line with budget and time requirements

- Evaluate key methods for measuring the success of marketing mix and communications activities

 EXAM TIP application

This set of learning outcomes gives a helpful overarching 'storyline' to the syllabus, which can be a bit fragmented in detail. It summarises the *process* of stakeholder relationship management, and any assignment is likely to reflect elements of each of its stages in some way. As you collect material in preparation for your work-based project, it would be helpful to keep coming back to some of these key elements.

- Are you prioritising the relevant stakeholder groups appropriately, according to their importance and impact?

- What opportunities are there to build relationship with relevant stakeholder groups – and with what aim or benefit in mind?

- What elements of the marketing mix (4Ps) or extended marketing mix (7Ps) can be co-ordinated to support stakeholder relationships?

- What elements of the marketing communications mix can be co-ordinated for effective stakeholder communication?

- What tools can you use to evaluate your organisation's current marketing mix and communications activities – and your own proposals?

- Have you taken both external *and* internal stakeholder groups into account? What internal stakeholder relationship marketing will be required to support external marketing efforts?

 EXAM TIP concept

Note that the entire syllabus content is covered in detail in the BPP Study Text for *Stakeholder Marketing*. This should not just be thought of as 'background reading': any or all of the theoretical concepts and models discussed may be useful (or required) to support your points or justify your proposals in an assignment.

Our Study Text coverage also clears up a few confusions of terminology and theory attribution, which may be raised by the syllabus: we recommend that, when you come to revisit Study Text material with the assignment in mind, you pay attention to the 'Assessment/Exam Tip' features for the relevant chapter(s).

SECTION 1 – The importance of stakeholders in the marketing process (Weighting 15%)

1.1 Assess the different categories of relationships that exist between organisations:

- One-to-one relationships
- Relationship channels
- Relationship networks

1.2 Assess the relative importance of the different stakeholder groups and consider the nature of stakeholder relationships and their influence and impact on the organisation:

- Stakeholder maps/matrices – Johnson & Scholes power/interest matrix, Freeman participant stakeholders
- Partners who support your agenda
- Allies who will provide support and encouragement
- Passive supporters
- Fence sitters whose allegiance is not clear
- Loose canons
- Opponents
- 'Voiceless'

1.3 Explain the nature of the interactions between the organisation and its different stakeholder groups:

- Partners – little interaction, but should not be ignored

- Allies – 'light touch' in terms of frequency of contact

- Passive supporters – build rapport and relationship

- Fence sitters – assess value that can be derived before deciding on level and type of interaction

- Opponents – structured approach eg formal meetings

- Voiceless – 'light touch' in event of coalition being formed

1.4 Explain the significance of the range of pressure groups as key stakeholders interested in the organisation and their potential impacts upon market-oriented organisations:

- Sectional pressure groups eg Marketing Society, Law Society, TUC, Chambers of Commerce

- Causal pressure groups eg welfare (NSPCC, Fair Trade) and environmental (Countryside Alliance, Greenpeace)

- Impacts – change in strategy, development of new products and services, process change, negative publicity, decrease in share prices

1.5 Specify the role of marketing in managing these pressure groups effectively:

- Planned marketing communications eg PR and advertising, brochures, encouraging interaction and dialogue

- Product messages – design, technical features, production process durability and distribution

- Service messages derived from interactions with pressure groups

- Proactive management of unplanned messages such as news stories, blogs – Hainsworth and Meng issue lifecycle model

1.6 Evaluate the different options to developing a Relationship Management (RM) approach within a market oriented organisation:

- Transactional

- Long term mutually beneficial relationship with a defined customer:

- Group

- Partnerships

- Strategic alliances

- E-relationships

- Networks

- Customisation

- Internal customer relationships

1.7 Specify the role of marketing in managing these pressure groups effectively:

- Planned marketing communications eg PR and advertising, brochures, encouraging interaction and dialogue

- Product messages – design, technical features, production process durability and distribution

- Service messages derived from interactions with pressure groups

 EXAM TIP

concept/application

CIM Guidance on this syllabus section emphasises the complexity of working with different stakeholder groups in the specific context of relationship marketing: that is, with the aim of obtaining their engagement with, commitment to or involvement in the organisation. 'Establishing the relative importance of stakeholders to the organisation and how they might impact upon the development of the marketing and communications mix will be essential': a helpful indicator as to what the examiners are looking for. Whether or not an assignment task explicitly addresses these concepts, you need to demonstrate your awareness of them.

This syllabus content will be particularly helpful for preparing a stakeholder audit and/or stakeholder analysis, and for recommending particular relationship strategies for different categories of stakeholder. It will also provide material for analysis and recommendations in regard to pressure groups, where this is the focus of an assignment.

Note that at no point does the syllabus explicitly name important stakeholder groups such as shareholders, suppliers, intermediaries or business allies (although it does specify customers, pressure groups and employees): they are 'understood' by references to various types of stakeholders and market relationships. However, you may well be asked to focus your analysis on a specific stakeholder group, such as the suppliers of your organisation. So as well as having a 'macro' view of stakeholders, you need to think about the full range of issues covered by the syllabus *in relation to each major stakeholder group* – and perhaps (as useful preparation for your assignment) in relation to *specific stakeholders in your organisation:* a major supplier, a promotional partner and so on.

SECTION 2 – Stakeholder relationship marketing (Weighting 20%)

2.1 Explain the position and importance of key stakeholders in the market oriented organisation and establish relationship priorities for the organisation:

- Stakeholder maps/matrices
- For stakeholders with little power/interest in project/programme – minimal effort
- For stakeholders with interest but little power – keep informed and nurture
- For stakeholders with little interest but high power – maintain relationships
- Key players – high level of interaction in developing and maintaining relationships
- Classic market relationships
- Special market relationships ie high income/high profile partners
- Green/mega/nano relationships (Gummesson, 2003)

2.2 Explain the concept of relationship marketing and its approach in developing customer retention, encouraging customer loyalty, stakeholder interest and engagement, both internally and externally:

- Relationship lifecycle model
- RM ladder of loyalty

2.3 Explain how relationship marketing is based on trust, commitment and co-operation and the importance of this concept not only to customers but the broader stakeholder audience:

- Service encounter
- Collaboration
- Transparency
- Creation of value

2.4 Explain how relationship marketing can contribute to both long-term and short-term customer retention:

- Improve customer experience and develop brand loyalty
- Superior service levels
- Develop stakeholders as advocates
- Profile strategies – sponsorship, use of celebrities versus advertising

  EXAM TIP

concept

CIM Guidance on this section emphasises the importance of relationship marketing, not just with customers but with all stakeholder groups. You must demonstrate that you appreciate the different nature (and impact on the organisation) of long-term loyalty-seeking versus short-term transaction-seeking marketing activities.

This syllabus content will be particularly helpful for justifying a relationship-marketing approach (with regard to high-priority stakeholder groups) in an assignment.

3.1 Explain how a co-ordinated marketing mix can be used to meet the needs of an organisation's broader stakeholder audience:

- Product development eg ethical clothing ranges, smoothies for children
- Renewable resources
- Price – value versus supply
- Place – direct distribution, e-distribution
- Promotion – Bluetooth, compliance with regulation eg football clubs sponsored by alcohol companies removing sponsorship on children's replica kits, not advertising foods high in fat, sugar and salt (HFSS0, products in children's programmes
- People – recruitment, working conditions and equal opportunities
- Process – recycling, alternative power sources, fair trade
- Physical environment (décor, corporate image, livery etc)

3.2 Analyse the behaviour and opinions of the decision making units in order to design and co-ordinate a marketing mix that is responsive to stakeholders' needs and adds value to them:

- Involvement theory
- Perceived risk – cost/value
- Attitudes
- Group influence and opinion leadership
- Organisational buying behaviour – stakeholders
- Personal buying behaviour and influence

3.3 Explain the dependencies of people, place and process in supporting relationship marketing approaches:

- Employees satisfaction versus customer satisfaction
- Reichheld Service Profit Cycle
- Customer and stakeholder management
- Product development
- Place

3.4 Explain the methods available for measuring the success of a co-ordinated marketing mix aimed at multiple stakeholders:

- Inquiry tests
- Recall tests
- Recognition tests
- Sales
- Tracking studies
- Financial analysis
- Media evaluation
- Stakeholder satisfaction surveys

CIM Guidance on this section emphasises the application of the marketing mix model (4Ps or 7Ps) to a broad range of stakeholders. You will be expected:

To 'differentiate between the marketing mix requirements for each stakeholder group or target audience': that is, to appreciate their different – potentially, conflicting – needs and priorities

To 'tailor the mix for different groups': that is, to come up with a co-ordinated marketing plan for one or more stakeholder groups, that can be justified by their specific mix requirements and the organisation's objectives

To 'describe how marketing mix activities can be measured': that is, to suggest what criteria and methods will be used to evaluate the marketing plan's success.

This syllabus content will be particularly helpful for preparing and justifying a marketing plan, or explaining how marketing mix elements can be tailored to wider stakeholder needs. It may also provide the theoretical framework for more detailed discussion points such as stakeholder decision-making units, or the importance of service elements (people, process, physicals) in relationship marketing.

SECTION 4 – Communicating with stakeholders (Weighting 40%)

4.1 Evaluate the extensive range of marketing communications mix tools and explain how they can be co-ordinated to contribute towards developing long-term sustainable stakeholder relationships:

- Advertising
- Public Relations
- New media
- Sponsorship and hospitality
- Personal selling
- Direct marketing
- Sales promotion

4.2 Identify and evaluate the range of tools available to support the communications relating to internal customer loyalty ie employee support, engagement and retention within the organisation:

- email
- Intranet
- Training –staff enrichment programmes
- Support – technical, management
- Flexible working: secondments, gap years
- Team meetings

4.3 Explain the challenges in communicating with stakeholders in international markets:

- Adaptation versus standardisation
- Culture – influence of religion, cultural norms and protocols
- Language and symbols
- Availability of technology
- Ensuring consistency of key messages
- Availability of media

4.4 Identify and evaluate the continuously evolving impact of new technologies and their contribution to economic and environmental sustainability of stakeholder relationships:

- Tele kits
- Virtual conferencing
- SMS
- Voice Over Internet Protocol (VOIP)
- Economic – reduction in overheads
- Environmental – CSR, carbon footprint

4.5 Explain approaches to managing budget resource for tactical communication activities:

- Marginal analysis
- Arbitrary
- Affordable
- Objective and task
- Percentage of sales
- Competitive parity
- Share of Voice (SOV)
- Centralised or decentralised management

4.6 Explain the methods available for measuring the success of co-ordinated marketing communications activities:

- Media exposure measurement
- Campaign measurement
- Increased sales
- Response rates
- Conversion rates
- Order values
- Repeat orders

 EXAM TIP

concept/application

CIM Guidance on this section emphasises the need to tailor communications media and messages to meet the different information needs of different stakeholder audiences. While in *Marketing Essentials* (Unit 1) you may have considered the broad marketing communications mix (ie what range of tools and media an organisation can or should use), here you will be focusing on the specific needs of one or more stakeholder groups, and formulating a co-ordinated mix for them.

This syllabus content will be particularly helpful for preparing and justifying a marketing communications plan for one or more stakeholder groups. It also provides underpinning content in regard to internal stakeholders (eg employee communication and internal marketing), international stakeholders and technology: these issues may be raised specifically in an assignment, or may be particularly relevant in the context of your project organisation.

Please note the difference in focus between Section 3 of the syllabus (marketing mix decisions) and Section 4 (marketing communications activities): confusion between the two is a classic exam pitfall – and the same applies to an assignment brief! Be clear whether it is the marketing mix (4Ps or 7Ps) *or* the communications/promotional mix (tools of communication) that you are being asked to discuss.

2 The project brief

The project brief is the document that sets out everything you need to know to complete your work-based project assignment:

- The submission date: when your project must be submitted (and when results will be released)

- A rubric or set of instructions in regard to the marks available, the maximum word count for the project, and the documentation which should accompany the assignment

- Guidance Notes on teaching, project preparation and assessment

- A choice of two Project Briefs on different topics (each set out separately), setting out:

  - Brief background context to the topic

  - The scenario or role in which you are required to present a report, presentation or other project format

  - A list of tasks to be worked through, in order to build up the content of the project

  - Maximum word and page counts for each task

  - A list of Syllabus References: that is, the learning objectives covered by the assignment

  - A list of the Assessment Criteria used to mark the assignment

- A Mark Scheme, with a breakdown of the marks available for each of the Assessment Criteria – cross-referenced to the CIM Magic Formula, discussed in Section 1.2 of this Workbook.

- Guidance on tackling the assignment, specifically related to the tasks and topics of the given Project Brief.

2.1 The exemplar project brief

In this section, we reproduce the Exemplar (Specimen) Work Based Project material published by the CIM, and provide some guidance to:

- Suggest how such material can be interpreted, for the best sense of what it is that examiners are really looking for

- Highlight key instructions which should form part of your 'compliance checklist' when planning, compiling and checking your assignment work

- Indicate how the format illustrated by the Exemplar could be used to target a range of syllabus themes, topics and types of task.

In section 5.4, we will give some general advice on research and assignment technique, and in section 5.5, we will work through the Exemplar Project Brief, giving guidance on how each of the tasks might be tackled – in such a way that you can apply the principles to your own work-based project.

In some instances, we have made slight alterations to the Exemplar Brief as published by the CIM, to correct typographical errors, and to reflect the formula subsequently adopted in the 'live' project briefs.

2.2 Rubic (front page instructions)

New syllabus specimen work based project

Project Brief and Mark Scheme

Candidates are required to choose ONE out of TWO of the following project briefs:

Option One – Relationship Marketing

Option Two – *[Second Option Title]* (detailed separately)

No second option was provided for the Exemplar, but when you are given the project brief for your sitting, there will be two options – covering two different themes. Each option is published as a separate set of documentation. The 'real' documentation also indicates submission dates for the project: one set of project briefs is relevant to projects to be submitted in December 2008 or March 2009, for example, and another to projects to be submitted in June or September 2009.

Report

- All tasks within the chosen project brief are compulsory
- 100% of the marks available for this paper
- Maximum word count – 4,000 words

Word Count

Candidates must adhere to the word count stated. No marks will be allocated for information contained in appendices, unless explicitly stated within the project brief. Appendices should be used for supporting information only. CIM reserves the right to return unmarked any project that exceeds the stated word count or contains, in the opinion of the examiner, excessive appendices.

EXAM TIP

format/presentation

Word count is obviously extremely important, and further guidelines on how to adhere to it are given below. There is less guidance on the use of appendices, however, it is worth bearing some key principles in mind:

- The Project Brief will clearly state what appendices are *required* (and at what length) as part of the assignment. One appendix will certainly contain your 'organisation background': a brief overview of the organisation which is the focus of your project. Another may be the detailed findings of a stakeholder audit or analysis, say.

- It would also be appropriate to use appendices to contain your list of references (sources referred to in the body of the report) and bibliography (books and other secondary sources consulted in preparing the report)

- Other appendices may be used to supply supporting information (such as research findings) or documentation (such as a stakeholder feedback questionnaire), a summary of which should be included in the main body of the report.

- Appendices are not included in the word count, but *do not* use them to try to squeeze in material for which you don't have 'room' in the body of your report. You won't gain any marks for the material – and 'excessive appendices' may disqualify your assignment altogether. (Examiners have long seen through the 'hide the extra 1,000 words in an appendix' ploy...)

Documentation

Candidates must register as a studying member and for this assessment with CIM by the required deadline(s). Prior to submitting the assignment for marking, candidates must complete the required declaration front sheet for this assignment. Tutors are also required to sign this declaration front sheeting stating that to the best of their knowledge the candidate's work is their own.

2.3 Guidance notes

Context

The assignment should be based on the candidate's organisation or an organisation of their choice, selected with tutor advice. A brief overview of each organisation chosen, including legal classification, product or service offered, target market and structure, should be included in the appendix. This information should *not* be included as part of the word count and *no* marks will be allocated to this section.

Candidates should ensure that sensitive data from the chosen organisation is not included *or* ensure the anonymity of the organisation used within the assignment.

Each assignment must be completed individually, not as part of a group.

  EXAM TIP application

Perhaps the most important aspect of this guidance is its indication of what examiners want included in the 'Organisation Background' appendix: we will use this mini-checklist as we work through the Exemplar brief in section 5.4.

Assessment Criteria

The assignment briefing documents include assessment criteria, which are designed to indicate to the candidate the types of information and format that are required. The assessment criteria should not replace any assignment briefing that is usually undertaken by the unit tutor. It is important that when assignments are issued, discussions take place between the group and tutor to clarify their understanding of the assignment brief and what is required.

Tutor Guidance to Candidates

Each candidate should receive a minimum of 60 minutes' individual tutorial time per unit. Tutors should be prepared to offer advice to candidates regarding the assignment, particularly with regard to the organisation(s) they choose to use.

Tutors can give feedback on one draft of an assignment and/or answer specific subject-related questions from a candidate related to their assignment. Tutors should not coach a candidate or return a marked assignment to the candidate for improvement. A tutor is not able to discuss with a candidate the marks or grades that a piece of work is likely to achieve.

  EXAM TIP application

Obviously, these matters will be negotiated between you and your unit tutor. The choice of organisation to use as the basis of your project will be particularly important. As you begin to think about this, bear in mind that an appropriate focal organisation will be: (a) one that you know well *or* one on which you will readily be able to access sufficiently detailed information; and (b) one whose environment, activities and stakeholders can be clearly related to the theme of the project (so that you have plenty of relevant material to work with).

Word Count

Candidates must comply with the recommended word count, within a margin of +10% where applicable. For some elements a maximum number of pages, rather than a minimum number of words applies.

Any assignments that exceed this will be penalised by candidates' forfeiting the marks for presentation. Work that grossly exceeds the recommended word count will be returned unmarked and candidates will be asked to complete and submit a new assignment.

Word count excludes the index (if used), headings, information contained within tables, references, bibliography and appendices.

The total number of words used for the whole assignment must be indicated on the front cover of the assignment.

Candidates should present their work professionally, using tables and diagrams to support and/or illustrate the text. If candidates present all/most of their answer in tabulated form, the words used will be counted and the rules relating to word count, as indicated above, will apply.

When an assignment task requires candidates to produce presentation slides, with supporting notes, the word count applies to the supporting notes only. The maximum number of slides indicated on the assignment brief excludes the title page slide and the contents page slide.

  EXAM TIP format/presentation

When you start work on your assignment, make yourself a checklist of all the elements (relevant to the type of task you have been set) which are *excluded* from the word count: this will enable you to make the most of your word count and check it accurately. Aim for the maximum word count (4,000 words), rather than the +10% margin (4,400 words): this will leave you more room for editing. To give you a broad idea, this page contains about 440 words (excluding headings): your report would be a maximum of 10 pages at this level of density: more, if you include diagrams, tables and so on. Tips for managing your word count will be provided in section 5.4.

Note also the helpful hints as to what the examiners expect to see in assignments: tables and diagrams to support and/or illustrate report text; and title and contents page slides as part of presentations.

Mark Schemes

CIM reserves the right to amend the mark scheme at standardisation. Tutors should not indicate to candidates whether a piece of work is likely to pass or fail or the likely allocation of marks. This applies to work in progress as well as final assignments that have been submitted to CIM for marking.

Final Grades

Final grades will be sent to the candidates from CIM by the usual process, depending on when projects were submitted for marking and/or moderation.

Referencing and Professionalism

A professional approach to work is expected from all candidates. Candidates should therefore:

- Identify and acknowledge all sources/methodologies/applications used

- Express their work in plain business English. Marks are not awarded for use of English, but a good standard of English will help express the candidate's understanding more effectively.

Plagiarism and Collusion

All work that candidates submit as part of the CIM requirements must be expressed in their own words and incorporate their own judgements. Direct quotations from the published or unpublished work of others, including that of tutors or employers, must be appropriately referenced. Authors of images used in reports and audiovisual presentations must be acknowledged. Tutors should ensure that candidates are appropriately briefed about how to avoid plagiarism and collusion, especially when using electronic sources or when working in a group. Candidates must sign the declaration front sheet with their membership number, confirming that the work submitted is their own. Tutors must countersign the documents to say that to the best of their knowledge the work submitted is the candidate's own work. CIM reserves the right to return assignments if the necessary declaration front sheets have not been signed.

Plagiarism is a serious offence and any candidate found to be copying another candidate's work or quoting work from another source without recognising and disclosing that source will be penalised. Situations where plagiarism or collusion are suspected will be taken very seriously. Candidates believed to be involved will have their work looked at separately by the senior examiner and/or another senior academic and plagiarism detection software may be used. Candidates found to be in breach of these regulations may be subject to one or more of the following: disqualification from membership; refused award of unit or qualification; disqualification from other CIM examinations/qualifications; refused the right to retake units/qualifications.

EXAM TIP

You might gather that plagiarism (claiming another person's work as your own) and collusion (working together with others on work that you claim as yours alone) are serious matters for the CIM! However, it is important to keep this in proportion: don't be prevented from using helpful sources of information by fear that you may be suspected of plagiarism. The key point is:

- To acknowledge the source of any concepts or models you refer to (eg Mendelow's stakeholder mapping matrix) in the text

- To acknowledge the source of any images you reproduce (eg photographs, drawings or diagrams) and any statistical data you use in tabular or diagrammatic form

- To provide detailed referencing for any material that is a direct citation or quotation (using the Harvard referencing system, discussed in Section 1.6 of this Workbook)

- To rephrase information you have read or heard, using your own words, where possible. Do this deliberately: be aware that it is easy to slip into reproducing text, when taking notes.

When dealing with basic theoretical material, it is inevitable that people will make some of the same points on a given topic: don't tie yourself in knots trying to come up with something different – just acknowledge the source from which you have derived your understanding.

2.4 The assignment brief

Stakeholder marketing

Option One: Relationship Marketing

Relationship marketing aims to form and sustain profitable, mutually beneficial relationships by bringing together the organisational stakeholders and resources to deliver the best possible value proposition for the organisation. Relationship marketing, through internal marketing, fosters the development of customer orientation, which facilitates market-led responses to change and thus improves competitiveness and positioning.

EXAM TIP

concept

Each project brief will start with a paragraph or two setting the context of the assignment: orienting you to its basic topic or theme. This is not just 'padding': it is important information about how the examiner defines key terminology and sees the overall purpose of the project tasks.

You have been asked to present a proposal to the Corporate Communications Manager that contains a set of recommendations for improving relationship marketing for your business unit or department.

EXAM TIP

application

Each project brief will contain a one- or two-sentence role and purpose description: what you have been asked to do (present a report/proposal, prepare a presentation), for whom (your organisation's Corporate Communications Manager or Marketing Manager, say), and for what purpose ('that contains a set of recommendations for...').

Again, this is important information, which you should use in planning your project and evaluating your first draft. The format and content requirements will be set out in more detail in the task descriptions, but you *don't* get much more detail about who your target audience is – and this will be vitally important: one of the underlying tasks of the assignment is to consider the information needs of your audience.

Don't worry if your chosen organisation doesn't have a Corporate Communications Manager. You are effectively being asked to treat your own organisation as if it were a case study scenario.

Task One

Undertake an audit of the stakeholders to:

- Identify the major stakeholders in your organisation
- Explain their level of influence and impact on relationship marketing.

Your audit findings should be included as an appendix to your report (maximum of four A4 pages).

 EXAM TIP application

The formula used in subsequent 'live' project briefs is: 'As background research to your report you will need to undertake an audit of your organisation (business unit or department) to:...' – which emphasises (a) the explicitly research-based nature of this task, and (b) the fact that the focus of the audit will not always be on stakeholders. The specific terms of reference for the audit will vary from brief to brief: they typically comprise two or three requirements, each very clearly stated in terms of instruction/command word (identify, explain, analyse, examine, assess) and topic.

Note that the audit findings have a page limit – and are not included in the word count.

Task Two

Produce a formal report for your Corporate Communications Manager in which you:

- Provide a brief background to your chosen organisation, its products/services, customer base and position in market (maximum two sides of A4, to be included as an appendix)

- Explain the concept of relationship marketing in the context of the organisation's stakeholders in achieving stakeholder interest, involvement, commitment and loyalty

- Summarise your audit findings, including the identification of key stakeholders, their level of influence and the impact on relationship marketing

- Select ONE internal and ONE external stakeholder group that you propose to develop a relationship marketing approach with, giving reasons for your choice

- Explain the benefits of relationship marketing to each of these stakeholder groups

- Develop a co-ordinated marketing and communications plan that is responsive to the needs of your identified stakeholder groups and adds value to the relationship

- Identify and evaluate a range of methods that you could utilise to measure the success of your marketing and communications mix.

 EXAM TIP concept/application/evaluation

This is your basic checklist for planning your project and evaluating each draft. You *must* fulfil the requirements of each of the bullet points, within your report – although you will not necessarily *structure* your report on a task-by-task basis: the structure of the report will be shaped by the particular issues drawn out of your audit analysis.

What this part of the brief *doesn't* tell you is the relative weighting (or length of coverage) of each topic within the report. This information is provided by the Mark Scheme, which we will look at later.

Appendix

In your appendix you should:

- Provide a brief background to your chosen organisation, its customer base, products/services and position in the market (maximum two sides of A4: no marks allocated)

- Include your audit findings (maximum four A4 pages)

Word count for report 4,000 words, excluding relevant appendices

Audit findings maximum four A4 pages, included in the appendix.

  EXAM TIP

add text + icon (lc)

Note that these aren't additional requirements. They merely summarise, for clarity, which parts of the task are to be separated out into appendices, and at what length (outside the word count).

Syllabus references

1.1, 1.2, 1.3, 1.4, 1.5, 1.6, 2.1, 2.2, 2.3, 2.4, 3.1, 3.2, 3.3, 3.4, 4.1, 4.2, 4.3, 4.4, 4.6

  EXAM TIP

concept

This might look of more interest to the examiner than to you – indicating which learning outcomes the project is supposed to assess. However, it is helpful information. It will point you to: (a) what the examiner considers appropriate underpinning content for the assignment tasks (ie which concepts, models and tools will be relevant); and (b) what chapters in the BPP *Stakeholder Marketing* Study Text will be most helpful (since the syllabus reproduced in the Text is cross-referenced to the chapters in which the content is covered).

It also provides useful reminders not to omit syllabus topics from your consideration: in the above case, for example, the inclusion of Learning Outcomes 4.3 and 4.4 should remind you to take *international* stakeholders (if any) into account, and to consider *technology-based* tools in your communication planning.

Assessment Criteria

- Explanation of the concept of relationship marketing in the context of the organisation's stakeholder in achieving stakeholder interest, involvement, commitment and loyalty

- Summary of audit findings, including the identification of key stakeholders, their level of influence and the impact on relationship marketing

- Selection of ONE internal and ONE external stakeholder group chosen to develop a relationship marketing approach with, giving reasons for choice

- Explanation of the benefits of relationship marketing to each of these stakeholder groups

- Development of a co-ordinated marketing and communications plan that is responsive to the needs of the identified stakeholder groups and adds value to the relationship

- Identification and evaluation of a range of methods that could be utilised to measure the success of the marketing and communications mix

- Presentation, format and style of the report

Note that the Assessment Criteria are very similar to the task description (with the addition of marks for the presentation, format and style of the report). Fulfil the task description – and you have fulfilled the assessment criteria...

2.4.1 Mark scheme

We have adapted the Exemplar Mark Scheme to include the CIM's Magic Formula, in the format used by the Mark Schemes of all subsequent 'live' project briefs. We have allocated marks to the Magic Formula elements based on these later Mark Schemes.

Mark Scheme – Relationship Marketing

Marking Criteria	Mark Allocation: Concept/Application/ Evaluation/Format	% Mark Available
Explanation of the concept of relationship marketing in the context of the organisation's stakeholders in achieving stakeholder interest involvement, commitment and loyalty	C = 10	10
Summary of audit findings including the identification of key stakeholders, their level of influence and the impact on relationship marketing	C = 15	15
Identification and justification of ONE internal and ONE external group chosen to develop a relationship marketing approach, with reasons for choice	E = 10	10
Explanation of the benefits of relationship marketing to each of these stakeholder groups	C = 10	10
Development of a co-ordinated marketing and communications plan that is responsive to the needs of the identified stakeholder groups and adds value to the relationship	A = 30	30 (2 x 15)
Identification and evaluation of a range of methods that could be utilised to measure the success of the marketing and communications mix	C = 5 E = 10	15
Presentation, format and style of the report	F = 10	10
Total Marks	100	100

Markers should use their judgement to reward answers that:

- Are relevant to the tasks
- Use concepts and frameworks to support arguments, points and recommendations
- Are presented in a suitably professional tone and in the required format
- Use examples appropriately to illustrate points
- Are appropriately referenced.

This is as clear a statement as you could wish of exactly what the examiner wants to see in your project: use it as a checklist for planning your work and evaluating your first draft.

The distinction between Concept, Application, Evaluation and Format/Presentation should be fairly clear cut. Note that having to select stakeholders for closer relationship, and justify your choice, would be an Evaluation task, as would making recommendations. Application tasks would include analysis of own organisation and/or its stakeholders (eg comparison of their information needs or responses to change, or explanation of how they might support a project or strategy).

2.4.2 Guidance on tackling the assignment

This assignment is an opportunity to use stakeholder analysis tools in relation to the impact and influence of an internal and external stakeholder group in relation to the development of relationship marketing at an operational level. Candidates are to recommend marketing and communications mix for each stakeholder group.

Your project brief will include a similar paragraph summarising the focus of your particular assignment.

Conducting the audit

When undertaking the audit, candidates should use stakeholder mapping techniques such as the power/interest matrix, Freeman participant stakeholders or other suitable mapping techniques, in order to establish the stakeholders and their level of influence and impact on relationship marketing.

The stakeholder audit may be supported by interviews with key stakeholders and consideration of relevant marketing theories and concepts. The stakeholder maps or matrices should be explained and stakeholder position justified. Generic stakeholder maps that reflect no application to the selected organisation will not be acceptable. Candidates must demonstrate knowledge and application of stakeholder theory.

The results should be included in the appendices, summarised within the findings the report and used to justify the recommendations made.

This section provides very helpful guidance on the requirements for the audit: notably, the need to use stakeholder mapping techniques; the kinds of supporting material that will be considered relevant; the need to explain any model used; and the need to justify your positioning of a given stakeholder group within a map or matrix.

The final paragraph sets out the purpose and uses of the audit task: make this a checklist for planning your work. In particular, note that any recommendations you make later in your report should be *justified* by reference to the your audit findings (eg the priority assigned to different stakeholder groups).

Some of the guidance is tailored to the specific terms of reference of the audit task: so, for example, the reference to 'relationship marketing' above will be replaced by comments on whatever audit themes and tasks have been set in your project brief.

Formal report

Information gathered from the audit should be analysed in relation to the chosen organisation and should reflect awareness of the key stakeholder issues in an original and innovative manner. Relationship marketing concepts and theories should be appropriately applied to reflect understanding.

The marketing and communications mixes should relate to operational marketing activity and it is not expected that candidates suggest strategic options. Moreover, candidates should be creative in their suggestions and how they communicate these, and this may include community projects eg sports initiatives, youth development programmes, educational initiatives, employees involved in mentoring and volunteer programmes within the local community, recycling etc.

The report should include marketing and communication mixes to develop long term relationships with an internal and external stakeholder group. This should include objectives, targets, tactics and proposed evaluation. Candidates should express their objectives as SMART objectives. Candidates should identify how to evaluate the success of their marketing and communications plans, and qualitative and quantitative methods should be considered. Candidates need to demonstrate the application of these measures in the context of the assignment. It is not sufficient to produce a generic series of measures, which may not be appropriate to the context.

In producing the report, it is important that candidates adopt a structure and style that naturally lend themselves to reporting on the outcome of their study. The format and approach used will be driven by the relevant themes and emerging issues arising from the research. A formulaic task-based approach should be avoided. The examiners will be looking for a more holistic approach where there is clear evidence of insightful analysis, originality and clarity of expression. The report should be in a professional style with references to conceptual marketing theory included as appropriate.

  EXAM TIP   concept/application/evaluation/format

Some of this guidance will obviously be specific to the report task set in a particular project brief. However, some common themes to highlight include:

- The need to apply relationship marketing concepts and theories appropriately

- The tactical or operational (rather than strategic) level at which you are expected to propose plans

- The need to be creative in developing and making suggestions

- The need to express SMART objectives, and to identify both qualitative and quantitative methods for evaluating success

- The need to develop a relevant, holistic approach to the structure and style of your report, based on the themes and issues arising from your research: *not* using a standard report 'formula' – or even, necessarily, the order of the Task Two bullet points.

2.5 Potential project themes

Each Project Brief will focus on a different theme or topic, which can be applied to a wide range of organisational contexts. The Exemplar Project Brief, for example, focused on Relationship Marketing.

- The December 2008/March 2009 options focused on (1) Improving Service Quality and (2) Developing Customer Retention and Loyalty.

- The June/September 2009 options are focused on (1) Reducing Organisational Carbon Footprint and (2) Supplier Relationships.

You can't afford to focus your study on particular areas of the syllabus, on the basis of these themes: the assignments are deliberately designed to test a wide range of Learning Outcomes. The more widely and holistically you study, the better prepared you will be to tackle the Project Brief when it is given to you.

So, for example, the theme of 'Service Quality' embraces a range of topics, including: the nature of service and the extended marketing mix; the importance of customer service in relationship marketing and customer loyalty; the importance of internal stakeholder marketing and relationships; Reichheld's Service Profit Cycle and other models which explain the link between employee satisfaction, customer satisfaction and organisational success; methods of improving service quality; the management of internal relationships; the use of technology in customer service and employee communications; the challenges of maintaining service quality in outsourced activity; the challenges of international employee communication; and so on.

Similarly, 'Reducing Carbon Footprint' (as with a focus on any other organisational or environmental 'issue') embraces a range of topics including: the wider ethical and corporate social responsibility of organisations; the nature, role and influence of stakeholders in global environmental issues; the role and management of pressure groups; organisational planning and how various stakeholder groups might support or contribute to an organisation's plans; internal, international and technological issues; and so on.

2.5.1 Further reading

Our coverage of Corporate Social Responsibility issues in the *Stakeholder Marketing* Study Text does not focus on carbon footprint in sufficient detail to provide you with a basis for tackling an assignment on the topic (indeed for all topics you are expected to contribute your own extensive research). If you are interested in this area, a wealth of resources and tools is available on-line. Plug 'carbon footprint' into your search engine. You might like to browse:

http://www.carbonfootprint.co.uk

http://www.nature.org/initiatives/climate change

http://www.footprint.wwf.org.uk

You might also like to check some corporate web sites for CSR or Environment statements which explain how the organisation is seeking to reduce its own carbon footprint.

Other potential themes, which similarly allow for both wide syllabus coverage *and* application to a range of organisations, include:

- A focus on any one of the major stakeholder groups (eg customers, suppliers, shareholders, pressure groups, employees, intermediaries or allies)

- Value creation: how different stakeholder relationships create or add value for both parties

- Corporate ethics and corporate social responsibility

- The marketing mix: its relevance to relationship marketing; how it can be tailored to different stakeholder needs; perhaps focus on specific elements such as product development

- Information and Communication Technology: its application in relationship marketing, customer service, employee communication, international trading and so on

- Stakeholder decision-making: influences on stakeholder opinions and decisions; Decision Making Units in different stakeholder groups; the importance of trust, communication and other dynamics in stakeholder relationships.

2.5.2 Potential project formats and tasks

In addition to potential *themes* on which future projects may be based, it is worth considering the range of *formats* and *tasks* that may be set.

So far, all Project Briefs published have followed the Exemplar in format, requiring: (a) a research/audit task and report on findings and (b) a formal report for a member of the management team. However, the guidance notes refer to other formats, including presentation slides and supporting notes, so this is a realistic possibility for future projects. These two formats are perhaps the most likely, since they allow for substantial work, creative thinking, professional approach, a realistic element of application and academic referencing.

In terms of tasks, the specific requirements vary according to the topic. However, some common elements have begun to emerge. Your Project Brief is quite likely to require:

- A brief overview of the organisation which is the subject of your project

- Some form of stakeholder research and mapping, *plus* analysis of particular aspects of stakeholder roles, influence, relationships and so on.

  [In the BPP Stakeholder Marketing Study Text, see Chapter 1 sections 6 & 7, and Chapter 3 section 5, for a range of stakeholder and relationship analysis tools.]

- A summary of your audit findings, *including* any particular point that needs to be drawn out

- Description, discussion or explanation of one or more models or concepts, in the context of your organisation and issues identified in your audit findings (related to the project theme).

  [The models and concepts specified by the syllabus are covered in the BPP Study Text. Use this coverage as a starting point for your further reading and thinking.]

- Production of a co-ordinated marketing mix and/or communications mix plan, outlining (or supporting) your recommendations for improving some aspect of stakeholder relations or stakeholder communication (relevant to the issues raised so far in the report). Alternatively, you may be asked to identify or recommend which elements of the mix may need to change in order to improve a situation (or in response to a changing situation): it would then be up to you whether you expressed these recommendations in the form of a mix plan.

  [In the BPP Study Text, Chapter 7 section 4 covers marketing mix planning, and Chapter 11 section 2 covers communications mix plans.]

- Identification and evaluation of methods which could be used to measure the success of your plan (if relevant).

  [In the BPP Study Text, see Chapter 7 section 5 and Chapter 11 section 4.]

One major application task that has not been set yet, but could well be set in the future, is identifying and evaluating different methods of setting budgets for marketing communications activity *[see Chapter 11 section 3]*.

3 Building a portfolio for your projects

3.1 Why build a portfolio?

You will have noticed that you are not required to *submit* any kind of portfolio to the CIM as part of your work-based project. So why are we suggesting that you prepare one?

- Preparing a portfolio is a helpful discipline which requires you to collect and record a range of secondary source materials, conduct research and analysis, and file topic notes. Any or all of this may be useful groundwork, or usable material, for your project.

- It is *not* advisable to focus your studies narrowly on the project theme, in the first instance: a wide-ranging and well-integrated understanding of stakeholder marketing is required in order to interpret and tackle project tasks effectively. Preparing a portfolio helps you to study broadly across the syllabus, while still compiling useful material for your project.

- You may not be given access to the project brief until a late stage of your studies: building a portfolio allows you to get a head start on important groundwork such as stakeholder analysis, so that you can maximise the time available, later, for more focused research.

3.2 Research strategy

A key skill in the 'Concept' area of the CIM Magic Formula is the ability to 'develop appropriate research strategies for secondary research' and to 'identify valid and relevant information from a suitable range of relevant sources for the discipline' (*Grade Descriptors for the Professional Certificate in Marketing*).

Compiling a secondary research strategy at the beginning of your studies, and refining it as you go along, will provide you with a range of useful material, and the basis for a comprehensive Bibliography for your assignment. Once you have received your project brief, you can refine your strategy further, focusing on the relevant themes and topics.

- Include a range of media: books (or chapters of books); newspaper and journal articles (printed or on-line); web sites; DVDs, videos or CD-ROMs; and corporate documents, outputs (eg advertising, stakeholder communications), public statements and research reports.

- Organise your list using appropriate headings: 'general' (eg for books on Relationship Marketing) and specific topic headings (eg Stakeholder analysis, CSR, Supplier Relationships)

- Start with your BPP Study Text and the Key Reading List titles (under the 'general' heading). As you pursue your studies, *add* sources from the Supplementary Reading list; Further Reading references; the CIM Knowledge Hub; your tutor's recommendations or handouts; and your own 'browsing'. *Delete* sources which, on closer inspection, lack relevance or credibility.

- When you actually consult a source:

    - Check or complete the reference details (title, author, publisher, date/edition, page numbers etc – or web address and date posted)

    - File your notes, or a copy or print-out of the information, in a Resource File for later use

    - Transfer the source reference to your draft Bibliography.

You might also draft an initial primary research strategy. For example, for your stakeholder audit, you may want to survey (using a questionnaire) or interview (one to one or in a group) colleagues, representatives of key stakeholder groups, or other relevant parties. Since this is a time-consuming approach, and involves other busy people, you should save primary research until you are able to focus on the project brief: however, it will still be useful to identify potential sources of information on different topics.

3.3 Portfolio-building exercises

Your unit lecturer or tutor may suggest portfolio-building activities at different stages of your course. The following are some general suggestions for the kinds of activities you might undertake to build a project-supporting portfolio, as you work your way through the syllabus. The BPP Study Text for *Stakeholder Marketing* includes Activities specifically designed to support portfolio-building, and we recommend that you attempt as many of these as possible during your studies: we have highlighted some of the most useful ones here.

Task	Comment	Study Text guidance
Compile an on-going Research Strategy ('reading list') and Bibliography	Discussed above	*'Key Text Links and Further Reading' features*
Open a Resource File	File (in an organised way, indexed by topic) your study notes; excerpts from books; cuttings from magazines and newspapers; print-outs from web sites; transcripts of interviews and discussions; copies of corporate documents; and so on, as you gather them. Please be aware of any copyright or confidentiality issues in storing, copying or using material.	
Collect examples of relationship marketing initiatives in the real world, for your Resource File	This will provide illustrative examples which you can use to underpin conceptual points in your project (an important skill in the 'Application' area of the Magic Formula).	
Draft your 'Organisational Background' or overview description	(If you know which organisation you will use for your project.)	

Task	Comment	Study Text guidance
Carry out a stakeholder analysis of your organisation	Use research techniques (brainstorming, observation, interviews, documentary evidence) to identify key stakeholders and analyse their power and interest.	*Chapter 1: Activities 2, 3, 5 and 8.*
	Draw a power/interest matrix.	
	Write notes justifying each stakeholder's position in the matrix.	
	Write notes explaining (a) the appropriate strategy and (b) the organisation's current strategy for each stakeholder.	
Draft a relationship analysis, and gather supporting evidence.	Focus on the 'Key Players' identified by your stakeholder analysis. Gather and file corporate value statements, policies, and observational/documentary evidence for each relationship.	*Chapter 3: Activities 1, 2, 7 and 8*
Gather evidence of your organisation's corporate social responsibility	Make a note-form appraisal and highlight any issues: these can be followed up later, if relevant to the Project Brief.	*Chapter 2: Activities 1, 3, 4, 5 and 6*
Gather evidence of your organisation's use of relationship marketing approaches and techniques	Make a note-form appraisal and highlight any issues: these can be followed up later, if relevant to the Project Brief. Don't forget internal marketing.	*Chapter 4: Activities 2 and 5* *Chapter 5: Activities 2, 7 and 9* *Chapter 9*
Gather evidence of your organisation's use of each element in the (extended) marketing mix	What is the organisation aiming to do with the mix, and how might it impact different key stakeholder groups? Identify any elements that might need to be changed to improve relationships with a key stakeholder: you can follow this up later, if it is relevant to the Project Brief.	*Chapter 6*
Gather evidence of, and appraise in note form, your organisation's marketing communications mix	How effectively does it reach different key stakeholder groups? Identify any elements that might need to be changed to improve relationships with a key stakeholder: you can follow this up later, if it is relevant to the Project Brief.	*See Chapter 8, and try Activity 1*
Gather evidence of, and appraise in note form, the methods your organisation uses for marketing planning and control	Focus on (a) budgeting for marketing communications activity and (b) measuring and evaluating marketing and communications plans.	*See the relevant sections of Chapters 7 and 11*
Identify (a) any international issues relevant to your organisation and (b) any technology used in its marketing mix and/or relationship marketing.	These points can be followed up in detail later, if relevant to the Project Brief.	*Chapter 10*

4 Tackling the project

4.1 Project technique

4.1.1 Writing an organisation background

The purpose of the organisation background or overview is:

- To brief the examiners on the context to which your project relates, so that they can judge whether your analysis and proposals are relevant and realistic in that context; and

- To save your having to describe and explain organisation details in the body of your report, which (a) would be poor communication practice in the context of a report to your own managers and (b) would waste word count!

Read the Context section of your Project Brief carefully for any instructions as to required content of the overview. So far, you have been asked to include: legal classification (eg partnership, charity, private limited company, public limited company), product(s) or service(s) offers, target market and organisation structure.

Further guidance on the kinds of information to include is provided in section 1.5 of this Workbook, and an example is given in section 5.5.1 below.

4.1.2 Conducting an audit and reporting audit findings

Read the Guidance section of your Project Brief carefully for any instructions as to the conduct of the audit task (see section 5.2.6 above for the Exemplar version). The following are just some suggestions for planning this task.

- Read the Task One brief carefully, to determine:

    - The level at which your audit should be undertaken: organisational, business unit and/or departmental

    - The focus of the audit: internal and/or external stakeholders, a particular stakeholder group – or perhaps an organisational process (eg purchasing, relationship marketing or change management) or issue (eg corporate social responsibility)

    - The terms of reference of the audit: identification of stakeholders; explanation of stakeholder influence and/or impact; description of a business process; analysis of stakeholder behaviour; examination of interactions and relationships between stakeholders; explanation of the impact of internal relationships on external relationships; or whatever is specified.

- Devise a research strategy that is appropriate for each of the terms of reference. If you are asked to analyse your organisation's supplier relationships, for example, you might need to interview or survey purchasing staff, as well as consulting available purchasing policies, supplier feedback forms and so on. If you are asked to assess the influence of a pressure group on your Industry sector, you might need to consult industry reports, news articles and case studies, say. You might also use various tools such as Ford *et al's* Relationship Analysis questionnaire or a Relationship SWOT analysis (Study Text Chapter 3).

- Use appropriate stakeholder mapping and/or classification techniques to support your analysis of stakeholder interest and influence, and appropriate management strategies. Examples which may be relevant, depending on the terms of reference, include:

    - Mendelow's power/interest matrix *(Study Text Chapter 1)*: this will almost always be a good starting place!

    - Freeman/Egan's classification of participant stakeholders *(Study Text Chapter 1)*

    - The Kraljic matrix, to analyse suppliers *(Study Text Chapter 5)*

    - Gummesson's 30R model, to distinguish relationship types and drivers *(Study Text Chapter 3)*

    - Relationship life cycle and/or ladder of loyalty models, to analyse relationship stage *(Study Text Chapter 3 for customers and Chapter 5 for suppliers)*

    - Christopher *et al's* classification of internal customers *(Study Text Chapter 9)*

    - Diagrams and flow-charts to illustrate internal structures, supply chains or networks, partnerships/collaborations or inputs-outputs to processes. *(In the Study Text, see Figures 3.2, 5.3, 5.4 and 9.1 for examples – but draw your own: don't use generic models.)*

Attribute and explain any map, matrix or classification scheme you use, and justify your decision to place stakeholders in particular classes or positions. Ensure that you apply the model using the specific stakeholders of your organisation, *not* generic categories.

- Compile your audit findings as an appendix to your report, to a maximum of four A4 pages. This appendix should include:

- A brief account of your research methodology

- Research findings: eg a digest of interview/survey results, process charts/diagrams, a summary of secondary research (correctly referenced) and so on

- Your map/matrix/classification analyses, with explanation and justification

- Discussion, description, explanation or analysis in line with each of the terms of reference of the task.

- Summarise your audit findings, for the body of your project report. Include any particular focus specified in the Task Two brief: this is likely to highlight an issue which will shape the rest of your report. For example, if you are asked to include your identification of key stakeholders and their level of influence/impact on organisational plans, this will provide a basis for later tasks: eg selecting stakeholder groups for further relationship development, or justifying resource allocations or changes to the marketing mix.

- Refer to the audit findings where necessary, in the body of your project report, to justify your arguments or recommendations (eg on the basis of the high priority of a stakeholder group, or identified barriers in a particular stakeholder relationship which need to be overcome).

4.1.3 Writing a formal report

Read the Guidance section of your Project Brief carefully for any instructions as to the content, structure and style of the formal report task (see section 5.2.6 above for the Exemplar version).

Further guidance is given in section 1.4 of this Workbook.

4.1.4 Managing your word count

We highly recommend that you take word count into consideration at the project planning stage. Your aim is:

- To ensure that your word count is appropriately distributed across the assessment criteria, in order to achieve a good balance and maximise the available marks *and*

- To get as close to the 4,000 word limit as you can, in your first draft – to avoid frustrating and inefficient padding or pruning at the second draft stage.

Read the Guidance Notes section of your Project Brief carefully for any instructions as to word count (see section 5.2.3 above for the Exemplar version). The following are some extra tips: use them if they suit your method of working.

- Start with a checklist of relevant maximum limits (in words, pages or slides) for different elements of the project, and of the *exclusions* from the word count (index, headings, diagrammatic and tabulated information, references, bibliography, appendices, title and contents page slides). Use this each time you check your count.

- Work out roughly how many words you present per average page of work, and therefore roughly how many pages your report will be: say, 9 pages densely typed.

- Check the Mark Scheme for your assignment. Leaving aside the 10 marks for format and presentation, there are 90 marks available for fulfilling the task criteria. For every 10 marks, therefore, you need to allow one-ninth of the total word or page count: about 450 words, or one page. Following the maths through:

Marks available for assessment criterion	Allocate:	
10	450 words	1 page
15	660 words	1 ½ pages
20	900 words	2 pages
25	1,110 words	2 ½ pages
30	1,330 words	3 pages

This is just a rough guide, but it will help with your word-count management, and ensure that you earn good marks across the assignment. (It should also be reassuring, since you don't have to write large volumes of material: the examiner is looking for quality, not quantity.)

- Don't try to 'hide' extra word count in appendices: this will not gain you marks. Use appendices only for legitimate supporting data, summarised in the body of the report.

- If you need to reduce your first-draft word count, look first for repetitions, superfluous illustrations/examples and irrelevant points: it may be easier to leave out a few short paragraphs than to cut words and phrases out of your writing style. (Unless you are a waffler, in which case, by all means: prune away!) Or consider whether some material might be conveyed in a diagram or table (excluding it from the word count) – with the added benefit of adding creativity and visual interest to your report.

- If you need to add to your first-draft word count, check whether you have *under*-written some parts of the task for the marks available, and add to those first. Add genuine content – *not* waffle!

- Don't forget to indicate your total word count on the front cover of your assignment.

4.2 Tackling the Exemplar Project

4.2.1 Specimen organisational background (Appendix 1)

The following overview, for the purposes of demonstration, is loosely based on a real-life organisation, but the case study organisation and its situation are essentially fictional.

Appendix 1: Organisation overview

The Wetland protection society

The Wetland Protection Society (WPS) is a leading UK conservation organisation, dedicated to preserving wetland ecosystems and habitats for the benefit of wildlife and human communities around the UK.

Background

Wetlands are areas of land saturated with moisture, providing a safe and supportive ecosystem for many different species of plants, fish, birds and insects. They perform useful functions in regulating local environments, but are also valuable as places for human recreational and educational activities such a wildlife observation, fishing, camping and field research.

By 1993, half the world's wetlands had been drained for development or flooded for use as recreational lakes (*New Scientist,* 1994). Since the 1970s, there has been a drive to preserve wetlands for their natural and educational functions.

Foundation and legal form

The WPS was founded in 1953 by a prominent ornithologist and nature writer, Sir Douglas Brown OBE. It was incorporated as a not-for-profit company limited by guarantee (with members acting as guarantors, rather than shareholders). It is defined as a voluntary organisation, set up for charitable purposes ('the advancement of environmental protection or improvement', as defined by the *Charities Act 2006*), and is registered as a charity in England, Wales and Scotland.

The Society has over 100,000 members, and enjoys the patronage of HRH Prince of Wales.

Aims and activities

The core aims of the Society are: to conserve wetlands and wetland species; to raise awareness of the issues that affect their survival; and to enhance people's lives through opportunities to learn about, be close to, and collaborate in the protection of, nature.

The key activities of the Society, in pursuit of these aims, include:

- *Wetland reserve management.* The Society manages six wetland reserves, with visitor centres enabling public access to designated areas, while restricting access to vulnerable areas. Together, these reserves cover some 1,500 hectares of wetland, receiving almost one million visitors per year. Some of the sites are designated as Special Protection Areas (under the EU directive on the Conservation of Wild Birds) or listed areas under the Convention on Wetlands of International Importance (Ramsar Convention, 1971).

- *Education.* The Society seeks to change public perception and foster public support for wetlands. Educational programs include guided tours for the general public, school visits, media liaison, visitor/information centres and information for Society members.

- *Research and environmental consultancy.* The Society conducts and publishes scientific research to enable conservation and planning bodies to understand and address the threats faced by wetland areas. Its consultancy division (WPS Consulting) is often contracted by corporations and government bodies to assess the impact of development plans and to recommend strategies for impact minimisation: all profits raised through the Consultancy are gifted back to the Society to support its conservation work.

- *Lobbying and influence.* The focus of lobbying is to secure protected status for key wetland areas and endangered species, and to oppose harmful development (eg the construction of dams) in sensitive areas.

Fundraising. In support of all the above activities, the Society raises funds via means such as: annual membership subscriptions (offering a range of member benefits, including free entry to WPS wetland centres and a free quarterly magazine); corporate membership and sponsorship; public donation appeals; events (including the annual Water Life Day volunteer fundraising day); government research and conservation grants; and commercial activities (such as consulting and merchandise sales).

In recent years, there have been increasing requests for the Society to participate in conservation ventures, lobbying campaigns and research programmes in overseas countries.

The UK charity sector

Each year, the British public gives nearly £5 billion to over 170,000 charities (Peck *et al,* 2004). According to the Charities Aid Foundation (CAF, 1996), the charitable categories which benefit most from voluntary donations in the UK include: health (eg cancer research), general welfare (eg the Salvation Army), international aid (eg Red Cross), heritage and environment (eg National Trust) and animal protection (eg RSPCA).

The WPS sees itself firmly in the heritage and environment category, but is often perceived as an animal protection charity. Environmental and wildlife charities tend to be supported by a younger and less well-off donor population than the national average (CAF, op cit), but also tend to have a good success rate in attracting corporate sponsorship, due to their positive and CSR-related associations.

Charities compete with each other for funds, and the charities that the WPS regards as its closest direct competitors are the Royal Society for the Protection of Birds (RSPB), the National Trust and the World Wide Fund for Nature (the top three conservation charities by voluntary income, [CAF, *op cit]*) as well as other conservation and wildlife charities. There is a positive level of co-operation between charities within this sector, however: major charities collaborate on lobbying and research funding, and even co-operate on marketing (eg holding bi-monthly meetings to co-ordinate their timetables of events and appeals).

Organisation structure

The Society employs a core of around 120 permanent staff, as well as volunteers (eg as centre guides) and contractors (eg on research projects and event management). The permanent management structure of the Society can be summarised as follows.

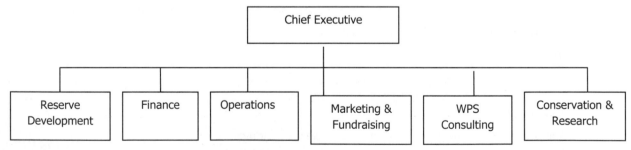

In addition, the Society has a Council, responsible for the general control and management of the charity, comprising a Chair, Treasurer and a number of other distinguished naturalists and academics.

 EXAM TIP

format/presentation

A few things to notice about our specimen overview:

- It occupies a maximum of two A4 pages.

- It gives a fairly broad overview, but because of the technical nature of the organisation's activities, it focuses in more detail on some areas (in order to brief the examiner) than another organisation might require. When writing your overview, you might have more room for a survey of organisation culture, key suppliers/distributors/allies, business processes, future plans and so on: see some of the other Case Study organisation backgrounds in this Workbook for examples. Be selective in the information you include.

- It covers the details required by the project brief – but not in a formulaic way: 'aims and activities' replaces 'products/services', for example, and 'the charity sector' replaces 'target market'. Be flexible in your thinking, and remember to contextualise your material to the particular organisation you are looking at.

- It deliberately includes elements which will support later discussion of relationship marketing (the theme of the project): mentioning a range of stakeholder audiences, the potential for an international element, and a number of potential RM activities (including fundraising and lobbying).

- It references sources of information (which would be cited in the References appendix of the report).

This task is worth doing well. Although it earns no marks, it may be the first thing the assessor reads, and therefore needs to create a good first impression of your clarity, judgement and professionalism.

ACTIVITY

application

If you haven't already done so, now would be a good time to attempt a first draft of your Organisation Overview. If you haven't chosen an organisation for your project, draft an overview of any organisation that interests you: still good practice. Consider what sorts of information are relevant – and at what depth, in order for you to keep to two pages and still give a good overview briefing.

4.2.2 Specimen stakeholder audit (Appendix 2)

Task One

Undertake an audit of the stakeholders to:

- Identify the major stakeholders in your organisation
- Explain their level of influence and impact on relationship marketing.

Your audit findings should be included as an appendix to your report (maximum of four A4 pages).

EXAM TIP

presentation/format

The following is a fairly generic audit of the 'Wetlands Protection Society' (overviewed in Section 5.5.1), with only partial content in some areas. It is designed to demonstrate the kinds of tools of analysis you might use, rather than focusing on content (which will be irrelevant to your own project). However, note how the content is intended to demonstrate attention to the Exemplar audit task requirements *and* to provide material in support of the project report tasks.

In fact, the Exemplar requirements are less specific, detailed and clear than any of the subsequent 'live' project briefs. What, for example, does it mean to address a stakeholder's 'impact on relationship marketing'? What if the organisation isn't currently doing any relationship marketing? We have tried to clarify and work with the requirement given, but be reassured: 'live' project briefs have been much more helpful!

Appendix 1: Stakeholder audit

Audit methodology

An audit of WPS stakeholders was undertaken, using the following methodologies.

- A survey of colleagues, conducted via the WPS Intranet discussion board.

- Perusal of WPS statements and documentary evidence in regard to the Society's relationships with stakeholder groups, stakeholder feedback and relationship performance measures.

- Personal interviews with the Operations Manager and Marketing & Fundraising Manager

- Secondary research on stakeholder theory and stakeholder analysis methodologies. (See the Selected Bibliography attached as Appendix 5 of this report.)

Identification of stakeholder groups

As for most public sector and not-for-profit organisations (Bryson, 2004), there are multiple diverse stakeholder groups with a legitimate (though not necessarily formal or contractual) stake in the organisation's activities. A number of stakeholder groups was identified by the in-house survey. The following table includes external stakeholders identified by all departments.

Table A1.1   Identified stakeholder groups in WPS

Internal stakeholders	Connected stakeholders	External stakeholders
Council	Members	Donors
Directors	Volunteers	Media and political audiences (MPs, MEPs, political press, political advisors)
Employees	Consultancy clients	Government
From Marketing & Fundraising Dept viewpoint:	Suppliers	Regulatory bodies (eg Charities Commission, conservation bodies)
Other functions/ divisions (See Appendix 1)		Direct beneficiaries (wetland species)
		Indirect beneficiaries (visitors, educators, society, local community, future generations)
		Other charities
		Land developers

Power and interest assessment

A systematic power assessment was conducted to identify stakeholders with high and low influence on WPS's relationship marketing, using a checklist of their 'indicators of power' (Johnson & Scholes, 2007):

Internal stakeholders were evaluated on the dimensions: status (position in hierarchy, average grade of staff); claim on resources (number of staff, budget as percentage of total); representation (number of Council members in the discipline, influence of the Director); and symbols (quality of accommodation, access to support services, profile in WPS culture).

External stakeholders were marked on the dimensions: status (WPS response to demands), resource dependence (size of donation/contribution, criticality of supplies), negotiating arrangements (preparedness of WPS to consult/negotiate on decisions) and symbols (hospitality offered, amount of communication, level of WPS staff dealt with).

 EXAM TIP

application

If you have fewer stakeholders to deal with, you might be able to include the power assessment findings in full. If suppliers are a major component of the stakeholder environment, you might choose to add a supporting Kraljic matrix analysis or supply chain map, to assess their power/importance to the organisation.

A qualitative assessment was also made of the 'interest' of identified stakeholder groups: that is, how likely they are to attempt to influence WPS to get their needs met or their interests protected, or to oppose or support a particular decision (Mendelow, 1985).

Stakeholder map: power/interest matrix

Mendelow (ibid) developed a simple matrix to plot two factors for each stakeholder: (a) how interested it is in influencing the organisation and (b) whether it has the power or influence to do so. On the basis of these two factors, the matrix recommends the most appropriate type of relationship to establish with each 'quadrant' of stakeholder group. The following figure shows the results of power/interest analysis for WPS stakeholders. The symbols [+] and [-] are used, according to whether each group is, broadly, a supporter or opponent of the aims and activities of WPS.

Figure A1.1   Power/interest matrix for stakeholders in WPS relationship marketing

Level of interest

	Low	High
Low	**Quadrant A** Donors [+] Indirect beneficiaries [+/-]	**Quadrant B** Volunteers [+] Direct beneficiaries [+] Other charities [+/-] Consultancy clients [+/-]
High	**Quadrant C** Media/political audiences [+/-] Government and regulatory bodies [+/-]	**Quadrant D** Members [+/-] Employees [+/-] Suppliers [+/-] Land developers [-] WPS functions/departments [+] Council and Directors [+]

Level of power

The current positioning of each stakeholder may be justified as follows.

- Influence is considered with particular reference to the stakeholder's potential impact on WPS's relationship marketing.

- Mendelow's recommended strategies for each quadrant are included. However, it may also be desirable to reposition stakeholders (Johnson & Scholes, 2007): eg to 'mobilise' high-power supporters by increasing their interest, or to reduce the power of highly-interested opponents.

Table A1.2   Explanation of power/interest matrix positionings

Quadrant A: Minimal effort

Stakeholder	Interest	Influence/power
Donors	Fairly low: Most 'occasional' (ie non-member) donors have only a passing interest in the cause and donate only on appeal.	Fairly low: Occasional donors are generally not sufficiently homogenous or organised to exercise collective influence. However, donors have individual power to withhold donations, which if exercised en masse would significantly impact on WPS funding.
Indirect beneficiaries	Fairly low: Many indirect beneficiaries are not aware of how they benefit from WPS activity: current marketing focuses on mass awareness campaigns to this group. Repeat	Fairly low: Most groups are insufficiently homogenous or organised to exercise collective influence, despite having the individual power to withhold or withdraw their use of WPS facilities (and therefore entrance fees). Conversely,

Stakeholder	Interest	Influence/power
	visitors and educators are perhaps closer to quadrant B, with targeted relationship marketing direct at these groups to maintain their interest.	however, as a target audience, this group has large potential to add support and revenue, and should therefore be an influence on WPS's RM planning.

Quadrant B: keep informed, to satisfy interest without arousing power-seeking opposition

Stakeholder	Interest	Influence/power
Volunteers	Fairly high: Regular volunteers are motivated by commitment to the Society and its cause, and by the extrinsic and intrinsic rewards of helping (merchandise, free membership, belonging, feel good factor). One-off volunteers may be less interested in on-going issues/participation.	Fairly low: Not sufficiently homogenous or organised to exercise collective influence, despite having individual power to withhold or withdraw their labour. WPS activities are not highly labour intensive, but experienced volunteers (eg to lead Clean Up days and act as guides in Wetland centres) have expert/ resource power (French & Raven, 1958): the need for a stable volunteer base should influence WPS's volunteer relations practices.
Direct beneficiaries	High: Wetland species are the raison d'être of the Society, and depend on its activities for their survival. They have a high – albeit unknowing – interest in WPS projects.	Low: Flora and fauna have no advocates or power to impact decisions: they are classified as 'voiceless' or 'silent' stakeholders (Freeman; Egan, 1994). However, they may be said to have high influence within WPS, by virtue of their importance to the Society's mission and values. RM, among other strategies, will be shaped to directly or indirectly support their interests.
Other charities	Fairly high: Other conservation charities are both partners in the cause and competitors in relation to funding, volunteers and media/public profile.	Fairly low: Other charities' activities will have some influence on WPS's RM plans, which are in part competitive in aim. There is also, however, an industry 'understanding' that outright competition (eg clashing appeal/event dates) is unhelpful to the cause, so major parties mutually adapt their RM and other marketing plans.
Consultancy clients	High: Clients are the most clearly identified 'customers' of WPS, and as such have a strong interest in the services, information and quality of relationship provided.	Fairly low: Most clients represent one-off projects and therefore do not have on-going influence on WPS policy (other than our learning from client feedback). Long-term clients (eg the Environment Agency) have considerable resource power (to award or withhold business), and would be positioned in Quadrant D.

Quadrant C: keep satisfied, to avoid arousal of interested opposition

Stakeholder	Interest	Influence/power
Media/political audiences	Fairly low: Both audiences have multiple interests, and wetlands issues will be low priority unless WPS works to raise their profile and urgency.	High: Both audiences are potential sources of influence for WPS, and therefore have considerable resource power (to give or withhold access to decision-making processes, public opinion etc). Since use of these resources depends heavily on relationship building, these have a strong impact on WPS's use of RM approaches.
Government and regulatory bodies	Fairly low: These bodies have an interest in WPS activity (use of funding grants, research information for policy-making, compliance with regulations and treaties etc), but this tends to focus on specific relevant projects or critical incidents, rather than continual activity.	High: These bodies have direct legitimate power to regulate WPS activity, plus resource power to give or withhold funding and support. The Charities Commission particularly exercises its power in regard to RM, with the requirements for transparency and reporting to stakeholders.

Quadrant D: Key players (high priority relationship management and communication)

Stakeholder	Interest	Influence/power
Members	Fairly high: Committed (repeat, life, active) members have a strong interest in the cause and WPS activity. One off members tend to have short-term self-interest (eg in membership benefits), and are less likely to seek to shape WPS plans.	Fairly high: Members have legitimate collective power to vote at annual general meetings, as well as resource power to give or withhold their subscriptions and volunteer labour. They are also a helpful source of feedback information for the Society, and a cost-effective (pre-identified, pre-motivated) audience for donation/volunteer appeals: they are therefore a key target of RM activity.
Employees	Fairly high: Staff have an interest in maintaining their employment, but also tend to be highly committed to the cause.	Fairly high: Staff have individual resource power to withdraw commitment and skills, and this is a strong influence where specialist professional staff are employed (eg in consultancy, research and conservation). At the interface with external audiences (eg education, media relations, consultancy), internal relationship management is vital to ensure that staff (otherwise scientific and internally focused in their outlook) are prepared to communicate effectively with external 'customers'. Staff effectively make up an internal market for RM activity (Peck et al, 1999).
Suppliers	Fairly high: For some suppliers (eg of research services), WPS represents a major proportion of their business, in ongoing partnership, and these firms therefore have a high interest. For others (eg large suppliers of one-off merchandise stocks), interest will not be as high.	Fairly high: Some suppliers (eg of research services) have high influence by virtue of providing (a) strategically important and (b) scarce/hard-to-source commodities, and therefore have a high degree of influence. In such conditions, supplier relationship development is a priority, in order to secure and develop supply (Kraljic,1983). Less important items can be sourced with a less relational approach. Supplier analysis will therefore influence RM priorities.
Land developers	High: Developers have a high financial interest in particular projects (eg construction of a dam or residential development) which may be opposed and defeated by WPS research and lobbying.	Fairly high: Although WPS often has political influence, conservation regulations and public opinion on its side in conflict with developers, they too employ researchers and lobbyists, and may have the support of investors, local governments, and potential beneficiaries. This primarily puts pressure on WPS's public, media and political relations activities, in order to compete successfully for decisions.
WPS functions/ departments	High: All functions have an interest in the success of the Marketing & Fundraising department, as a driver of funding and public awareness for their activities.	High: Marketing & Fundraising sees the other departments as internal customers of their activity (including RM): their needs, and the information flowing from them, are essential components in RM planning and decision-making.
Council & Directors	High: These teams are ultimately responsible for (and evaluated according to) the management and performance of WPS. They may not have a detailed interest in day-to-day RM issues, but they are strongly invested in its long-term results.	High: These groups have legitimate power or authority ultimately to direct organisational (and RM) activity at a strategic or policy level, and to hold managers accountable for results. All RM activity must be aligned with strategies and policies set at the board/council level.

Critical incidents in stakeholder relationship management

Interview respondents identified a number of critical incidents illustrating relationship management issues.

- The declaration of Carmarthen Bay as the UK's first marine Special Protection Area in 2003, after WPS surveys demonstrated its importance for Common Scooters, and the dropping of plans to build a dam at the main area for breeding Pink-footed Geese in Thjorsarver, Iceland in 2004, after successful lobbying by WSP. These incidents were interpreted as demonstrating successful use of relationship marketing in the areas of corporate consultancy, media relations and lobbying initiatives.

- A purchasing and public relations 'disaster' in which WPS's Chinese supplier of 'Their Future Our Future' merchandise was found to have been polluting rivers in the area of its factories. This was interpreted as highlighting financial and reputational risks arising from WPS's supplier selection and supplier management practices.

- A disappointing response to the 2006 'Their Future Our Future' fundraising appeal. Street collections, letter box drops, raffle ticket sales and general donations were down 14% on previous years, and traditionally account for some 10% of total value of donations by non-members. Attributed to 'compassion fatigue', fears of economic recession, increasing competition and public assumptions as to the charitable funding now provided by National Lottery, this was interpreted as highlighting the need to secure more stable funding by 'leveraging' memberships: focusing on recruiting, retaining and upgrading members to maximum their loyalty and lifetime value to the cause.

 EXAM TIP

application

We have added these findings because they contribute to the stakeholder analysis – but also, specifically, because they will support the selection of key stakeholders and relationship management priorities, for the body of the report. In other words, they provide good raw material for the report. You will need to be selective about what information you gather for your audit, and what findings you choose to include (and at what level of detail) in your appendix: remember, you only have four A4 pages...

4.2.3 Formal report

 EXAM TIP

application

We are not going to present a full formal report, the contents of which will be largely irrelevant to your actual project. We will simply highlight how you might go about tackling each component of the task set in the Exemplar Project, with reference to the specimen organisation and stakeholder audit findings set out in Sections 5.5.1 and 5.5.2, and provide note-form specimen points for an answer.

We will also add notes on how different types of organisations or findings might have led to different approaches. Remember, the key point is that you will need systematically to fulfil the specific task requirements and assessment criteria for your own project brief.

Task Two

Produce a formal report for your Corporate Communications Manager in which you: ...

 EXAM TIP

format

We have already discussed suggestions for structuring and presenting a formal report. You might like to have a look at some real-life examples, in order to avoid a formulaic approach.

- See if you can get hold of some formal in-house reports compiled for or by your work organisation: if the 'house style' is helpful, why not adopt it?

- For more creative report presentations, check out corporate reports aimed at stakeholders. For example, from the Marks & Spencer website (http://www.corporate.marksandspencer.com) you can download the company's 'How we do business' report.

Provide a brief background to your chosen organisation, its products/services, customer base and position in market (maximum two sides of A4, to be included as an appendix)

Already completed: see section 5.5.1.

Explain the concept of relationship marketing in the context of the organisation's stakeholders in achieving stakeholder interest, involvement, commitment and loyalty

  EXAM TIP

concept/application

This is mostly bookwork, but remember that you have been asked to apply the concepts in the context of *the* organisation's stakeholders – not just 'any organisation's stakeholders'. Make sure that your points are relevant to the context (type of organisation, sector, policies) and use illustrative examples from the organisation.

- Define relationship marketing: eg 'The process of creating, maintaining and enhancing strong, value-laden relationships with customers and other stakeholders (Kotler et al, 1999, p 11) or 'All marketing activities directed towards establishing, developing and maintaining successful relational exchanges' (Morgan & Hunt, 1994, p 22)

- Explain broadly why stakeholder interest, involvement, commitment and loyalty are important, using examples from WPS: for example, media and visitor interest in the cause raising awareness/revenue; involvement of members as volunteers enabling activity; commitment of members enhancing lobbying, and maintaining membership despite competition from other causes/charities; and loyalty supporting repeat on-going donation for stable and predictable funding.

- Describe the key features and characteristics of relationship marketing, using examples of stakeholders and activities drawn from WPS:

  - A shift from marketing activities which emphasise acquisition to retention: not just gaining new members, but retaining and deepening involvement of existing members (up-selling and cross-selling membership, prompting advocacy)

  - The development of on-going (and if possible, constantly deepening and improving) relationships as opposed to one-off transactions: converting one-off street donations to memberships, and moving members to higher 'grades'

  - The maximisation of life-time value: prioritising potentially profitable donor/members (eg lifetime, corporate and educational members)

  - The encouragement of cross-functionally-based marketing: all contacts (eg with consultants, researchers, conservationists) are seen as stakeholder marketing opportunities

  - The development of supportive network relationships with other internal and external stakeholders: eg Marketing and Fundraising working with other departments to enhance member experience; working with other charities on lobbying programmes; developing suppliers to enhance services and merchandise.

- A distinctive feature of the stakeholder audit (Appendix 2, section 4) was the number of stakeholder groups identified as either ambivalent about WPS (eg local communities torn between wetland preservation and the benefits of development), or generally supportive but identified as potential opponents of particular WPS plans or conduct (eg competitors with specific conflicts of interest, or members who might agree with some of our policies and not others). This prioritises stakeholder relations and communication: a key driver for relationship marketing.

  EXAM TIP

application

There is other content you could include here – but you have to be careful not to pre-empt your content for following sections: eg by discussing benefits or relationship marketing, or including too many suggestions which you might need for your marketing/communications plan.

This content should be useable for other types of organisation, except that you might include 'customers' in a more explicit way in your examples.

Summarise your audit findings, including the identification of key stakeholders, their level of influence and the impact on relationship marketing

 EXAM TIP

concept/application

This is designed to test your ability to select the most relevant material from your findings, and to draw out key points in a way that will provide a justification for the following section of your report. Don't just repeat your audit findings verbatim. And don't forget to cross-reference your summary to your Appendix, clearly numbered.

- An audit was undertaken to identify key stakeholders in WPS, and to assess the nature and level of their impact on WPS's relationship marketing and potential future use of relationship marketing. (For research methodology and detailed findings, see Appendix 2.)

- Key stakeholders identified by the audit, with short explanations where necessary.

- Donors and indirect beneficiaries (including visitors to the wetland centres) have relatively little power or interest to influence current relationship marketing (or other) plans. However, since these groups are broadly supportive of WPS and its cause, there might be a case for increasing relationship marketing to these groups, in order to mobilise their support.

- Volunteers, other charities and consultancy clients have a high interest in influencing WPS strategy, but generally (with the exception of major long-term clients) have little power to do so. However, again, since these groups can be of benefit to WPS in various ways, there may be a case for increasing relationship marketing to these groups: to increase volunteer loyalty/commitment, to minimise harmful competition with other charities; and to retain profitable clients.

- The direct beneficiaries of our activity have no 'direct' influence, as 'voiceless' stakeholders (Egan, 1994), but due to the Society's mission, all relationship marketing (and other) activity is directed to their benefit: the test of any relationship marketing initiative should be its long-term benefit to wetland species.

- Media, political audiences, government and regulatory bodies have high potential influence on WPS policy, because of their legitimate power and ability to mobilise public opinion. They will mainly impact on relationship marketing as key audiences for such activity: Peck et al (1999) emphasise the importance of the 'influence market' as part of the network of relationships.

- Members, employees, suppliers, other WPS functions and the WPS council and directors all have a high degree of influence on policy, through legitimate power, resource power and/or expert power (French and Raven, 1958). They impact on relationship marketing as key internal, supply and customer markets (Peck et al, op cit). Internal stakeholders are also likely to be implementers of cross-functional relationship marketing activity, or suppliers of information and support for relationship marketing by the M & F function.

- WPS's relationship marketing was found to be effective in the area of media and lobbying management, but less effective in the areas of supplier relationship management (creating financial and reputational risk) and the conversion of one-off and occasional donors to membership (failing to protect and maximise donations and donor profitability).

Select ONE internal and ONE external stakeholder group that you propose to develop a relationship marketing approach with, giving reasons for your choice

EXAM TIP

concept/application

You will often be asked to select a stakeholder or aspect, in order to allow more detailed focus. There is no right or wrong choice: just make sure that you 'give reasons for' or 'justify' your choice. In this case, it is an important choice of which stakeholders to prioritise (part of the process of relationship management) for relationship marketing, arising from your stakeholder analysis – and it is worth demonstrating your awareness of this too.

- Not all stakeholder groups are worth investing attention and money in relationship marketing: there is a need to prioritise relationships and develop a portfolio of relationship types (Ford et al, 2003).. The process of relationship management begins with this process of analysing and prioritising customers or other stakeholders: this is one outcome from a Mendelow power/interest analysis (see Appendix 2, section 4).

- Priority should be given to stakeholders who are most potentially beneficial or profitable to the organisation, or offer a high return on relationship investment; stakeholders who present a potential risk to the organisation, its brand or reputation, which must be managed; and relationships which offer realistic potential for adding value with on-going development.

- In addition, relationship marketing requires certain conditions in order to be effective: access to stakeholders' contact details (in order to facilitate contact); stakeholder permission to receive on-going contact; and potential for mutual benefit (in order to develop genuine relationship and stakeholder willingness).

- Internal stakeholder group selected: employees, with specific focus on the staff at the wetlands reserve centres. They are the staff most regularly at the interface with external 'customers' (visitors, educators) and motivated donors (captured at the point of awareness/enjoyment). They are therefore a key source of leverage to convert one-off and occasional visitors to repeat visitors and, where possible, members, through their customer service; ability to communicate enthusiasm for wetlands; ability to cross-sell and up-sell memberships; ability to implement donation appeals and promotions on-site.

  This is an aspect of internal marketing: 'the acknowledgement of the impact of employee behaviour and attitudes on the relationship between staff and external customers' (Peck et al, op cit, p 313). There are well-established channels of contact with these employees, which can be used for more relational purposes, and significant opportunities for mutual benefit: better performance in return for extrinsic and intrinsic rewards (for which suggestions are made below).

- External stakeholder group selected: one-off and occasional donors, including visitors to wetland reserve centres. Although not featuring highly on the priority list (arising from the Mendelow matrix), this group has been identified as a significant source of wasted potential contribution.

  With relatively little extra effort and expense, street/appeal donors and visitors may be converted into members and up the 'ladder of loyalty' (Kotler 1997) to lifetime members. WPS's has existing contact details, or the potential to gather them, for this group, at the point at which they are most motivated/interested (having experienced a wetland or received information prior to donation). This potential may be leveraged for significant added donations, greater predictability of funding, advocacy and involvement. The decline in non-member donations identified in the stakeholder audit (see Appendix 2, Section 6) makes this an immediate priority to protect funding: it is less costly to retain donors than to repeatedly acquire new ones (Reichheld, 1996).

EXAM TIP

concept/application

Building on the stakeholder audit, you might equally well have chosen suppliers as a priority external stakeholder group, because of the identified problems and their negative impacts.

Similarly, if you had separately analysed different internal departments of WPS, you might have selected a particular function as your internal stakeholder: if the Finance function often conflicts with Marketing & Fundraising over the cost of its activities, say; or if M & F depended on Research and Conservation function for information and success stories to use in its marketing.

Explain the benefits of relationship marketing to each of these stakeholder groups

 EXAM TIP

concept/application

This is more or less straight bookwork on the benefits of relationship marketing, except that you need to apply your points to each of the specific stakeholders you have selected. We have just given a brief checklist of the kinds of points you might make. Note that, in your report structure, you could have included this section within the previous one: identified your internal stakeholder, explained why you chose it, and then enumerated the benefits of relationship marketing to it – and then gone through the same three processes for your external stakeholder.

Benefits of relationship marketing to wetland centre staff:

- Loyalty and retention: reduced staff turnover and costs of recruitment/training

- Empowerment of staff to offer better levels of service to visitors: competitive advantage over other recreational/educational venues

- Enhanced 'employer brand' as good employer: attract quality staff

- Compliance with legal requirements for staff consultation and involvement

- Improved multi-directional communication throughout the organisation

- Improved employee morale and employee relations: stable and co-operative relationships, commitment and mutuality (Armstrong, 2000).

 EXAM TIP

concept/application

You might choose to support your argument about the staff with an illustration and explanation of Reichheld's 'service profit cycle' or loyalty-based cycle of growth (see Figures 6.3 and 9.1 in the Study Text) – perhaps placing this analysis in an Appendix.

Benefits of relationship marketing to one-off and occasional visitors to centres

- Ladder of loyalty: illustrate with diagram, and explain desirability of each stage

- Economics of retention v acquisition (Reichheld, 1996): lower costs of contact and donation (eg by legacy, direct debit); potential for increased revenue (through cross-selling and up-selling of membership); cost-effective source of word-of-mouth referrals to potential new members

- Increased loyalty and commitment: reduced risk of switching to other charities, or ceasing donation

- Cost-effective marketing communication channels can be established (with greater openness to further contact and appeals)

- Information on donor/visitor needs and wants can be more effectively gathered, for improved planning and value/reward creation

- Enhanced issues and crisis management (eg re supplier 'Their future, our future' merchandise), by personal contact

- Positive word-of-mouth promotion and advocacy with family and friends, or co-option into political advocacy

EXAM TIP

concept/application

You might choose to support your argument about the donors with a 'donor pyramid' analysis (in an appendix) showing how people are moved up the ladder of loyalty from potential members, to occasional visitors/donors, to members and then to increasing levels of committed/involved membership. (See the RSPB example in chapter 4 of the Study Text.)

Develop a co-ordinated marketing and communications plan that is responsive to the needs of your identified stakeholder groups and adds value to the relationship

EXAM TIP

concept/application

This is an unusually complex requirement, in asking for both a marketing (mix) and a marketing communications plan: 'live' project briefs will probably ask for one or the other. Remember, only 15 marks is available for each task. Try not to duplicate your points for the 'Promotion' part of the marketing mix when you come to marketing communication.

This is your opportunity (a) to show your ability to *apply* theory in practice, with realistic and cost-effective planning, and (b) to be creative. You might use illustrative examples from other charities or corporate practice, for example, with copies of advertisements or analyses in numbered/referenced appendices. We have just given some brief note-form ideas here.

Note also that you could structure this task in different ways: a combined marketing/communication plan for each stakeholder separately; or a marketing plan for both followed by a communications plan for both; or even a combined marketing/communication plan for both. It will depend on how different the needs of your stakeholder groups are.

Marketing & Communications Plan: Wetlands Reserve Staff

I. Marketing objective

Increase percentage of reserve staff demonstrably exercising front-line marketing roles (signing up volunteers, cross-selling and up-selling memberships, adjusting customer complaints) by 20% in next nine months.

EXAM TIP

concept

Note that we have attempted to draft a SMART objective, as recommended in the brief guidance.

II. Key needs and drivers of the staff

Brief explanation of:

Information needs (to perform front-line marketing tasks, to feel confident and satisfied in their work)

Training needs, focusing on core competencies for customer service, front-line PR and membership sales

Motivators: growth in the job, fair pay and benefits, opportunity to contribute meaningfully to the cause, enjoyment of contact with the public

Concerns: risk of error when using initiative to serve customers; risk of alienating customers by 'pushing' membership

You might back up these points with an internal customer segmentation: eg Christopher *et al*'s matrix using the dimensions closeness to external customers and involvement in marketing activity (see the Study Text, Chapter 9). Reserve staff would be 'contactors': frequent customer contact and heavy involvement in conventional marketing activities. Contactors need to be well versed in the firm's marketing strategies, and trained, prepared and motivated to serve customers on a day-to-day basis in a responsive manner.

You might also include the results of staff attitude survey in an appendix, giving actual data on employee's perceived needs, concerns and expectations about their roles.

Magic formula icons are: format, concept, application or evaluation. Exam tip text.

III. Internal marketing action plan

The framework of the marketing mix has been applied to internal customers, using the method suggested by Jobber (2007, p 864).

(i)   Product: the marketing plan and strategies being proposed to staff, together with the resources necessary to make the plan successful

Prepare a relationship marketing plan for visitors to wetland centres (see section IV) below

Ensure that support and resources are available: M & F staff for briefing and coaching, administrative support (eg brochures, membership information and registration forms)

Prepare processes to motivate and capture visitor sign-up: loyalty programmes, promotional competitions (to capture contact details)

(ii)   Price: what staff are being asked to pay or sacrifice as a result of accepting the plan

Minimise perceived sacrifice/risk on part of staff, by emphasising support, training and resources available

Emphasise value gained in return for extra effort: new skills, greater contribution to the cause

Add rewards/incentives (without incurring cost): eg Marketer of the Month award (eg for most members signed up), Visitor award (for most commendations in visitor feedback forms) and Centre of the Month (for reserve with most members signed up)

Address identified concerns: emphasise support for initiative, tolerance of learning curve; re-define perceptions of 'pushy' marketing as 'helping customers to maximise contribution to the cause'

(iii)   Promotion/communications: the media and messages used to inform, persuade and gain the support of staff for the plan

Place: how the plan and communications are delivered to staff.

Set up a staff briefing at each reserve centre, covering: the visitor relationship marketing plan, the nature and importance of the front-line marketing role, the importance of converting visitors into members

Follow up with on-the-job coaching programme and mentoring system (using more confident/experienced staff to support others)

Issue staff briefing pack, setting out visitor marketing plan in user-friendly language; emphasising the importance and contribution of the front-line role; including guidelines for staff

Set up dedicated intranet pages for reserve centre staff: on-going guidance and tips, news of staff awards, blogs by award winners, discussion boards for good news and advice swapping

Feature centre staff members in the WetLife Newsletter, Society web site and reports: emphasise importance and inclusion within 'family' of WPS (despite geographic isolation)

Gather and feed back membership sign-up numbers and donation value for each centre on a monthly basis, so that staff can monitor and celebrate their financial contribution to the cause.

Use email for on-going mentoring, supporting and question-answering by a member of the Marketing & Fundraising team.

IV   Timetable

Set up plan and resources for visitor/donor marketing: months 1-3

Implement briefing and coaching programmes: month 4

Results/progress measurement: months 6-9

V   Monitoring and control

See Section X below.

Marketing & Communications Plan: One-off and occasional visitors/donors

I. Marketing objective

Add 5,000 new WPS members within the next twelve months; increase percentage of 5-year, 10-year and life memberships by 3% within the next twelve months.

II. Key needs and drivers of non-member donors/visitors

Brief explanation of:

Information needs (to motivate to become members: need for and use of membership finds; benefits of membership; benefits of long-term membership)

Expectations of value: feel good factor (from donation); life-enhancing, fun leisure experience (from visits); educational value (from information obtained); tangible value in exchange for donation (eg photos, merchandise, entertainment, information).

Concerns: uncertainty of priority of wetlands in face of human welfare needs, disasters etc; lack of trust re use of charitable funds; perception that National Lottery and government/EU grants cover the need; economic uncertainty re long-term financial commitment.

 EXAM TIP

 concept

You might back up these points with a donor segmentation, published data on charitable giving or visitor survey results in an appendix, giving actual data on donor's perceived needs, expectations and concerns.

III. Donor/visitor marketing action plan

(i)   Product

Define bundle of benefits exclusive to members (membership card, magazine, free entry to wetland centres, priority booking for events, 'adopt a species' programme) and higher classes of membership (gold card, badge, acknowledgement, VIP entry to special events, naming rights)

Emphasise symbolic aspects: maximised contribution, part of a prestigious society, special access

(ii)   Price

Price incentives to become member: more cost-effective donation via credit card, direct debit, covenant; discounted annual fee for 5/10 year and life membership

Price incentives to sign up now: discounted annual membership during promotion/appeal period.

Reassurance re: use of funds; ability to cancel membership at any time if necessary; amount of government grants in relation to need

Emphasise added value benefits received.

  EXAM TIP ▪▪▪▪▪▪ concept

You may want to add a table (or appendix) showing the actual grades of membership, membership fees, and associated benefits.

(iii)   Promotion/communications

Advertising (within current plan/budget) to raise awareness of the cause : discuss with advertising agency the possibility of adding messages re importance and benefits of membership (contribution, feel-good, belonging, special access). TV advertising is currently used only in the run up to major appeals; magazine advertising regularly, targeting pre-motivated audiences (nature, leisure, travel, bird-watching, conservation titles) with full-colour images for high interest/impact.

Web site (as currently) to inform potential donors, visitors and educators: add stronger incentives to click on 'Membership' link. Emphasise special benefits of membership, contribution ('if you want to do more...'), belonging ('join us') etc. On membership page, emphasise product/price messages outlined above. Consider adding interactive on-line games (eg 'find the crested grebe'), virtual tours etc to motivate repeat visits/exposures.

Direct selling by street collectors and visitor centre staff: opportunity to persuade pre-motivated donors of the benefits of upgrading to membership, and/or to capture contact details.

Direct permission-based marketing to database of pre-qualified targets (donors, visitors, enquirers): via mail, e-mail and SMS (according to preference)

Visits and community projects by members, researchers, conservation and visitor centre staff: eg school presentations (to sign up individual, family and/or school membership); community 'clean up' projects; individual member initiatives in schools, workplaces etc (eg 'adopt a species' programmes, corporate days out at the wetland)

Sales promotion: devise limited-time-only incentives to sign up for membership eg discounted membership; free 'endangered species' screen saver, or branded pen/baseball cap with membership. Consider a promotional competition (requiring web site visit to answer questions), gathering contact details and permission-to-contact.

Special events: in addition to current appeal-related events, consider offering entertainment/education special events at reserves eg 'Dawn Chorus' or 'Twilight Tours', or outdoor concerts and theatrical presentations. Entry could be offered to members only, or at a reduced rate for members, or with VIP booking for members. This would also create opportunities for members of the public to experience the wetland, and for the promotion of membership by centre staff and event MCs.

  EXAM TIP ▪▪▪▪▪▪ concept

We have given as broad a range of suggestions as we can. You may want to be more selective at greater depth. You may also want to add an appendix with examples of advertisements or web pages used by WPS or other similar charities.

(iv)   Place

Membership sign-up or contact details gathered in person at point of donation (eg street collectors, events) and visitor centres; and via direct response mechanisms (eg letter box appeals, web donations and promotional competitions)

Once contact details and permission-to-contact obtained: direct mail, e-mail and SMS contacts to send information, offers and invitations, feedback questionnaires etc

Collaborative 'donation/sign-up' centres (using info desks and forms): eg at branches of supermarkets or banks

(v)   Process

Prepare information/forms for contact details gathering and membership signup, and web equivalents

Ensure that forms are promptly returned to WPS, contacts databased and memberships actioned

Assign responsibility for driving potential member, new member and upgraded member contacts

(vi)   People

Brief, train and empower visitor centre staff (see separate marketing plan), volunteer collectors, membership co-ordinators, database co-ordinators etc.

(v)   Physicals

Add tangible value to membership offering: membership card, information pack, newsletter, branded badge/merchandise (for purchase, or free to higher-grade members)

Ensure that WPS collectors and staff are recognisable and present the brand appropriately: eg logo on shirts and caps; ID cards and so on.

IV   Timetable

Implementation: 6 months

V   Monitoring and control

See Section X below.

8.   Identify and evaluate a range of methods that you could utilise to measure the success of your marketing and communications mix.

 EXAM TIP   concept

The content of this section will obviously vary according to the nature of the plan you are trying to measure; what marketing objectives you have set; and what kind of organisation you are focusing on. (For example, is it meaningful to talk about 'sales volume' or 'repeat sales'? Are media exposure, share of voice or market share a priority?) Even if you *know* that objectives-based evaluation is the most effective method, given your SMART objectives, note that you need to 'identify and evaluate a range of methods'... Note also that you could have included this section within your marketing plans for each stakeholder, under the 'monitoring and control' headings, if you wished.

This is more or less straight bookwork, as long as you ensure that all the methods you choose are relevant. We've just skimmed a range of possibilities, to show how broad your thinking needs to be – and how you need to tailor your methods to the circumstances.

Measuring the donor/visitor marketing plan

Response/enquiry measurement. WPS currently uses response coupons in direct mail and print advertising: coupons can be counted and data broken down according to medium (via identification code) and respondent segment (eg visitor, first-time donor, repeat donor, member). There is little additional cost, other than staff/computer time, in conducting this analysis, and it will be particularly helpful in measuring progress towards the stated objective of the plan. Data should also be monitored on conversion of enquiries to memberships; numbers of new memberships; and numbers of upgraded memberships contained in responses. The member database should also be able to provide the membership figures and changes for stated periods.

Similar measurement can be made through response/enquiry telephone lines (using computer telephony integration to input caller details direct to database) and web site traffic and transaction analysis (carried out automatically by the software)

It would also be helpful to run inquiry tests as new marketing initiatives are introduced, to identify the success of particular tools or promotions, and progress over the period of the plan, in terms of number of inquiries and cost per inquiry.

Media exposure and share of voice measurement, and recall and recognition testing, are already utilised by WPS's advertising agency to cover advertising and PR, but these are of less relevance, as the marketing objective is focused on conversion to memberships.

Internal financial analysis should track measurable increases in membership fees and contributions over time. This will be a useful measure, to demonstrate that discount incentives (and other costs of motivating membership) are 'profitable' in terms of increasing overall contribution through memberships. Extrapolations may also be made to estimate the 'lifetime value' of membership contributions, with the increase in 5/10 year and lifetime memberships.

Qualitative measures might also be helpful in order to support the further refinement of the plan. For example, feedback forms, survey questionnaires (administered by post or on-line) and perhaps focus group interviews (with new corporate or educational members) could be used to analyse: what attracted new members to the membership proposition; where/how they signed up; whether they feel membership is good value for money; what their experience of WPS membership has been like for them so far; and so on.

Over time, WPS will also have information in regard to retention rates (percentage of new members remaining after one year) and defection rates (percentage of members not renewing after one year, two years etc). This will also help to indicate whether the membership proposition is sufficiently attractive, and relationship marketing sufficiently effective, to retain members.

WPS already monitors its 'market share', that is, its share of total donations to conservation charities in the UK (using published survey data). However, share of donations does not necessarily correlate with number of members, which is the objective of interest.

Measuring the internal marketing plan

Staff turnover and retention rates, absenteeism and dispute rates. These are general indicators of morale and esprit de corps, which might help to suggest whether staff are satisfied, secure and supported in their work. However, they are only indirect indicators, which may not correlate meaningfully to the internal marketing programme: other problems may be responsible for the figures.

Post-training observation by coaches and mentors can be used to measure the success of the learning exercise and transfer of learning to the job.

Feedback forms and attitude surveys (as well as informal feedback gathering and/or formal interviews by mentors and centre managers) may be used to gain feedback from participating staff: how effective they thought the briefing/coaching and communication was; what information needs were or were not met; what effect the new role emphasis has had on their job satisfaction; and so on.

Critical incident analysis may be used to identify examples of best practice and success or problems and further training/support needs.

Performance data will be gathered using the forms and systems provided: how many potential membership enquiries and new or upgraded memberships were signed up by each centre, and by each member of staff. This is a useful results-based measure of the success of internal marketing, according to the plan's objective, but it poses a motivational risk. It should be emphasised that results monitoring is for the purpose of support planning and award-giving: individual staff members will not be 'judged' or penalised for low sign-ups, and awards are celebratory, rather than purely competitive.

Review form & Free prize draw

All original review forms from the entire BPP range, completed with genuine comments, will be entered into one of two draws on 31 January 2009 and 31 July 2009. The names on the first four forms picked out on each occasion will be sent a cheque for £50.

Name: _____   **Address:** _____

_____

_____

1.How have you used this Text?
(Tick one box only)

☐ Self study (book only)

☐ On a course: college_____

☐ Other _____

3. Why did you decide to purchase this Text?
(Tick one box only)

☐ Have used companion Assessment workbook

☐ Have used BPP Texts in the past

☐ Recommendation by friend/colleague

☐ Recommendation by a lecturer at college

☐ Saw advertising in journals

☐ Saw website

☐ Other _____

2. During the past six months do you recall seeing/receiving any of the following?
(Tick as many boxes as are relevant)

☐ Our advertisement in *The Marketer*

☐ Our brochure with a letter through the post

☐ Saw website

4. Which (if any) aspects of our advertising do you find useful?
(Tick as many boxes as are relevant)

☐ Prices and publication dates of new editions

☐ Information on product content

☐ Facility to order books off-the-page

☐ None of the above

5. Have you used the companion Assessment Workbook?   Yes ☐   No ☐

6. Have you used the companion Passcards?   Yes ☐   No ☐

7. Your ratings, comments and suggestions would be appreciated on the following areas.

	Very useful	Useful	Not useful
Introductory section (How to use this text, study checklist, etc)	☐	☐	☐
Introduction	☐	☐	☐
Syllabus linked learning outcomes	☐	☐	☐
Activities and Marketing at Work examples	☐	☐	☐
Learning objective reviews	☐	☐	☐
Magic Formula references	☐	☐	☐
Content of suggested answers	☐	☐	☐
Index	☐	☐	☐
Structure and presentation	☐	☐	☐

	Excellent	Good	Adequate	Poor
Overall opinion of this Text	☐	☐	☐	☐

8. Do you intend to continue using BPP CIM Range Products?   ☐ Yes   ☐ No

9. Have you visited bpp.com/lm/cim?   ☐ Yes   ☐ No

10.If you have visited bpp.com/lm/cim, please give a score out of 10 for it's overall usefulness   /10

Please note any further comments and suggestions/errors on the reverse of this page.

Please return to: Dr Kellie Vincent, BPP Learning Media, FREEPOST, London, W12 8BR.

If you have any additional questions, feel free to email cimrange@bpp.com

Marketing essentials

Review form & Free prize draw (continued)

Please note any further comments and suggestions/errors below.

Free prize draw rules

1   Closing date for 31 January 2009 draw is 31 December 2008. Closing date for 31 July 2009 draw is 30 June 2009.

2   Restricted to entries with UK and Eire addresses only. BPP employees, their families and business associates are excluded.

3   No purchase necessary. Entry forms are available upon request from BPP Learning Media. No more than one entry per title, per person. Draw restricted to persons aged 16 and over.

4   Winners will be notified by post and receive their cheques not later than 6 weeks after the relevant draw date. List of winners will be supplied on request.

5   The decision of the promoter in all matters is final and binding. No correspondence will be entered into.

Marketing essentials